A Comprehensive Guide to Shakespeare's Sonnets

Related titles

On Shakespeare's Sonnets: A Poets' Celebration
Edited by Hannah Crawforth and Elizabeth Scott-Baumann
978-1-4742-2158-0

Shakespeare's First Folio 1623-2023: Text and Afterlives
Edited by Matthias Bauer and Angelika Zirker
978-1-3504-3636-7

Shakespeare's Sonnets: Revised
Edited by Katherine Duncan-Jones
978-1-4080-1797-5

The Poetry Toolkit: The Essential Guide to Studying Poetry
Rhian Williams
978-1-3500-3220-0

The Sonnets: The State of Play
Edited by Hannah Crawforth, Elizabeth Scott-Baumann and
Clare Whitehead
978-1-3500-9485-7

A Comprehensive Guide to Shakespeare's Sonnets

Roland Weidle

THE ARDEN SHAKESPEARE
LONDON • NEW YORK • OXFORD • NEW DELHI • SYDNEY

THE ARDEN SHAKESPEARE
Bloomsbury Publishing Plc, 50 Bedford Square, London, WC1B 3DP, UK
Bloomsbury Publishing Inc, 1385 Broadway, New York, NY 10018, USA
Bloomsbury Publishing Ireland, 29 Earlsfort Terrace, Dublin 2, D02 AY28, Ireland

BLOOMSBURY, THE ARDEN SHAKESPEARE and the Arden Shakespeare logo
are trademarks of Bloomsbury Publishing Plc

First published in Great Britain 2025
Reprinted in 2025

Copyright © Roland Weidle, 2025

Roland Weidle has asserted his right under the Copyright, Designs and Patents
Act, 1988, to be identified as author of this work.

Cover image © MarcoMarchi/Getty Images

All rights reserved. No part of this publication may be: i) reproduced or
transmitted in any form, electronic or mechanical, including photocopying,
recording or by means of any information storage or retrieval system without
prior permission in writing from the publishers; or ii) used or reproduced in any
way for the training, development or operation of artificial intelligence (AI)
technologies, including generative AI technologies. The rights holders expressly
reserve this publication from the text and data mining exception as per Article
4(3) of the Digital Single Market Directive (EU) 2019/790.

Bloomsbury Publishing Inc does not have any control over, or responsibility for,
any third-party websites referred to or in this book. All internet addresses given
in this book were correct at the time of going to press. The author and publisher
regret any inconvenience caused if addresses have changed or sites have ceased
to exist, but can accept no responsibility for any such changes.

A catalogue record for this book is available from the British Library.
A catalog record for this book is available from the Library of Congress.

ISBN: HB: 978-1-3503-8283-1
ePDF: 978-1-3503-8285-5
eBook: 978-1-3503-8284-8

Typeset by RefineCatch Limited, Bungay, Suffolk
Printed and bound in Great Britain

For product safety related questions contact productsafety@bloomsbury.com.

To find out more about our authors and books visit www.bloomsbury.com
and sign up for our newsletters.

For Carolanne

Love is not love
Which alters when it alteration finds,
Or bends with the remover to remove.
O no, it is an ever-fixed mark,
That looks on tempests and is never shaken

CONTENTS

List of Illustrations x
List of Tables xi
Preface xii

Introduction 1

Part I Contexts and Forms

1 Sonnet Tradition 15

2 The Text 29
Date 30
The 1609 Quarto 33
Early Editions of the *Sonnets* 35
The *Sonnets* as Biography? 37

3 The Sequence, Dramatis Personae, and Form 43
The Sequence 43
Dramatis Personae 51
The Speaker 52
The Youth 52
The Mistress 53
The Rival Poet 59
The Shakespearean Sonnet 60

Part II Themes

4 Preservation 69
Procreation 75
The Limits of Procreation 84

5 Writing 89
Imitatio vs. *Inventio* 90
Uses of Poetry 95
The Rival Poet and the Marketplace 100
Petrarchism 104

6 Desire 109
Irrational and Infectious Desire 112
Desire for the Youth 116
Desire for the Mistress 127
Triangular Desire 131

7 Deception 143
Deceptive Desire 143
Deception: Speaker and Youth 147
Deception: Speaker and Mistress 152
Poetry as Deception 155

8 Imagination 157
The Imagined Youth 161
The Imagined Mistress 170

9 By Way of a Conclusion 173

Appendix

1   Pairs, Sequences, Groups and Theme Clusters   183

2   Conjectured Dates of Composition for the Sonnets   190

3   Addressees of the Sonnets   191

4   A Step-by-step Approach to Sonnet 75   196

5   Model Interpretation of Sonnet 106   202

References and Commentary on Key Works   207
Index of Sonnets   229
General Index   235

ILLUSTRATIONS

2.1. Shakespeare, William. [*Sonnets*] Shake-speares sonnets. Neuer before imprinted. (London: G. Eld for T[homas]. T[horpe]. and are to be solde by William Aspley, 1609), title page. STC 22353, A1r, title page, image 1356, Folger Shakespeare Library.   30

2.2. Shakespeare, William. [*Sonnets*] Shake-speares sonnets. Neuer before imprinted. (London: G. Eld for T[homas]. T[horpe]. and are to be solde by William Aspley, 1609), dedication page (directly following title page). Call #: STC 22353, A2r. Image: 7917. Folger Shakespeare Library. STC 22353, A2r, dedication page (directly following title page), image 7917, Folger Shakespeare Library.   39

3.1. Shakespeare, William. [*Sonnets*] Shake-speares sonnets. Neuer before imprinted. (London: G. Eld for T[homas]. T[horpe]. and are to be solde by William Aspley, 1609), leaf H2 verso ‖ leaf H3 recto. STC 22353, leaf H2 verso ‖ leaf H3 recto, image 19641, Folger Shakespeare Library.   64

6.1. John de Critz, (attr.) Henry Wriothesley, 3rd Earl of Southampton in his youth, *c.* 1592, Cobbe Collection, Hatchlands Park.   126

9.1. Pyramid Model of Theme Clusters. Illustration by Christian Fittinghoff.   177

TABLES

1	Connected pairs and sequences	183
2	Separated pairs and groups	188
3	Theme clusters (as identified in this *Guide*)	189
4	Conjectured dates of composition	190
5	Male addressee (thirty-six sonnets)	192
6	Female addressee (twenty-one sonnets)	194
7	Male and female addressee (five sonnets)	195
8	Male or female addressee (eighty-four sonnets)	195
9	No specific addressee (eight sonnets)	195

PREFACE

Shakespeare's sonnets dazzle. They dazzle you with their phonetic effects, their imagery and word choices. They invite you to stay and engage with them. At first, they seem like manageable texts, consisting (in most cases) of only fourteen lines suggesting brevity and clarity. A second reading, however, reveals that the poems are not as clear as one initially thought. In their density and compactness they present the reader with a number of challenges: they often begin in the middle of an action asking you to infer what had happened before; they are often characterized by an elliptical and inverted syntax which, in order to fit the metre and rhyme scheme, omits and rearranges words; they regularly employ unusual metaphors, metonymies, similes and wordplay which require decoding; they interrupt and continue narratives, ideas and themes, or feature characters and motifs from other sonnets in the sequence which one is not aware of; they refer to specific historical and cultural contexts or expressions one is not familiar with; and they often contain complex arguments.

So, why bother then with these complex texts? The answer is, for the very characteristics just mentioned, since the intellectual challenges the poems pose contribute to their fascinating and intriguing quality. To be able to fully appreciate the sonnets, one needs to accept these challenges. Engaging with these intellectual demands enhances if not constitutes the aesthetic and also sensual experience of the 'passionate rationality' (Burrow 2002: 91) of the sonnets. Just as the unwrapping of an exquisite chocolate is not only the prerequisite for enjoying it, but also part of the entire gustatory experience, investing time and effort in 'unwrapping' a sonnet is both precondition and part of the aesthetic sonnet experience.

Joseph Pequigney's *Such Is My Love: A Study of Shakespeare's Sonnets* was published in 1985 and was the first scholarly monograph to pursue a homoerotic reading of Shakespeare's *Sonnets*. Since then, and especially in the last two decades, scholars have put questions to the collection that not only resonate with the concerns of our own times, but which also call upon us to reassess our view of the *Sonnets* and of Shakespeare as a canonical author. For example, what does the speaker's treatment of the 'woman coloured ill' (144.4) who is 'as black as hell, as dark as night' (147.14) tell us about early modern (and Shakespeare's) views of race and how does this relate to the cultural value attached to the notion of 'fairness' in the *Sonnets*? What exactly is the nature of the relationship between speaker and youth, and how does this play out in the context of early modern attitudes to same-sex relationships? Do the hermaphrodite features of the 'master mistress' (20.2) imply that we need to correct our assumption that gender was conceived of in binary terms at Shakespeare's time? Asking questions like these and studying the recent contributions in these fields have challenged some of the notions I had taken for granted about the *Sonnets*, but at the same time have also proved very fruitful and productive in making me re-evaluate my own position and background as a white male European Shakespeare scholar who received his academic training during the 1980s and 1990s. You will no doubt bring your own questions to these works by Shakespeare and it is my hope that this book will help you as you engage with these and with Shakespeare's collection.

This book has its origins in the Covid pandemic that hit the globe in 2020. During the recording of the podcast for my lecture 'Introduction to Shakespeare's Sonnets' in the winter term 2020/21 I realized that talking into a microphone alone in my study was quite different from live communication with students in a lecture hall. My preferred way of using slides with keywords and key phrases to communicate what I believe to be the most important and interesting aspects of the *Sonnets* simply did not work vis-à-vis a microphone. I decided therefore to write down word for word what I wanted to say in the lecture. After about three lectures I felt that I wanted to give the 'story' I had begun to tell about the sonnets, their tradition, features and themes, a more lasting form that would also be accessible to a wider audience. As the term went along, I

xiv PREFACE

continued to write the lectures with the possibility of publication in the back of my mind. In the final weeks of term, I asked my students for their feedback and gave them a questionnaire to complete with questions on the content, structure and language (English) of the lecture and what suggestions they might have regarding a published version. The students' responses reinforced my decision to go ahead and approach potential publishers.

In writing this book I have benefited immensely from the work by others. The editions of the *Sonnets* by Booth ([1977] 2000), Burrow (2002), Burto ([1964] 1999), Duncan-Jones (2010), Edmondson and Wells (2020), Evans (1998), Ingram and Redpath ([1964] 1978), Kerrigan ([1986] 1999), Mowat and Werstine (2004), Paterson (2010) and Vendler (1999) have been of invaluable help in shedding light on some of the poems' more obscure moments. I also benefited greatly from, among others, the essay collections by Crawforth, Scott-Baumann and Whitehead (2018), Cheney (2007), Fielitz (2010), Schiffer (2000) and Schoenfeldt (2007), the introductions by Blades (2007), Callaghan (2007), Innes (1997), Matz (2008), and Edmondson and Wells (2013), and the more general introductory works to Shakespeare's poetry by Hyland (2003), Post (2017) and Schoenfeldt (2010) that deal with all of Shakespeare's poetry, i.e. the *Sonnets* plus the narrative poems.

Francis Bacon famously wrote in his essay 'Of Studies' that there are different ways to read books: some 'are to be tasted, others to be swallowed, and some few to be chewed and digested; [. . .] some books are to be read only in parts; others to be read, but not curiously; and some few to be read wholly, and with diligence and attention' (Bacon [2002] 2008: 439). Although I would wish that this *Guide* will be 'read wholly' and fully 'digested', it can also be read 'in parts' as a reference work. For example, if you are only interested in the textual history or the structural design of the *Sonnets*, you may want to begin with Chapter 2 or 3. Or you may want to use the book's additional features in your selective reading. In that case the index will help you in finding discussions of particular sonnets you are looking for, and the tables in the appendix will provide an overview of the groups and themes, dates of composition and the addressees for each sonnet along with a step-by-step approach to and model interpretation of two sonnets. In the further reading sections at the end of each chapter and the partially

PREFACE

annotated list of references you will find additional sources on matters that this book was only able to treat in a cursory manner.

I would like to thank various people who were involved in the writing of this book. First, I should like to thank the students in my lecture on Shakespeare's *Sonnets* in the winter term 2020/21 at the Ruhr University Bochum without whom the idea for this *Guide* would not have emerged and been realized. They have been my implied readers from the start and their ideas on what a guide to the *Sonnets* should offer have been immensely helpful in turning the lecture series into a book. I also would like to thank Burkhard Niederhoff, Claudia Olk, Anette Pankratz, Gary Soska and Carolanne Weidle for the time and effort they took in reading parts of the manuscript and sharing their thoughts with me. Preparing a book for publication is an onerous task, and the meticulous editorial work by Anke Baumann, Christian Fittinghoff, Jan Mosch, Sara Tuckwell, Jan Willing and Anthea Ziermann at the English Department were invaluable in finalizing the manuscript. It goes without saying that any remaining faults are my own. Among the many people at Bloomsbury Arden Shakespeare, I would like to thank Mark Dudgeon for supporting this book project from a very early stage and Ella Wilson for guiding me through the 'House Style Guidelines for Authors and Editors' and answering my many questions with admirable patience.

A brief note on the use of the terms 'black' and 'dark' in my discussion of the mistress: when referring to the physical features of a non-Black woman, I will use these words without quotation marks. However, when the speaker employs these terms to describe character traits and attributes that have socially and historically been associated with darkness and blackness, these words will be used with quotation marks ('black', 'dark'). In those instances, in which she is meant to be conceived of as a person of colour, I will refer to her as 'Black'.

All quotations from Shakespeare are from the Third Series Arden edition of Shakespeare's *Complete Works*, edited by Richard Proudfoot et al. (2021). In the following, publications by Edmondson and Wells will be abbreviated as E/W, and Duncan-Jones's edition of the *Sonnets* as KDJ.

Roland Weidle
Bochum

Introduction

Although I argued in the preface above that the challenges the *Sonnets* pose, such as their density and 'passionate rationality' (Burrow 2002: 91), provide enough reason to engage with them, this may not immediately convince all readers, especially of the younger generation. Why should one read, let alone study Shakespeare's *Sonnets* in the twenty-first century when there are much more interesting, topical, relevant and also more accessible texts and media around than these over 400-year-old poems in which a speaker (who also happens to be a poet) expresses his love and desire for different love objects? Moreover, Shakespeare employs a literary form that was already considered outdated by some of his contemporaries (the sonnet was established in the thirteenth century), adheres more or less rigidly to the genre's rules of metre and rhyme, uses complex and arcane metaphors, and often expresses his ideas in an intractable and at times confounding syntax. When one adds to this the historical distance between Shakespeare's and our own period and the differences in society, outlook, ideology, and political structure, the *Sonnets*, one might think, have nothing really relevant to tell us.

However, this is a misconception, for these poems speak to us in many ways. We will see, for example, that the *Sonnets* explore ideas about gender and sexuality that are strikingly modern, especially when it comes to the relationship between the speaker and the young man. The poems address the performative and 'fluid nature of gender practices' (Joubin 2023a: 70), show that 'early modern gender was not always imagined in strictly binary terms' (Chess, Gordon and Fisher 2019: 14) and may even 'predict, push past, or resonate powerfully with contemporary theorizations of trans life'

2 A COMPREHENSIVE GUIDE TO SHAKESPEARE'S SONNETS

(ibid., 13), as Colby Gordon's (2020) analysis of Sonnet 20 attempts to show. It will also become evident how, by placing the speaker in sexual relationships with both a young man and an older, more experienced woman, Shakespeare addresses and interrogates moral and sexual norms of his time: the unreproductive heterosexual relationship with the woman is shown to be more 'unnatural' than the homoerotic relationship with the young man.

The *Sonnets* also alert us to the fact that aspects of gender and sexuality intersect with concepts of race and class. In the sonnet collection, the woman is repeatedly referred to as possessing 'black' or 'dark' qualities. Although it does not become quite clear whether this darkness indicates her geographical or cultural origin, the speaker's predominantly negative associations with the colour black do tell us something about the cultural value of whiteness ('fairness') and darkness in Shakespeare's England, in which Black people could be seen and heard about and in which notions of 'race' and 'racism' already existed (cf. Little 2016). As Caroline Spurgeon already argued in 1935, and Arthur J. Little (2021: 274) reminds us, Shakespeare 'is just as sensitive to the colour and tint of flesh, and the contrasts of the various shades which are called "white"' (Spurgeon [1935] 1960: 66) as his plays and poems are embedded in what Ayanna Thompson has called early modern 'race-making' (2021a: 7).

Before I comment in greater detail on some of these more recent approaches, however, let us first take a look at Sonnet 21 which not only illustrates some of the more elementary characteristics and difficulties addressed in the preface but also features the central dramatis personae of the collection.

Sonnet 21

So is it not with me as with that Muse,
Stirred by a painted beauty to his verse,
Who heaven itself for ornament doth use,
And every fair with this fair doth rehearse,
Making a couplement of proud compare
With sun and moon, with earth and sea's rich gems;
With April's first-born flowers and all things rare
That heaven's air in this huge rondure hems;
O let me true in love but truly write,
And then believe me: my love is as fair

INTRODUCTION

As any mother's child, though not so bright
As those gold candles fixed in heaven's air:
    Let them say more that like of hearsay well,
    I will not praise, that purpose not to sell.

How do we approach such a poem? To get to the heart of this sonnet, we need to address some of the *Sonnets*' problems addressed in the preface. The very first word 'So', for example, indicates that what the speaker is going to say in this poem, picks up an idea expressed earlier (in this case the idea of preserving the desired other's beauty in verse, discussed in sonnets 15–19), a clue which helps us to understand the main argument of the poem (that the speaker rejects traditional ways and forms of expressing his love for the object of desire). Elliptical expressions such as 'that Muse' (v. 1) and 'every fair with his fair doth rehearse' (v. 4) require clarification and can be paraphrased with the help of annotated editions, in these two instances as meaning 'the poet inspired by *that Muse*' (KDJ 2010: 152) and 'describes *every* beautiful thing in the world alongside his own beautiful (love object)' (ibid.). Similarly, the meaning of some of the imagery is ambiguous. The metaphor 'painted beauty' (v. 2) could refer to the love object's artificially enhanced beauty by the use of cosmetics, the (stale) poetic metaphors employed to describe that object, or to both. Also, words such as 'couplement' (v. 5) or 'rondure' (v. 8) may pose a problem and consulting the entries for both terms in glossaries like Onions (1994) or Crystal and Crystal (2004) will be of help.

Another difficulty one is confronted with when dealing with a Shakespeare sonnet is simply to follow its argument. As sensual as the experience of reading, speaking or hearing a Shakespeare sonnet may be, one of the *Sonnets*' most defining characteristics is their syllogistic and cerebral quality. Following a sonnet's argument and appreciating its logic therefore depends to a great extent on being able to identify what Paul Edmondson and Stanley Wells identify as the '"When"/"Then" strategy' (2013: 53) which I will discuss in greater detail in this *Guide*. While it is fairly easy to identify the individual steps of the argument in some sonnets, following the logic in others becomes more difficult.

In Sonnet 21, it is fairly easy to trace the three stages of the argument. In the first part (vv. 1-8), the speaker tells us how he does not want to write about his love. Unlike other poets before him, the speaker does not want to use exaggerated praise and comparisons to celebrate his beloved. He does not want to compare the addressee to 'heaven' (v. 3) or to all the other many beautiful things one can think of (v. 4): neither to the planets, the riches of the sea (v. 6), April's flowers (v. 7) nor to all the other beautiful things in the world (vv. 7-8). In the second part of the argument, introduced after the traditional *volta* between verses 8 and 9, the speaker then specifies how his poetry will be different from other poets' verse. He wants to write 'truly' (v. 9) because his 'love' (v. 10) does not need exaggerated praise and 'couplement' (v. 5) with sun, moon, earth and sea. The desired other is as natural and beautiful as any child (vv. 10-11) and, as the speaker admits at the end of the second part, cannot be expected to shine as bright as the stars.

In the final part of the argument, the couplet, we are given yet another reason why the poet-speaker rejects traditional hyperbolic poetry. Not only does the desired other's natural beauty need no hyperbolic praise, the speaker also does not feel the need to advertise his love (in the sense of both his feelings and the object of his desire) to the public. This professed restraint is ironically undercut by the fact that the speaker does in fact advertise his love by writing about it, resulting in a self-reflexive and contradictory engagement with previous literary traditions that is characteristic of the *Sonnets* and also adds to their appeal.

Sonnet 21 is also indicative of another remarkable feature of Shakespeare's *Sonnets*: the speaker's palpable presence and how he confides his feelings and thoughts to us. He comes across as a confident poet who believes in his abilities and who refers to himself at various moments in the sonnet: 'not with me' (v. 1), 'O let me true in love' (v. 9), 'believe me: my love' (v. 10), 'I will not praise' (v. 14). As we will see, this self-reflexive gesture, this connection between writing and loving, between beauty and poetic style, is a feature that characterizes many sonnets in the sequence.

What this sonnet also illustrates is the fact that we are dealing with a number of different characters in the sequence. Apart from the speaker, who is a poet and who loves someone, there is 'my love' (v. 10), who, as we will see, is not only one person, but in the course of the sequence refers to at least two-character constructs, a young man and a more experienced woman. Finally, there is 'them' (v. 13), the other poets who are the speaker's rivals in both poetry and love, and who keep reappearing in the sonnets.

INTRODUCTION

In exploring these features and qualities this book hopes to show that investing time and energy into unlocking the hidden secrets of these dense and sensual poems can be extremely rewarding. This *Guide* attempts to assist the reader in this endeavour by providing literary, cultural and historical contexts, offering close readings of more than 100 sonnets, explaining the most important structural features and stylistic devices, and by suggesting grouping the sonnets into five primary theme clusters. Additionally, this book aims to provide concrete interpretative tools needed to approach the sonnets and the sequence as a whole. This *Guide*'s aim then is to offer a more all-encompassing approach to the *Sonnets* than previous introductions which either predominantly focus on themes and ideas (Blades 2007; Callaghan 2007) or on historical contexts (Matz 2008). Edmondson and Wells' particularly helpful *Shakespeare's Sonnets* (2013) comes closest to my approach since it also combines a historical with a theoretical, thematic, and structural perspective although it provides less practical information on how to approach and analyse the sonnet collection.

As already briefly referred to above, the last years have seen what can be considered a sea change in Early Modern and Shakespeare Studies with scholars drawing our attention to the many blind spots of its inherent 'institutionalized cis-sexism' (Joubin 2023a: 65). A 'white-dominated Shakespeare scholarship' (Park 2023: 269–70), so the argument goes, has, consciously or unconsciously, reproduced heteronormative views on sex(uality) and gender and neglected to ask critical questions about early modern 'race-making and racecraft' (Park 2023: 269).

When Thomas Laqueur in his highly influential study *Making Sex: Body and Gender from the Greeks to Freud* (1990) popularized the notion of the one-sex model for early modern England, this proved to be a watershed moment in early modern studies. By demonstrating that men and women were believed not to be separate sexes but different versions of just one human sex, and that females were understood as 'unfinished' men who, by being subsequently exposed to heat and movement could eventually develop into men, Laqueur alerted us to the early modern idea that sexual categories are not fixed but fluid and unstable.

More recent approaches have come to question the binary categories of female and male still underlying this model and have argued for an even more radical understanding of sex outside these categories. Taking their cue from the idea that sexual difference is a matter of degree and not opposites implied by Laqueur's one-sex model, Simone Chess, Colby Gordon and Will Fisher, for example, refute the notion that 'transition [between the sexes] was unthinkable' (2019: 1) in early modern England and refer to terms such as '"transfeminate" and "transsexion"' (ibid.) that were in use for gender transition at the time. Critics have also identified 'queer residues' (ibid., 8) in boy actors, '"soft" angels' (ibid., 7) in Milton and 'trans and nonbinary residues in the history of science and across literary and dramatic representations' (Chess 2019: 243) of the Renaissance. Alexa Alice Joubin applies a 'theory of trans lens' (2023a: 65) to Shakespeare's works and their performance and contradicts those who assume 'the cis status of even those characters with fluid gender' (ibid.). In this way we are asked 'to consider what changes if the body of the female character and the actor's somatic presence exist on a continuum rather than in contrary fixations' (Joubin 2023b: 9).

Sonnet 20, discussed below, is a case in point. Colby Gordon in his reading of this famously ambiguous poem has suggested that by 'adding one thing' (20.12) to the youth, the poem implies 'that the addition of a prick expands the menu of erotic possibilities available to the youth's lovers, but it does not necessarily channel that desire into a cisnormative frame' (Gordon 2020: 281). Similarly, Goran Stanivukovic has drawn our attention to the possibility that the young man of the *Sonnets* can be perceived as 'cross-gendered' (2020: 184) and 'lure[s] both men and women into its erotic space, even if the tone and spirit of the poem is homoerotic' (ibid.).

The idea of a fluid biological sex for early modern subjects might be unfamiliar and challenging for a male white Shakespeare scholar like myself who was brought up in the 'institutionalized cis-sexism' of late twentieth-century academia, and who may have, consciously or subconsciously, perceived Shakespeare as his 'property'. However, applying such a 'trans lens' to early modern texts invites one at least to explore the notion of fluid sexual categories and the idea that gender can be perceived 'as social practices that evolve over time and in different performance settings and social spaces' (Joubin 2023b: 5).

There is, of course, always the danger of presentism when looking at the past through our own lenses. As Ania Loomba reminds us, is 'it really possible to recover the early modern meanings of raced

INTRODUCTION

and gendered bodies in terms untouched by the [. . .] subsequent histories' (2016: 234) and 'how can we perform the task of recovery without fetishizing the past and remaining alert to our reasons for asking of the past the questions that we do?' (ibid., 234–5). As critics, then, we must find the right balance between leaving our own assumptions and perspective behind and not assuming a past that is totally disconnected from the present. Or, as Ania Loomba and Martin Orkin have argued, it 'is certainly true that we must not flatten the past by viewing it entirely through the lens of our own assumptions and imperatives. However, neither is it desirable, or even possible, entirely to unhook the past from the present' ([1998] 2008: 5–6).

Looking at the developments in recent Shakespeare scholarship, the task to see the past as not entirely separate from the present seems to be even more pressing when it comes to the topic of race. For far too long, as proponents of Premodern Critical Race Studies (PCRS) and White Studies argue, the working assumption has been 'simply that the early modern period isn't *about* race but that it is also, as a field, white property' (Little 2016: 88; cf. Smith 2022). Calls have been made to remind Shakespeareans of their 'ethical responsibility' (Brown, Akhimie and Little 2022: 20) to make visible the hidden racial discourses of the early modern era and thereby also to reflect on their own (racially inflected) perspectives (cf. Grier 2023; Little 2021; Park 2023). Initiatives and projects like the British Black and Asian Shakespeare Project, the RaceB4Race Mentorship Network and #ShakeRace give evidence of this wide interest. To what extent each scholar feels inclined to follow the call 'to sing a new scholarly song' (Erickson and Hall 2016: 13) is, of course, a different matter; but there is certainly a growing realization that 'Shakespeare is indeed on the border of having real meaning for an audience who might not readily see him as relevant of issues of immigration, assimilation, cultural integrity, and social and racial inequities' (Espinosa 2016: 66).

Admittedly, the exact nature of the mistress's darkness and black features in the *Sonnets* remains much less clear than, for example, Othello's or Aaron's in *Titus Andronicus*. Is the speaker in the *Sonnets* referring to her skin colour, exposure to the sun, the use of cosmetics, or to her dark eyes caused by the use of the drug *atropa belladonna*? But even only associating the woman with dark and black properties in unspecific terms at a time when blackness was

8   A COMPREHENSIVE GUIDE TO SHAKESPEARE'S SONNETS

equated with 'promiscuity' (Sanchez 2019a: 72), as well as faithlessness, religious difference and Islam (cf. Loomba 2016: 235, 237), racializes and places her, at least implicitly, in the discourse of '[x]enophobia [that] did indeed inform not only anti-immigrant polemics but also the theater of the period' (Espinosa 2016: 63). As we will see, engaging with these perspectives will help deepen our understanding and appreciation of the *Sonnets*, but also alert us to some of their more problematic and even disconcerting aspects that resonate with our own times.

This book is divided into two sections. The first of these, 'Contexts and Form', consists of three chapters and deals with the literary tradition of the sonnet (Chapter 1), the composition and early publication history of the sequence (Chapter 2) and the structure of and main figures in the *Sonnets*, as well as the features of the Shakespearean sonnet (Chapter 3). The second section is divided into chapters on each of the five theme clusters (Chapters 4–8) I identify in the collection (preservation, writing, desire, deception, imagination) and discusses the sonnets in each theme cluster.

The first chapter in the section on 'Contexts and Form' traces the history of the sonnet from thirteenth century Italy to sixteenth century England. It describes the main features and elements of the Italian sonnet, introduces the works of its main proponents da Lentino, Dante and Petrarch, and comments on the most prominent features in terms of form as well as themes and argumentative structure. The chapter then charts the development of the English sonnet and how poets like Thomas Wyatt, Henry Howard and Philip Sidney adapted the sonnet to suit their own needs and those of the English language. It shows how the English sonnet gained a greater intellectual flexibility, how it became more diverse in terms of themes and argumentation, and how it culminated in the sonneteering craze of the 1590s when Shakespeare was working on his sonnet collection.

The second chapter focuses on the *Sonnets*' time of composition and publication, and their biographical relevance. While the first part of the chapter discusses the probable chronological order in which the poems were written, the next part delineates the different publication stages the author's manuscript went through before it was printed and what the collaborative publication process can tell us about Shakespeare's involvement in the design of the collection. A brief section on the early publishing history of the sonnet

INTRODUCTION 9

collection focuses on the key features of the early editions by John Benson (1640), Charles Gildon (1710) and Edmond Malone (1780). The final section introduces some of the most prominent theories regarding possible biographical contexts of the *Sonnets* with regard to the dedicatee, speaker, young man, woman and rival poet figure.

The concluding chapter of the first section discusses the patchwork structure of the *Sonnets*. It addresses the arguments for and against differentiating between a youth sequence and a mistress sequence, explains why it makes sense to operate with such a distinction, and introduces some of the most apparent groups, mini-narratives and linking devices that can be identified. The chapter then introduces the principal character constructs (speaker, youth, mistress, rival poet) and identifies their main traits. The chapter's last section summarizes the most common features of the Shakespearean sonnet but also discusses those sonnets in the collection that deviate from this norm.

The book's second main section begins with a chapter which, after introducing the five theme clusters that organize the sonnet collection, explores the theme of preservation and how it relates to some of the other clusters. It focuses on the procreation sonnets and how and why the speaker implores the youth to preserve not only his beauty but also other aspects of his personality, including his faults and weaknesses. These sonnets not only thematize the reasons why the young man should have children, but also the speaker's own investment in the latter's procreation. The chapter concludes by drawing attention to the limits of the procreation argument and to the fact that some of these sonnets already point to an alternative strategy of preserving the young man: writing poems about him.

This strategy and its various forms and functions are explored in Chapter 5. After discussing sonnets in which the speaker reflects on the relationship between memory and writing in a 'table' (notebook), the chapter examines how the speaker-poet employs the poetic traditions of *imitatio* and *inventio* to find a unique way of expressing his desire for the young man. The chapter then discusses the speaker's reflections on the different objectives and consequences of writing about the youth and concludes with a discussion of two sonnets that illustrate Shakespeare's engagement with the literary tradition of Petrarchism.

Chapter 6 on desire begins by discussing its physical, irrational, contagious and uncontrollable nature in the collection, as opposed to the Petrarchan model of love. The next section analyses the speaker's longing for the young man and its various aspects: the symbiotic quality of the relationship, the paradoxical claim that the desire is constant whilst at the same time ever increasing, its sinister aspects, its homoeroticism, and how it is influenced (and staged) by separation and reunion. The third section explores the speaker's relationship with the mistress, and the role her darkness/'darkness' plays in the speaker's desire for her. The chapter's closing section examines the sonnets on the triangular desire between speaker, youth and mistress, and how in the end the speaker's heterosexual desire for the mistress is considered a far greater threat than the homoerotic desire for the young man.

Chapter 7 on the theme of deception first looks at sonnets from the cluster of desire in which betrayal and deception play an important, although subordinate role in the speaker's desire for the young man. The next section focuses on those sonnets that thematize deception itself. It will be shown that while the speaker assumes a fairly conciliatory tone towards the deceptions of the youth, the mistress's acts of betrayal are viewed in a more critical light. The chapter's final section explores the relation between writing and deception in the collection, showing that the speaker-poet finds a middle ground between Plato's critique of art and Sidney's apology of poetry.

The final chapter discusses the sonnets in the theme cluster of imagination. Beginning with the sonnets to and about the youth, the chapter reveals that the speaker reflects on various aspects and functions of imagination while being separated from his object of desire, such as the energy and effort involved in imaginative work, the healing powers of imagination and its ability to bring back past emotions, absent or dead friends. The second section is devoted to the sonnets that are concerned with the mistress and which show a less optimistic view of the faculties of imagination.

A short concluding chapter summarizes some of the central ideas developed in the book and also reflects on the importance of the *Sonnets* for today. Five appendices provide (1) a survey of the pairs, mini-sequences, groups, and theme clusters in the collection, (2) a possible timeline for the poems' composition, (3) tables identifying the addressee's gender for each sonnet, (4) a step-by-step approach to preparing a sonnet for interpretation, using Sonnet 75 as an example, and (5) a model interpretation of Sonnet 106.

Further reading

Anthologies of sonnets: Hirsch and Boland 2009; Levin 2001. **Editions of Shakespeare's** *Sonnets*: Booth 2000; Burrow 2002; Burto [1964] 1999; KDJ 2010; E/W 2020; Evans 1998; Ingram and Redpath [1964] 1978; Kerrigan [1986] 1999; Mowat and Werstine 2004; Paterson 2010; Vendler 1999. **Essay collections on Shakespeare's** *Sonnets*: Crawforth, Scott-Baumann and Whitehead 2018; Cheney 2007; Fielitz 2010; Schiffer 2000; Schoenfeldt 2007. **Essay collections on the sonnet:** Cousins and Howarth 2011. **Glossaries and lexicons:** Schmidt 1971; Rubinstein 1984; Onions 1994; Crystal and Crystal 2004. **Introductions to Shakespeare's poetry:** Dubrow 1987; Hyland 2003; Post 2017; Schoenfeldt 2010. **Introductions to Shakespeare's** *Sonnets*: Blades 2007; Callaghan 2007; E/W 2013; Innes 1997; Matz 2008; Monte 2021; Rudenstine 2015. **Introductions to the sonnet:** Hirsch and Boland 2009: 39–54, 365–80; Levin 2001, xxxvii–lxxiv; Petzold 2022; Regan 2019; Spiller 1992. **Premodern Critical Race Studies and White Studies:** Brown, Akhimie and Little 2022; Erickson and Hall 2016; Espinosa 2016; Grier 2023; Little 2016; Little 2021; Loomba 2016; Loomba and Orkin [1998] 2008; Park 2023; Sanchez 2019a; Smith 2022. **Trans and Queer Studies:** Chess, Gordon and Fisher 2019; Gordon 2020; Joubin 2023a; Joubin 2023b; Sanchez 2019b; Stanivukovic 2020; Traub 2016.

PART ONE

Contexts and Forms

1

Sonnet Tradition

When the English poet George Gascoigne in 1575 defined the sonnet in his *Primer of English Poetry* as consisting 'of fourteen lines, every line containing ten syllables' (2004: 170) and rhyming 'in staves of four lines by cross metre, and the last two rhyming together do conclude the whole' (ibid.), he provided a definition which is more or less still taught today. Shakespeare's sonnets, as a rule, observe this definition, as the following example demonstrates:

Sonnet 18
Shall I compare thee to a summer's day?
Thou art more lovely and more temperate:
Rough winds do shake the darling buds of May,
And summer's lease hath all too short a date:
Sometime too hot the eye of heaven shines,
And often is his gold complexion dimmed;
And every fair from fair sometime declines,
By chance, or nature's changing course, untrimmed:
But thy eternal summer shall not fade,
Nor lose possession of that fair thou ow'st,
Nor shall death brag thou wander'st in his shade
When in eternal lines to time thou grow'st:
    So long as men can breathe or eyes can see,
    So long lives this, and this gives life to thee.

The sonnet is written in iambic pentameter (five disyllabic metric feet with a stress on the second syllable) and consists of three stanzas, each comprising four verses (quatrains) in cross rhymes, followed by a rhyming couplet, resulting in the rhyme scheme *abab cdcd efef*

16   A COMPREHENSIVE GUIDE TO SHAKESPEARE'S SONNETS

gg. As we will see in the course of this *Guide*, this 3x4+2-structure lends itself particularly well to developing a logical argument. In our case, we can see how the first two quatrains claim that the addressee surpasses the imperfection of summer. A turn, also known as the volta (see below), after the eighth line changes the focus to the addressee's perfection and explains how the addressee is superior to summer. The final couplet presents the conclusion and further explains this superiority: unlike summer, the beauty of the beloved is made to last forever by immortalizing it in the sonnet.

Let us take a closer look at how Shakespeare develops his case. The main point of the sonnet is that the addressee's beauty will be preserved by the speaker's poems. The speaker begins by rejecting traditional methods of comparison because comparing the addressee to a summer's day would not be appropriate since summer is characterized by extremes (v. 2), 'rough winds' (v. 3), 'too short a date' (v. 4) and hot temperatures (v. 5). The addressee's beauty on the other hand is 'eternal' (v. 9) or rather will be eternalized through the poet by writing about it 'in eternal lines' (v. 12), although, as Ronald Gray suggests, the 'lines' can also refer to 'lines of descent, through which beauty is preserved from one generation to another' (2011: 4–5). The final couplet proves the speaker's claim: as long as we, the readers, continue to read this and the other sonnets, so long will the addressee's beauty continue to live and never die.

Although the sonnet as a form was well established and defined in England by the time Shakespeare wrote his sonnets at the end of the sixteenth century, it was still fairly new, at least when compared to such poetic genres as the eclogue, the ode, the epyllion or the epos which had been around since antiquity. The sonnet came to England in the early sixteenth century, roughly fifty years before Gascoigne defined it in his *Primer*. It arrived from Italy, where it originated in the early thirteenth century at the court of Frederick II (1194–1250), king of Sicily.

Giacomo da Lentino, one of the attorneys at the Sicilian court, is credited with having invented the form (cf. Levin 2001: xl). At the time, poetry 'was part of the culture of the court, composing and exchanging poems a form of intellectual entertainment' (ibid.), a cultural practice that would continue to be performed well into the seventeenth century.

The first sonnets written by da Lentino were different from the English sonnets written 300 years later. He used a traditional stanza,

SONNET TRADITION

the eight-line *strambotto* (an octave rhyming *abab abab*) and added six more lines to it, a sestet rhyming *cde cde*, resulting in the prototypical Italian 8+6-structure. In the following, we will see how this Italian 8+6-structure developed into the 3x4+2-structure used by Shakespeare, although the 8+6-form has survived in English sonnets well into the present day.

Much has been said and written about the possible reasons for the asymmetry between the octave and the sestet in the Italian sonnet, which makes it 'top-heavy' (Levin 2001: xxxviii) and endows it with a specific dynamic, restlessness (cf. ibid., xl) and momentum. While some have identified the Fibonacci sequence (in which each number is the sum of the two preceding ones) as a possible origin, others have argued for the number of notaries at Frederick's court (fourteen), biblical references or the octagonal shape of one of Frederick's castles (cf. ibid., xlii–xliv).

One of the more convincing explanations seems to me that the 'Pythagorean-Platonic theory of numbers' (ibid., xli) influenced da Lentino, and more specifically Pythagoras' theory of the Golden Mean, a 'mathematical expression present in architecture, painting, and throughout the natural world' (E/W 2013: 52) which describes the following phenomenon: 'If an area is divided into two sections according to the ratio 1:1.6 (approximately), then the lesser of the two sections is in precisely the same ratio to the greater, as the greater is to the area of the whole' (ibid.).

Applied to the sonnet form this means that the ratio between sestet and octave is the same as that between octave and the entire sonnet. In constructing his poems in such a way, da Lentino brought two dissonant parts into 'dynamic harmony' (Levin 2001: xlii) thereby imitating the creator's skill in harmonizing the different 'vibrations in the world soul' (ibid.).

It is perhaps no coincidence that da Lentino as an attorney and notary specialized in the preparation of legal documents, which are characterized by a rational and logical structure and argumentation similar to that of a syllogism, in which two propositions are followed by a conclusion (for the influence of the tradition of the syllogism on da Lentino cf. Sprang 2016: 46). Many Shakespearean sonnets begin with a hypothesis, which in the course of the poem is tested and, in the end, often refuted. As Kurt Tetzeli von Rosador argues, 'the antithetical form and argumentation become constitutive of the sonnet' (2000: 578; my translation). For E/W, this antithetical quality is one of the defining features of the Shakespearean sonnet and expresses itself most notably in what they call the '"When"/"Then" strategy' (2013: 53). Similarly, John Archer refers to the *Sonnets* as 'philosophical poetry' (2012: 1) because of their 'complex argumentation' (ibid.). This syllogistic quality also explains why the sonnet form is not necessarily only 'a matter of 14 lines' (Zukofsky [1948] 2000: 67). As Edward Hirsch and Eavan Boland demonstrate in their anthology of sonnets, it is foremost this argumentative structure and the 'mathematical possibilities' (2009: 297) of the sonnet that have given poets room to 'tinker [. . .] with the fourteen-line formula' (ibid., 295) and allowed the form to 'travel [. . .] remarkably well' (ibid., 39) throughout the ages and cultures.

Apart from the 8+6-structure, it is also the volta which contributes to the sonnet's dynamic and dialogical quality. In Italian sonnets, the volta, the 'turn', traditionally occurs after the octave and 'introduces into the poem a possibility for transformation, like a moment of grace' (Levin 2001: xxxix). In narratological terms, the volta is the event of the poem, 'an unexpected, exceptional or new turn in the sequential dimension, some surprising "point", some significant departure from the established course of incidents' (Hühn 2010: 2).

The volta initiates 'a "turn" or change in tone, mood, voice, tempo, or perspective – a shift in focus, a swerve in logic; a change of heart' (Levin 2001: xlix); it is 'the seat of its [the sonnet's] soul' (ibid., xxxix). Felix Sprang stresses the importance of the volta as the 'juncture of the argument' (2016: 40; my translation), which 'abruptly ends a line of reasoning, forces the recipient to change the perspective and thereby lays the foundation for the genre's self-reflexive mode; because in reflecting on the sonnet the recipient has to relate two separate lines of reasoning to each other' (ibid., 43; my translation).

This integral function of the volta may also be the reason why it has survived to the present day although the sonnet form has changed considerably over the last 800 years. As we will see, many of Shakespeare's sonnets even feature two voltas.

The term 'sonnet' derives from the Italian *sonetto* (plural *sonetti*), meaning 'little song' or 'little sound' (cf. Levin 2001: xli). It may have its origin in *suonare* or *sonare*, meaning 'to sound', 'to ring' or 'to play'. The term was first used by the Italian poet Dante Alighieri, himself the author of sonnets, to refer to poems 'that make a "soft noise," their words arranged harmonically but not necessarily set to music' (ibid.). The reference to music here is a little misleading, as the sonnet was one of the first lyrical forms since late antiquity which was not set to music but intended for silent reading. The 'soft noise' comes from the sonnet itself, its play with words and how they are arranged in the fourteen-line stanza.

The term 'stanza' refers to a group of verse. Its Italian meaning 'room' is actually quite helpful in conceptualizing the stanza as a space or stage for the speaker's presentation of his argument and as a site for the speaker's introspection, meditation and self-reflection. The line 'We'll build in sonnets pretty rooms' (v. 32) from Donne's poem 'The Canonization' (2007: 77–8) should be understood in this sense. Conceiving the sonnet as an actual room or stage also highlights its similarity to a soliloquy spoken on stage which provides a 'space for the self to hold audience with the "inmost" self we may take for granted but often have trouble naming – a psychological or metaphysical entity called soul, mind, the *cogito*, consciousness' (Levin 2001: xliv).

After da Lentino, Dante Alighieri continued the sonnet tradition in his *Vita Nuova*, a collection of twenty-five sonnets and six songs, composed at the end of the thirteenth century. The main subject of this sequence of autobiographical sonnets is the speaker's love for a woman named Beatrice who had died only a few years earlier. About half a century later another Italian poet, Francesco Petrarca, composed his *Canzoniere*, a sequence of 317 sonnets and forty-four other poems, a work which has been viewed as the foundational text of continental and English love poetry. Just like Dante in his *Vita Nuova*, the speaker in Petrarch celebrates his unrequited love for an unattainable woman, the married Laura. By this time, expressing (and also celebrating) male unrequited love for a distant female love object had become the central feature of the continental sonnet.

Although the English poet and diplomat Geoffrey Chaucer (1953: 18–19) adapted one of Petrarch's sonnets in his *Troilus and Criseyde* (Book I, stanzas 58-60) in the fourteenth century, the actual rise of the sonnet in England did not occur until the beginning of the sixteenth century when English courtiers and diplomats travelled to the continent and were exposed to the sonnets of Dante and Petrarch. Although Anne Locke's *A Meditation of a Penitent Sinner* (1560) is the first sonnet sequence written in English (cf. below), Thomas Wyatt, courtier, ambassador, and poet in the reign

20   A COMPREHENSIVE GUIDE TO SHAKESPEARE'S SONNETS

of Henry VIII, is widely recognized as the founder of the English love-sonnet tradition. From his travels to the European continent, he brought back and modified the sonnet form by dividing the sestet into a quartet (quatrain) and a concluding couplet. Both the octave and the quatrain, however, still consisted of embracing rhymes, resulting in the rhyme scheme *abbaabba cddc ee*.

Henry Howard, Earl of Surrey, and friend of Wyatt, modified the sonnet further by introducing another rhyme in the octave, thereby splitting it into two quatrains, and by using both alternating and embracing rhymes, resulting in the patterns *abba cddc effe gg* and *abab cdcd efef gg*. The latter scheme with three quatrains in alternating rhymes and a concluding couplet is commonly referred to as the standard English sonnet form.

But why did Wyatt and Howard change the sonnet form once they wrote in English? The first answer to this question could simply be the English poets' need to establish their own sonnet tradition, distinct from the Italian. Gascoigne's definition of the sonnet, cited above, shows that early modern poets saw themselves very clearly as poets who were indebted to and aware of literary traditions whose boundaries they wished to stretch.

Another probable reason for changing the form is the difference between the Italian and the English language. In Italian, most nouns end on vowels, often an *a*, *o*, *e* or *i*, which correspond to an adjective and article of the same gender and ending. For example, the English phrases 'the spacious room' and 'comfortable bed' become the more poetic *la camera spaziosa* and *letto commodo* in Italian because of the assonances on *a* and *o*. But what sounds like a natural poetic advantage can also be seen as a disadvantage. Italian poets have fewer choices when it comes to rhymes. For example, in Petrarch's 'Rime 140' from his *Canzionere* every verse ends with either an *e* or *a*, and the whole poem consists of only four different end rhymes: *-egna*, *-ene*, *-ore* and *-ema*. In fact, as Phyllis Levin argues, in Italian 'it is difficult not to rhyme' (2001: li).

The English language, on the other hand, offered early modern sonneteers a wider range of rhymes to choose from which in turn necessitated a different rhyme scheme. Instead of merely using two end rhymes in the first octave, English poets introduced four, and the Italian sestet was further divided into a quatrain and a couplet consisting of three instead of only two end rhymes. While the Italian form only consists of two large units (octave and sestet), the English form contains four smaller ones (three quatrains and a couplet). In the English sonnet,

> these four-line units [the three quatrains] have the potential to build to a momentum that will fulfil itself in the rhyming couplet of the final two lines, whose force and wit must close the poem convincingly, maintaining a separate identity by virtue of their radical (within the system of the sonnet) departure from the pattern of the preceding lines. Because the rhyme scheme of each quatrain in the English sonnet is distinctly different from the one before it, there is space in each to introduce a new set of sounds, images, and thoughts. These the reader will perceive as more clearly demarcated than in the Italian sonnet, because no rhymes overlap. (ibid.)

The English sonnet not only allows for more rhymes, but it is also characterized by a greater intellectual diversity and flexibility, as we can see in Howard's translation of Petrarch's 'Rime 140':

> **Henry Howard, Earl of Surrey**
> Love that liveth and reigneth in my thought,
> That built his seat within my captive breast,
> Clad in the arms wherein with me he fought,
> Oft in my face he doth his banner rest.
> She that me taught to love and suffer pain,
> My doubtful hope and eke [also] my hot desire
> With shamefast cloak to shadow and refrain,
> Her smiling grace converteth straight to ire;
> And coward love then to the heart apace
> Taketh his flight, whereas he lurks and plains
> His purpose lost, and dare not show his face.
> For my lord's guilt thus faultless bide I pains;
> Yet from my lord shall not my foot remove,–
> Sweet is his death that takes his end by love. (qtd. in ibid., 7)

The difference in form is obvious. Instead of the four rhymes in the Italian original, Howard's version employs seven rhymes across three quatrains and one couplet rather than the Italian 8+6-structure, thereby drawing more attention to the distinct stages of the lover's conflict and suffering. In the first quatrain the speaker claims that

22   A COMPREHENSIVE GUIDE TO SHAKESPEARE'S SONNETS

he cannot hide his love. The second quatrain states that the beloved is displeased about this. Consequently, the third quatrain argues, the speaker hides his love in his heart and suffers from it.

In both the Petrarchan original and Howard's version, the speaker stages himself as the suffering lover, whose rejection by Laura defines his whole existence. Laura acquires the status of a goddess, and the process of unrequited courting becomes the centre of attention. The main focus in Petrarch's sonnets is therefore not Laura but the speaker's unrequited desire for her and his experience. Desire becomes, in Catherine Bates's words, 'intransitive' (2011: 108; see also Chapter 6 below). For the speaker's poetic project, it is vital that his desire is not consummated. Only the fact that the love object is unattainable guarantees that the poet will continue to love and express his love through poetry. The consummation of that desire would mean the end of the speaker's love and of his sonnets – although, as Richard Strier has noted, in Petrarch's sonnets we also find 'a sustained insistence on the importance and value of the bodily and the mortal' (2007: 73).

In this respect, the name 'Laura' is revealing as it not only refers to the unattainable love object but also to the laurel wreath (*lauro*) a poet received when being crowned poet laureate in recognition of his literary skill and craftsmanship, the gold (*l'auro*), and the aura (*l'aura*) the poet-speaker desires to gain: 'The Petrarchan lover is always also a poet, who describes and dissects loving and writing poetry in equal measure. Sexual and textual desire are mutually dependent, homologous, or exchangeable' (Tetzeli von Rosador 2000: 585; my translation. Cf. also Bates 2011: 114, 116, and Braden 2000: 173).

Petrarch's 'Rime 140' as well as Howard's translation (see above) illustrate this quality and also the typical features of a Petrarchan sonnet discussed earlier. Laura is presented as a cruel figure, who teaches the speaker 'to love and suffer' ('Quella ch' amare e sofferir ne 'nsegna', v. 5), asks him to control his 'doubtful hope' and 'hot desire' ('e vol che 'l gran desio, l'accesa spene,/ ragion, vergogna, e reverenza affrene', vv. 6-7) and rejects the speaker's advances by turning her 'smiling grace [. . .] straight to ire' ('di nostro ardir fra se stessa si sdegna', v. 8). The volta after the octave introduces the consequences of the speaker's dilemma: Laura's rejection of the speaker leads to 'coward love' taking 'flight' to the speaker's heart ('Onde Amor paventoso fugge al core', v. 9) and makes him abstain from any further attempts to woo her and 'show his face' ('lasciando ogni sua impresa, et piange et trema;/ ivi s'asconde et non appar più fore', vv. 10-11). Desire becomes self-reflexive: instead of directing his love towards the object (Laura), the speaker surrenders to a new 'lord' ('il mio signore', v. 12) to whom he vows eternal loyalty ('se non star seco infin a l'ora estrema?/ ché bel fin fa chi ben amando more', vv. 13-14), Love itself.

While Howard chose the English sonnet form for his translation, Petrarch's 'Rime 140' with its octave and sestet conforms to the 8+6-structure we know from da Lentino, with a slight change in the rhyme scheme, however: where da Lentino uses alternating rhymes in the octave, Petrarch uses two sets of embracing rhymes (*abba abba*). The rhyme scheme in the sestet with its alternating rhymes *cde cde* remains the same. Whenever we speak of the Italian or Petrarchan sonnet, we refer to this form.

Petrarch's *volta*, the speaker's turn of argument after the octave, is kept in Howard's poem. After describing the inability to hide his love and the beloved's displeasure, the speaker turns to the pain his love gives him. The poems' conclusions are, however, different. While the speaker in Petrarch's sonnet concludes that he has no other choice than to stay true to his love until death, the speaker in Howard's translation is more determined. Instead of merely asking what he could do except be loyal to his master Love (as in Petrarch's sonnet), he defiantly announces '*Yet* from my lord *shall* not my foot remove' (my emphasis). He thereby shows a greater resolve than Petrarch's speaker, which is further underlined by the introductory 'Yet' and the fact that the last two lines constitute a couplet separated from the previous quatrain.

Wyatt's and Howard's sonnets were published in Richard Tottel's anthology *Songes and Sonnettes* in 1557, closely followed in 1560 by the publication of the first sonnet sequence in English, Anne Locke's *A Meditation of a Penitent Sinner*. The latter is a series of altogether twenty-six religious sonnets, including twenty-one sonnets paraphrasing Psalm 51 with one sonnet for each of the nineteen verses and one additional sonnet each for verses one and four. Like Howard's translation of Petrarch's 'Rime 140', all twenty-six sonnets follow the rhyme scheme of the English sonnet form with three quatrains in alternating rhymes and a concluding couplet.

Wyatt's, Howard's and Locke's sonnets popularized the form and led to the publication of a number of sonnet cycles and

24 A COMPREHENSIVE GUIDE TO SHAKESPEARE'S SONNETS

collections, the most widely known of which are given here (for a more comprehensive list with publication dates of 'British Sonnet Sequences' from 1560 to 1634 see Spiller 1992: 198–9):

- Anne Locke, *A Meditation of a Penitent Sinner* (1560): twenty-six religious sonnets, including twenty-one paraphrasing Psalm 51
- Thomas Watson, *The Hekatompathia, or, Passionate Century of Love* (1582): 100 poems (each consisting of three stanzas of verses) which Watson calls 'sonnets'
- Philip Sidney, *Astrophil and Stella* (1591): 108 sonnets and eleven songs
- Samuel Daniel, *Delia* (1592): fifty sonnets, one ode, one complaint
- Giles Fletcher, *Licia* (1593): fifty-two sonnets, one ode, one dialogue
- Thomas Lodge, *Phillis* (1593): collection of poems, some of them being sonnets
- Michael Drayton, *Ideas Mirrour: Amours in Quatorzains* (1594): fifty-one sonnets (expanded in several versions from 1599 to 1619)
- Edmund Spenser, *Amoretti* (1595): eighty-nine sonnets addressed to an Elizabeth
- William Shakespeare, *Sonnets* (1609): 154 sonnets about the speaker's relationship with multiple (female and male) addressees
- Mary Wroth, *Pamphilia to Amphilanthus* (1621): eighty-three sonnets and twenty songs; strongly influenced by *Astrophil and Stella*
- John Donne, 'La Corona' (1633): 'crown' of seven religious sonnets; the last line of each sonnet is repeated in the first line of the following sonnet
- John Donne, *Holy Sonnets* (1633): nineteen religious sonnets

Of these, seven were published between 1590 and 1610, the height of what is often considered the 'sonneteering craze' (Levin 2001: liv) of the time.

Sidney's *Astrophil and Stella* is the first English sonnet cycle with Petrarchan features. It consists of 108 sonnets and eleven songs in which Sidney engages creatively and flexibly with the Petrarchan tradition. While every sonnet consists of an octave with two end rhymes, some finish with a quatrain and a couplet, others with a sestet (for example sonnets 3, 4, 6, 15, 29). The rhyme patterns vary; some octaves are written in alternating rhymes (for example in sonnets 1, 3–7, 10, 20), others in embracing rhymes (for example in sonnets 2, 8, 9, 11–19). The rhyme scheme of the sestet also varies, with patterns such as *ccdccd* (sonnets 4 and 40), *cddece* (sonnet 29) or *ccdeed* (sonnets 48, 58). While most of the sonnets are in iambic pentameter, a few of them consist of iambic hexameter (sonnets 1, 6, 8, 76, 77, 102).

The title *Astrophil and Stella* refers to the typical asymmetrical relationship in Petrarchan poetry between the friend or lover of the star (Astrophil) and the unattainable star (Stella). (The name 'Astrophil' can also be understood, as some critics have pointed out, to refer to Sidney's first name. For the biographical context of the sequence cf. Sidney 2008: 357.) The lover looks up to, idolizes and idealizes the love object, but this love is a love from afar which is not reciprocated. In his cycle, Sidney describes various stages of wooing, hoping, frustration and failure, and employs typical Petrarchan topoi, such as the blazon which is a catalogue describing the appearance and demeanour of the beloved in detail. An example can be found in Sidney's 'Sonnet 77', written in iambic hexameter:

> Those *looks*, whose beams be joy, whose motion is delight;
> That *face*, whose lecture shows what perfect beauty is;
> That *presence*, which doth give dark hearts a living light;
> That *grace*, which Venus weeps that she herself doth miss;
>   That *hand*, which without touch holds more than Atlas' might;
> Those *lips*, which make death's pay a mean price for a kiss;
> That *skin*, whose pass-praise hue scorns this poor term of 'white';
> Those *words*, which do sublime the quintessence of bliss;
>   That *voice*, which makes the soul plant himself in the ears;
> That *conversation* sweet, where such high comforts be,
> As construed in true speech, the name of heaven it bears,
> Makes me in my best thoughts and quiet'st judgement see

That in no more but these I might be fully blessed:
Yet ah, my maiden muse doth blush to tell the rest.

> Sidney 2008: 185; my emphasis

The speaker lists and praises Stella's features one after the other: her eyes, her face, lips, skin and voice. Stella is perfect: her face betrays 'perfect beauty' (v. 2), Venus, the goddess of love, envies Stella for her grace (v. 4), her skin is whiter than white (and thereby embodies quintessential beauty), and Stella's soul speaks through her voice. While the blazon subscribes to and confirms Petrarchan conventions and ideals of beauty, it is not used without irony: the last verse 'Yet ah, my maiden muse doth blush to tell the rest' refers to another aspect of the beloved which the speaker seems to value most and which refers to the more physical and sexual aspect of the desired relationship with Stella. The rest is something the speaker, or rather the muse, would blush to speak of. This tension between the idealized and non-physical nature of love of the Petrarchan tradition on the one hand and the (desired) physical nature of the relationship between speaker and beloved on the other, characterizes many English sonnets, and to a great degree Shakespeare's sonnet cycle.

This conflict between the platonic and the physical, between the rejection and the consummation of love, can also be found in Edmund Spenser's sonnet cycle from 1595. Unlike in Sidney's sequence, however, Spenser's speaker is eventually successful in his wooing of the beloved Elizabeth, and the cycle ends with an epithalamion, a wedding song.

The English adaptation of Petrarch's *Trionfo della Morte, The Triumphs of Death* (written *c.* 1595) by Mary Herbert, Countess of Pembroke constitutes quite a different engagement with the Petrarchan tradition. Unlike her male fellow poets before her, she does not focus on the first part of the *Canzoniere*, in which Laura's voice is given very little room. Instead, Herbert allows the spirit of Laura to speak about the joys of heaven and her love for Petrarch.

While Herbert's translation follows the *terza rima* structure of the original *Trionfo*, Herbert's niece Mary Wroth returned to the sonnet form in her *Pamphilia to Amphilanthus,* a collection of 103 sonnets and songs, published in 1621. Like her aunt, Wroth shifts the attention to the female lover Pamphilia, celebrating 'the woman lover-poet's movement from the bondage of chaotic passion to the freedom of self-chosen constancy' (Roberts [1983] 2000: 1422).

Further reading

Development of the sonnet: Levin 2001: xxxvii–lxxiv; E/W 2013: 12–21; Hirsch and Boland 2009: 49–59; Hyland 2003: 125–47; Kennedy 2011; Spiller 1992; Tetzeli von Rosador 2000. **Petrarchism:** Bates 2011; Braden 2000; Strier 2007. **Volta:** Sprang 2016.

2

The Text

What do we know about the writing and publication of Shakespeare's *Sonnets*? In 1609, T. T., whom we know to be the publisher Thomas Thorpe, published a book in quarto format (slightly smaller than A5 size), called 'Shake-speares Sonnets. Never before Imprinted.' This volume contains 154 sonnets and the 329-line poem *A Lover's Complaint*.

Thomas Thorpe was a respectable publisher who had already published Ben Jonson's Roman tragedy *Sejanus* in 1605 and his comedy *Volpone* in 1607. Thorpe established his right to publish the *Sonnets* on 20 May 1609 by the following entry in the Stationers' Register: 'Entred for his copie under the handes of master Wilson and master Lownes Warden a Booke called SHAKESPEARES *sonnettes* vjd' (qtd. in Burrow 2002: 92). The Stationers' Register provided an early form of copyright law. By entering titles to be published or printed in this record, publishers, printers, booksellers and bookbinders in England documented their right to produce a particular printed work (the idea of intellectual property did not yet exist at the time).

No manuscripts of either the *Sonnets* or *A Lover's Complaint* survive, so the 1609 Quarto is the earliest text that exists of the *Sonnets*, with the exception of the unauthorized volume *The Passionate Pilgrim* which was published in 1599 and includes versions of sonnets 138 and 144, as well as passages from *Love's Labour's Lost* (cf. E/W 2013: 3–4). Consequently, there is not a lot we know for certain about the *Sonnets*. We can only conjecture the dates or order of composition, Shakespeare's intentions, the identity of the dedicatee and the gender of the addressee for every sonnet. We do not even know whether the male and female characters addressed are always the same (cf. ibid., xiii and Chapter 3 below).

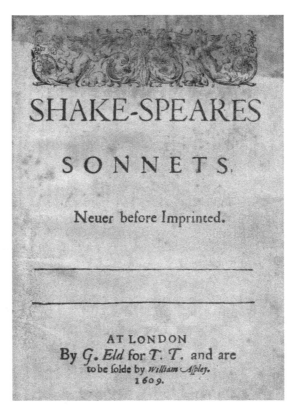

FIGURE 2.1 *Shakespeare, William. [Sonnets] Shake-speares sonnets. Neuer before imprinted. (London: G. Eld for T[homas]. T[horpe]. and are to be solde by William Aspley, 1609), title page.*

In the following I will therefore focus on 'what is known and what is fairly safely conjectured' (Spiller 1992: 150) about the composition and publication of the *Sonnets* (cf. also Evans 1998: 111–15; Hyland 2003: 148; Schiffer 2000: 6–15; Spiller 1992: 151–2).

Date

To establish when a work was written it is common to differentiate between external and internal evidence. External evidence refers to

THE TEXT

documents outside the work which help us to define the time of composition. In the case of the *Sonnets* we have two such documents. The first is Frances Meres' *Palladis Tamia, Wits Treasury*, a book published in 1598 which mentions Shakespeare's 'Sonnets to his private friends' (qtd. in Burrow 2002: 103). We do not know, however, how many of Shakespeare's sonnets were completed at the time and how many of them Meres really knew. The other text is the second edition of Shakespeare's poem *The Passionate Pilgrim* from 1599, mentioned earlier, which includes versions of two of the sonnets from the 1609 Quarto, namely sonnets 138 and 144. Thorpe's claim 'Never before Imprinted' on the title page of the *Sonnets* is therefore not quite correct. This is as much external evidence as we have.

Internal evidence on the other hand refers to signs and clues from within the text, most often consisting of references to events, texts, and contexts as well as stylistic properties. A lot of stylometrical work has been done on the *Sonnets*, especially regarding the use of specific words that Shakespeare used in different stages of his literary career. The analyses conducted so far suggest that the *Sonnets* were not composed in the order they were printed. Referring to research by MacDonald P. Jackson, Colin Burrow suggests the following approximate order of composition:

Sonnets 1–60: composed *c.* 1595–6 (possibly revised thereafter)
Sonnets 61–103: composed *c.* 1594–5
Sonnets 104–26: composed *c.* 1598–1604
Sonnets 127–54: composed *c.* 1591–5. (2002: 105)

E/W only slightly revise this order by suggesting that Sonnet 154 was Shakespeare's first sonnet, closely followed by Sonnet 153, both composed before 1582, and by proposing that sonnets 78–86 were written at a later stage (cf. Appendix 2 below).

Although estimates vary as to the dating of specific sonnets and smaller groups, the stylometrical analyses referred to above suggest that sonnets 127–154 were written first (cf. Burrow 2002: 103–8; E/W 2020: 23–6; Jackson 1999b and 2002). However, Burrow also warns us that there is no certainty about when Shakespeare wrote which sonnets. Instead, he suggests thinking of the groups as 'sections which may contain greater or lesser concentrations of early and late periods of work' (Burrow 2002: 105). The fact,

32   A COMPREHENSIVE GUIDE TO SHAKESPEARE'S SONNETS

however, that earlier versions of sonnets 138 and 144 were published in 1599 as part of *The Passionate Pilgrim* seems to corroborate the theory that sonnets 127–154 may have been written first, and maybe even as a separate entity. This is further supported by the fact that this mini-sequence of twenty-eight sonnets includes Sonnet 145, which – because of its 'comparative inferiority' (Evans 1998: 263) – some critics assume to be the first sonnet Shakespeare ever wrote (cf. Gurr 1971; Burrow 2002: 106).

Sonnet 145 stands out for many reasons. First of it all, it is not written in iambic pentameter; each line consists of only eight syllables. But what also makes this poem unusual, especially compared to most of the other sonnets in the sequence, is the 'surface simplicity of its wordplay' (Burrow 2002: 670). The first quatrain has only one end rhyme (*make, hate, sake, state*) and the imagery employed is very conventional. In typical Petrarchan fashion, the speaker stylizes himself as the rejected, languishing lover, uses stale expressions and tropes such as 'my woeful state' (v. 4) and 'gentle day/ Doth follow night' (vv. 10-11), and the final twist is rather contrived: '"I hate" from "hate" away she threw,/ And saved my life, saying "not you"' (vv. 13-14).

Andrew Gurr (1971) has suggested that the sonnet was written in 1582 when Shakespeare was eighteen, still living in Stratford and courting the eight-years older Anne Hathaway. According to Gurr, '"hate" away' in verse 13 is a pun on 'Hathaway', and Stephen Booth in his commentary on the sonnet goes even further by identifying another instance of word play in the last line. He argues, '[s]ince *And* was regularly pronounced "an" [. . .], there may be a pun on Shakespeare's wife's first name as well' (Booth 2000: 501). The last two lines could then be paraphrased as follows: '"I hate" from Hathaway away she threw,/ Ann saved my life, saying "not you"', meaning it was Anne, the private woman the speaker got to know, who turned the statement made by the public persona Hathaway (that she did not love him) into its opposite and acknowledged and reciprocated his love. As intriguing as such a biographical reading might be, it remains highly speculative and lacks dependable evidence (see below).

At any rate, critics agree that this poem is not one of Shakespeare's finest. They refer to it as 'the slightest of the sonnets' (Booth 2000: 500) or even suggest (or rather hope) that it is not by Shakespeare

THE TEXT 33

at all (cf. ibid.). The fact, however, that it connects nicely with the heaven-and-hell theme in the previous sonnet, makes this claim implausible and rather suggests that Shakespeare either might have simply had a 'bad day' or included an older sonnet which he then touched up for circulation or publication.

The 1609 Quarto

Before a text was published in Shakespeare's time, it went through several hands and stages. The first stage is the author's manuscript. Unfortunately, no manuscript of an original Shakespeare poem or play has survived. Next, the author would have revised the first draft. Only few of these revisions by authors of that period have survived. A manuscript with revisions to a scene from the collaboratively authored play *Sir Thomas More*, very likely to be written by Shakespeare (cf. Jowett 2011: 18–22), is the only hand-written document we have of a work by Shakespeare. The revised authorial draft was then given to professional scribes who would produce a 'rough working manuscript copy' (Burrow 2002: 95), the so called 'foul papers' (ibid.). The publisher's compositors would then use these foul papers to produce a compositor's text. This text in turn was used as the basis for the printed text. In the case of the first edition of the *Sonnets*, the printer's name is G. Eld.

As one can easily imagine, the many stages allowed for many errors to occur in the transmission of the text from manuscript to printed book. One should therefore never assume that the Quarto from 1609 represents *the text* that Shakespeare wrote and wanted to release to the public. The 'printed copy always and necessarily reflects not just what its author may have intended, but also the material business of printing it' (Burrow 2002: 95). One must also bear in mind that once a publisher obtained the manuscript or foul papers of a work and entered the title into the Stationers' Register, he would not have needed the author's final consent to print and publish the book.

It is generally assumed that two compositors prepared the *Sonnets* for printing and that, because of a number of irregularities and differences in spelling, Shakespeare did not personally oversee (and maybe did not even intend, in light of the explicit sexual and homoerotic content of the poems) the publication (cf. Burrow 2002: 99; Booth 2000: 545; E/W 2013: 10–11; Evans 1998: 275–82; Schiffer 2000: 9). Some of these irregularities include imperfect rhymes, identical couplets in sonnets 36 and 96, Sonnet 99 with fifteen lines, and an evidently misprinted second verse in Sonnet 146 (cf. Burrow 2002: 92).

There are, however, two other explanations for these irregularities. They could either merely be mistakes on the part of the typesetter or they could be regarded as evidence of an intentionally heterogeneous and ambiguous text inviting 'readerly activity' (ibid., 110). The fact that the sequence, much more than any other sonnet sequence at the time, lacks a clear linear narrative and often leaves the reader in doubt as to the gender of the desired person or the exact nature of the relationship between the characters, supports this impression.

Therefore, this lack of narrativity does not necessarily prove that the Quarto's order of poems is not Shakespeare's. As Heather Dubrow has argued, perhaps Shakespeare 'did not arrange these sonnets in a way that tells a clear story' (1996: 293). The lack of narrativity and the fact that the sequence demands 'readerly activity' would actually speak for the Quarto's order being Shakespeare's, as such a more demanding arrangement invites us to take a more active part in the production of meaning, as is also the case in his plays, I would argue. Moreover, as the discussion of narratives and mini-narratives in the next chapter will reveal, a narrative quality is not entirely absent from the sequence.

For the reasons given and since '[n]one of the proposed rearrangements has been more satisfactory than Q's' (Booth 2000: 546) I follow those critics who accept the Quarto's order of the sonnets. While Matz believes the 1609 order to be 'roughly correct' (2008: 15) for stylistic reasons, Burrow says about his own edition of the *Sonnets*: 'for me it was axiomatic that the artifact called Q "was" the sonnets, and that this physical thing, rather than any abstract conception of Shakespeare's intentions, or any hypothetical authorial manuscript, was what it was my job to present to readers' (2007: 161). In the end, the Quarto 'provides us with a remarkably stable text – one that is inclusive, well printed, and, for the majority of poems, without a textual rival. [. . .] it is the only Shakespearean "sonnet sequence" we have' (Traub 2003: 280).

Early editions of the *Sonnets*

The Quarto, apparently, did not sell well as no second edition was published until 1640 (the *Sonnets* were not included in the First Folio edition of the plays) and since copies of the 1609 edition show 'that the first printing was not read to pieces' (E/W 2013: 117). KDJ speculates that '[e]arly readers, like later ones, may have found the collection disconcerting, disappointing or even shocking' (2010: 69). One early annotator wrote in his copy after the final sonnet 'What a heap of wretched Infidel Stuff' (qtd. in ibid.).

When John Benson published his edition of the *Sonnets* in 1640, he included 146 of the original 154 sonnets, 'but in a jumbled order, intermingled with "The Phoenix and the Turtle," *A Lover's Complaint*, and the entire 1612 *Passionate Pilgrim* (most of which is not by Shakespeare) and other works by numerous poets, including Herrick, Jonson, Beaumont, and Milton' (Schiffer 2000: 17).

Benson sometimes also combined up to five sonnets into a single poem to which he gave titles like 'An Invitation to Marriage', 'Love's Relief', 'The Picture of True Love' and 'Self-Flattery of her Beauty' (cf. E/W 2013: 118). He also changed the addressee from male to female (cf. KDJ 2010: 74). E/W have pointed out, however, that Benson did not 'attempt to give the impression that the poems are addressed to a woman' (2013: 118; cf. also de Grazia 2000: 90).

After Benson's edition in 1640 no edition of the *Sonnets* appeared in print throughout the rest of the seventeenth century (E/W 2013: 119, 131). When Charles Gildon published his edition of the *Sonnets* in 1710, he used Benson's edition as his main source (cf. ibid.) which in turn led to numerous reprints and revisions of Benson's 1640 text over the course of the eighteenth century (in 1714, 1725, 1728, 1741, 1771, 1774 and 1775). Although the 1609 Quarto was reprinted in 1711 and further editions and reprints appeared in the course of the eighteenth century (for example, Bernard Lintot's edition in 1711 and George Steevens' reprint in 1766; cf. also the list of editions in Ingram/Redpath [1964] 1978: xxiv–xxv and E/W 2013: 119), Benson's edition remained the standard text until Edmond Malone published the *Sonnets* as a supplement to the Johnson and Steevens edition of Shakespeare's plays in 1780 (followed by a second edition in 1790). Since Malone's edition, the *Sonnets* have been mostly reprinted in the order of the 1609 Quarto although repeated attempts to reorder them have been undertaken.

Malone is credited with being the first modern editor of the *Sonnets* who provided his readers not only with the texts of the sonnets but also with 'textual notes and critical commentary, thus for the first time bringing the Sonnets into the Shakespearean canon' (Schiffer 2000: 20; cf. also E/W 2013: 119–20). While editors like George Steevens found many of the sonnets offensive and of questionable aesthetic and moral value (cf. Schiffer 2000: 21 and E/W 2013: 133), Malone showed a less normative attitude, as can be witnessed, for example, in his attempt to defend the homoerotic content of the *Sonnets* against charges of immorality by his contemporaries:

> Some part of this indignation might perhaps have been abated, if it had been considered that such addresses to men, however indelicate, were customary in our authour's [*sic*] time, and neither imported criminality, nor were esteemed indecorous. [. . .] To regulate our judgment of Shakspeare's [*sic*] poems by the modes of modern times, is surely as unreasonable as to try his plays by the rules of Aristotle. (1790: 207)

In trying to contextualize and historicize the *Sonnets*, and by not applying eighteenth-century moral standards to them, Malone may have been the first Shakespeare critic in a modern sense. At the same time, however, he was also the first editor who argued that the speaker in the sonnets and Shakespeare were the same (ibid.) and in doing so, rather ironically exposed Shakespeare to the moral criticism of those contemporaries he tried to defend him from.

The biographical interpretation may also explain why Steevens decided in 1793 to publish *The Plays of William Shakespeare* without the *Sonnets*. Responding to the strongly homoerotic Sonnet 20 with 'an equal mixture of disgust and indignation' (Malone 1780: 596), he defends his omission in the preface:

> We have not reprinted the Sonnets, &c. of Shakspeare [*sic*], because the strongest act of Parliament that could be framed, would fail to compel readers into their service; notwithstanding these miscellaneous Poems have derived every possible advantage from the literature and judgement of their only intelligent editor, Mr. Malone, whose implements of criticism [. . .] are on this occasion disgraced by the objects of their culture.—Had Shakspeare [*sic*] produced no other works than these, his name

would have reached us with as little celebrity as time has conferred on that of Thomas Watson, an older and much more elegant sonnetteer [*sic*]. (Steevens 1793: vii–viii)

The only value which the *Sonnets* have for Steevens derives from the critical work of his fellow editor Malone. Had Shakespeare written nothing else except the sonnets, he would have been nearly forgotten, Steevens concludes. Just as Malone was the first critic with a more objective approach to the *Sonnets*, Steevens can be credited with being the 'first writer to voice more or less explicit objections to the poems on moral as well as aesthetic grounds' (E/W 2013: 133).

The *Sonnets* as biography?

Do the *Sonnets* tell us something about Shakespeare's life? This question has occupied generations of readers and critics. But, as critics keep reminding us (and as Gurr's and Booth's readings of Sonnet 145 above have shown), we should be very careful equating the speaker with the poet Shakespeare (cf. E/W 2013: 22; Kerrigan [1986] 1999: 11; Callaghan 2022: 14). What is interesting about the question, however, is what it tells us about our readiness to assume that poems (unlike novels or plays) are immediate expressions of the author's feelings and that the events, figures and locations referred to must have a biographical relevance. The possibility that these poems, just like novels, plays and short stories could simply be just made up is all too often ignored. As the British poet Gavin Ewart wryly remarked in his 'Sonnet: Shakespeare's Universality': 'A playwright's material (unless it's outrageously slanted)/ usually deals with a group of opinions; people can never say/ "Of course this play is entirely autobiographical"' (vv. 6-8; qtd. in Gross 2003: 27). Why should the same not hold true for poems? Moreover, the notion that poems must be based on the author's life, was anything but accepted in Shakespeare's time. Jochen Petzold has recently drawn attention to Giles Fletcher's dedication prefaced to his sonnet sequence *Licia, or Poems of Love* (1593), where he writes 'a man may not be in love, and write of love, as well as of husbandry, and not go to plough: or of witches and be non: or of holiness and be flat profane' (qtd. in Petzold 2022: 24).

38   A COMPREHENSIVE GUIDE TO SHAKESPEARE'S SONNETS

The desire to equate the lyrical speaker with the author is very much indebted to the still very popular Romanticist understanding of poetry and the poet, according to which poems are the author's unmediated expressions of their feelings and thoughts. In Shakespeare's time, poetry was seen to serve a different function. According to Philip Sidney in his *Defense of Poesy*, poetry has an ethical function to 'delight and teach; [. . .] delight, to move men to take that goodness in hand, which without delight they would fly as from a stranger; and teach, to make them know that goodness whereunto they are moved' (2008: 218). A poet, as the name with a Greek origin implies, is a maker, an inventor. Consequently, poems are things made up and fabricated:

> The sonnet's lyric voice is a dramatic construct: authors refract their /I/ in different ways. The sonneteer may have his or her speaker narrate, to tell in effect a short story about a character distanced from /I-who-speaks/ at least as far as /I-that-was/ [. . .] he or she may dramatise, by inventing dialogue or creating the illusion of a hearer or interlocutor [. . .] he or she may indeed make the /I/ speak of itself in an unlocated present – the archetypal lyric position – but this last is only one of the possibilities open, and is thus a constructed choice, like any other stance the poesis creates. (Spiller 1992: 6)

The sonnets constantly draw attention to the fact that they are poems by way of metre, rhyme and a highly foregrounded language. To view the texts as unmediated expressions of the author's thoughts and feelings would negate their constructed character. The speaker in the sonnets is *not* Shakespeare, although critics like Don Paterson (2010: xiv), Robert Matz (2008: 11), P. D. McIntosh (2013) and, more recently, Steven Monte (2021) would like to convince us of the opposite.

Admittedly, 'all significant art is autobiographical' (Evans 1998: 111), at least to some extent. However, the fact that literature is always informed by biographical and historical contexts is different from equating a voice in the text with the voice of the author. As John Kerrigan has poignantly argued, although the distance between speaker and poet can vary, it is always there: 'The text [i.e. the *Sonnets*] is neither fictive nor confessional. Shakespeare stands behind the first person of his sequence as Sidney had stood behind

Astrophil – sometimes near the poetic 'I', sometimes farther off, but never without some degree of rhetorical projection' ([1986] 1999: 11).

Despite this *Guide*'s primary interest in the sonnets as textual artefacts and how they engage with themes and issues of their time, I will summarize, for the sake of completeness, some of the most often voiced theories on the identities of the main figures as well as the dedicatee.

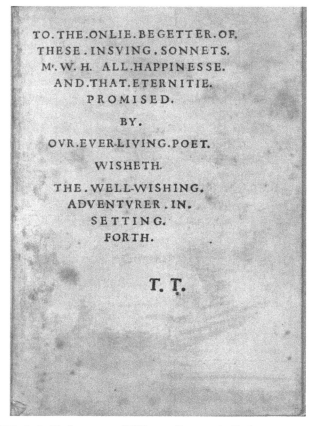

FIGURE 2.2 *Shakespeare, William. [Sonnets] Shake-speares sonnets. Neuer before imprinted. (London: G. Eld for T[homas]. T[horpe]. and are to be solde by William Aspley, 1609), dedication page (directly following title page).*

40   A COMPREHENSIVE GUIDE TO SHAKESPEARE'S SONNETS

The dedicatory page of the quarto edition has given rise to a lot of speculation. The fact that the publisher Thorpe signed it, supports the view that Shakespeare was not in London when the Quarto was published, otherwise he may have signed the dedication himself. The sonnets are dedicated to 'the only begetter [. . .]. Mr. W. H.,' which begs several questions. Who is the begetter? Is W. H. the begetter or are they different people? Could the 'youth' in the sonnets be modelled on W. H.? Could the other figures appearing in the sonnets, the woman and the rival poets, also be modelled on people Shakespeare knew?

These questions have been addressed independently although most critics assume that W. H. is the same person as the begetter. Nathan Drake, in 1817, was the first to propose Henry Wriothesley, Earl of Southampton as a candidate. Southampton had already been the dedicatee of Shakespeare's poems *Venus and Adonis* (1593) and *The Rape of Lucrece* (1594). Although there is no evidence that Shakespeare had any contact with Southampton since the publication of *The Rape of Lucrece*, it is possible that those sonnets which were most likely written at an earlier stage, in the 1590s, may also have been dedicated to or intended for the Earl.

Another candidate is William Herbert, third Earl of Pembroke, to whom the First Folio of Shakespeare's plays in 1623 was later dedicated. What could speak for Pembroke is the fact that he, like the youth in the *Sonnets*, was a confirmed bachelor and that he resisted marriage four times to four different women between 1595 and 1599.

There are also arguments, however, that speak against these candidates. In the case of Southampton, the initials H. W. only work if they are reversed (although this was in fact sometimes practised in prefatory matters, cf. Evans 1998: 116). A stronger argument against both Southampton and Pembroke is that it would have been very unlikely to address an Earl as 'Mr.' and, moreover, to associate an Earl with the strong homoerotic content that we find in many of the sonnets, as for example in Sonnet 20.

Apart from Southampton and Pembroke many other candidates have been suggested for the dedicatee (cf. Booth 2000: 547–8). Some of the most interesting suggestions include an actor by the name of Willy Hughes, first suggested by Edmond Malone and made famous by Oscar Wilde in his short story *The Portrait of Mr. W. H.* (cf. E/W 2013: 25 and Ellmann 1988: 279–82), Shakespeare's

THE TEXT   41

brother-in-law William Hathaway or even Shakespeare himself, 'W. H.' being a misprint for 'W. S.' or 'W. SH.' Another, more absurd theory claims that the *Sonnets* were written by an Anne Whateley who dedicated them to Shakespeare, 'using the second letter of his last name in order to confuse people' (Booth 2000: 548).

One should not forget, however, that the dedication, just like the lack of a linear narrative in the sequence, may have also been intentionally employed to add to the mystique and 'structural complexity' (Vendler 1999: 22) of the sequence. Burrow argues that this 'targeted anonymity' (2002: 101) as a strategy of intentionally obscuring the identity of the dedicatee was a common practice in Elizabethan erotic poetry. The use of misleading and obscure initials and hints could therefore have been intentional on the side of the publisher, a marketing scheme to increase the attraction and selling value of the volume (cf. Burrow 2002: 102–3). While Burrow jokingly suggests that 'W. H.' may stand for 'Who? He?' (ibid., 103), Orgel, based on a conversation he had had with the bibliographer Arthur Freeman, more earnestly suggests 'Whoever He (may be)' (2007: 143).

Similarly inconclusive are the (possible) real life identities that have been suggested for the speaker, the young man, the woman and the rival poets. Among those who have preferred an autobiographical reading, many assumed that the dedicatee of the *Sonnets* is also the young man, which, however, does not have to be the case. A lot depends on the meaning of the word 'begetter' in the dedication and the signature 'T. T.' beneath it. 'Begetter' could refer to the person who inspired the poems or to the author as procreator who 'begot', i.e. authored them. In the first case, it is possible that the dedicatee could also be the young man and that Thorpe signed the dedication in lieu of Shakespeare. In the latter case, Thorpe as publisher would have signed the dedication himself to dedicate the whole volume to the author, i.e. Shakespeare. The fact, however, that the term 'begetter' was rarely used in this context, makes this reading rather unlikely.

Many candidates have also been suggested for the female addressee in the sonnets (for an overview cf. Schoenbaum 1980: 228–36 and Hunt 2000: 371–8). Among them we find Mary Fitton, one of Queen Elizabeth's maids of honour and mistress of William Herbert (Schoenbaum 1980: 229), Elizabeth Vernon, a lady-in-waiting to Queen Elizabeth (Fleissner 2005: 86), Queen Elizabeth herself (Schoenbaum 1980: 228), Lucy Baynam aka Lucy Negro aka Black Luce, a dark-skinned prostitute (Schoenbaum 1980: 231; Salkeld 2023; MacDonald 2021), Emilia Lanier, mistress of Henry Carey, 1st Lord Hunsdon, Shakespeare's wife (Schoenbaum 1980: 229) and the wife of a former Stratford neighbour of Shakespeare's. However, and this may not come as a surprise, 'we have no clue whatsoever as to the woman's identity. Speculation on her identity has ranged from wanton to ludicrous and need not be illustrated' (Booth 2000: 549).

Similarly, some of Shakespeare's fellow playwrights and poets have been mentioned as possible candidates for the rival poets in the sequence who compete with the speaker for the love or patronage of the young man, the leading candidate being George Chapman, followed by Christopher Marlowe, Edmund Spenser, Thomas Nashe, and many others (cf. Booth 2000: 549; Evans 1998: 193–4; Matz 2008: 10). Again, '[t]here are no grounds for certainty that Shakespeare had any real particular poet(s) in mind' (Booth 2000: 549; cf. also Jackson 2005). Ultimately, biographical speculation on the identity of the addressees rests on the assumption that the speaker always addresses the same male or female person, an idea that is possible and probable, but also contested, as the next chapter will show.

Further reading

Dating: Burrow 2002: 103–11; Hieatt, Hieatt and Prescott 1991; KDJ 2010: 1–28; E/W 2020: 21–6; Jackson 1999b; Jackson 2002; Schoenfeldt 2010: 57–60. **Manuscript circulation**: Marotti 2007; Marotti/Freiman 2011. **Publication history**: Acker 2021; Burrow 2002: 91–103; KDJ 2010: 29–45; E/W 2013: 3–21, 117–30; Orgel 2007; Post 2017: 71–7.
Reception: E/W 2013: 131–76; Kingsley-Smith 2019; Kingsley-Smith and Rampone (eds) 2023; Pfister and Gutsch (eds) 2009; Schiffer 2000: 3–71.
Biographical contexts: E/W 2013: 22–7; KDJ 2010: 50–69; Dutton 2007; Hunt 2000; MacDonald 2021; Salkeld 2023; Schoenbaum 1980.

3

The Sequence, Dramatis Personae, and Form

After discussing the sonnet tradition and the early textual history of the *Sonnets* in the first two chapters, this chapter considers the structural aspects of both the sequence as a whole and the individual Shakespearean sonnet. It will do so by first approaching the structure and organization of the sequence, then by introducing its principal figures and the way in which their relationships affect the layout of the collection, and finally by describing the general formal features of the Shakespearean sonnet as well as its variations.

The sequence

Notwithstanding the lack of information we have about Shakespeare's involvement in the publication of the 1609 Quarto (see above), many critics identify a narrative order in them. While MacDonald P. Jackson argues that the 'sonnets are placed as Shakespeare intended' (1999a: 114), Joseph Pequigney, who is also credited with being the first critic to champion a homoerotic reading of the *Sonnets* (see below), claims that 'the Sonnets in Q are unimpeachably ordered' (1985: 213). He divides the sequence into four groups. While the first 126 poems are addressed to a young man describing 'the growth of love (Sonnets 1–19), its maturity (Sonnets 20–99) and its decline (Sonnets 100–126)' (ibid., 5), the final twenty-eight sonnets are addressed to a woman and focus on the cycle of lust with its circular stages of desire, consummation, aftermath and resuscitation of desire, epitomized in Sonnet 129

44   A COMPREHENSIVE GUIDE TO SHAKESPEARE'S SONNETS

(ibid., 155–88). Neil L. Rudenstine sees an even more detailed narrative. According to him, the *Sonnets* tell the story of 'betrayals or transgressions by the two main figures [the speaker and the youth], from the beginning to the end of the work' (Rudenstine 2015: 13). He identifies a narrative that begins with an acknowledgement of love between speaker and young man (sonnets 1–20), continues with doubts regarding the latter's faithfulness (sonnets 21–32), the youth's betrayal and abandonment of the speaker, the youth's admission of regret (sonnets 33–36), a phase of separation (sonnets 37–39) and the introduction of the speaker's mistress who is unfaithful to both youth and speaker (sonnets 40–42). The speaker then attempts to discover the youth's true nature (sonnets 43–75), with the latter temporarily rejecting the speaker for a rival poet (sonnets 76–86). Consequently, the speaker oscillates between hope and despair and criticizes the young man (sonnets 87–96). After a longer separation, the speaker is reconciled with the youth, becomes unfaithful himself and is eventually reunited with the youth (sonnets 97–120), which causes the speaker to make new professions of love (sonnets 121–126). The speaker's attention then returns to his desire and lust for the mistress in sonnets 127–154 (cf. Rudenstine 2015: 11–13; cf. also Appendix 1 below).

Another design of the sequence was recently propounded by Steven Monte who, inspired by Alastair Fowler's (1970) reading, argues that the collection 'has a pyramidal organisation' (Monte 2021: 29) based on numbers and recurring keywords, and that it 'consists of seventeen groups of poems whose first group contains seventeen sonnets, and whose subsequent groups decrease in size incrementally from sixteen sonnets to one poem' (ibid., 2).

Burrow, on the other hand, argues the *Sonnets* are 'a structured miscellany of recurrent themes, passions, and thoughts, rather than a story or a mathematically ordered sequence' (2002: 118). They contain in fact 'many possible stories' (ibid.). For Burrow, it is this lack of structure and of an overall narrative that must be seen as the *Sonnets'* most outstanding and intriguing quality, and not as their deficit.

James Schiffer sees five main functions in the *Sonnets'* 'anti-narrativity' (2007: 48): it heightens the poems' dramatic effect, it creates in the (early modern) reader a 'voyeuristic pleasure' (ibid., 50), it stimulates the readers' 'pleasures of detection and invention' (ibid.), it 'replicate[s] in the reader the speaker's experience of disorientation, confusion, and uncertainty' (ibid., 51), and, finally, by 'arousing and then frustrating the desire for story and narrative closure' (ibid., 52), Shakespeare forces the reader into 'lyric attentiveness' (ibid.). In this regard, Burrow reminds us that the term 'sequence' which suggests 'linearity and its promise of unity was not used of sonnet books in the period' (2002: 110). E/W therefore suggest to rather view the *Sonnets* as a 'collection' (2013: 28) with an 'impressionistic narrative [, . . .] a patchwork composed of separately woven pieces of cloth [. . .] that has only a deceptive, though at times satisfying, unity' (ibid., 46; cf. Edmondson 2013). In the following, I shall supply an overview of some of the most apparent groups and narratives that have been identified in the collection up to now.

The division most widely accepted since Edmund Malone's edition in 1780 (cf. Burrow 2007: 159) is between two large groups: the sonnets addressed to or about a young man (sonnets 1–126) and the sonnets addressed to or about a woman (127–154), the latter group ending with two sonnets (153 and 154) written in a highly erotic style. Both are revisions of an epigram on the god of love by the Byzantine sixth-century poet Marianus Scholasticus (cf. KDJ 2010: 422) and argue that the speaker's love for his mistress cannot be quenched. The two poems are characterized by a bawdy tone with references to sexually transmitted diseases.

John Kerrigan ([1986] 1999) adds a further group, the poem *A Lover's Complaint* with which the *Sonnets* were published in the 1609 Quarto. It consists of forty-seven rhyme royal stanzas (containing seven verses in iambic pentameter with the rhyme scheme *ababbcc*), and there are in fact many reasons why viewing it as an integral part of the *Sonnets* makes sense. As Burrow (2002: 140) and Dubrow (2007) have pointed out, many sonnet sequences of the time are followed by poems which can be understood as providing variations of the collection's main theme.

In *A Lover's Complaint* we find a young woman who complains to an old man that she was pursued, seduced and finally abandoned by a young man, only to conclude that she would succumb to his charms again. The triangle of young woman, young man and old man seems like a comment on and variation of the triangle which we can also identify in the *Sonnets*. Moreover, the narrative structure of the poem creates similar problems and ambiguities to those found in the *Sonnets*. For example, often it is not clear who is speaking in the *Complaint*: the old man who falls upon the young woman complaining, the young woman who tells her story to the old man, or the young man speaking to the young woman.

The division into a group of sonnets addressed to a male (1–126) and a group addressed to a female (127–154), however, is not as neat as one may think or wish. First, we do not really know whether the sonnets in each group are all addressed to the same person. E/W argue that it remains unclear whether the first seventeen sonnets, the so-called procreation sonnets (see Chapter 4), 'are all directed towards the same man, or to several men, or to men in general' (2020: 29; cf. also ibid., 2013: 23).

Secondly, we cannot be certain that the addressees are always male in the first group and female in the second group, 'for what Malone's clear-cut division has obscured is the astonishing number of sonnets that do not make the gender of the addressee explicit. Shakespeare is exceptional among the English sonneteers [. . .] in leaving the beloved's gender unspecified in so many of the sonnets: about five-sixths of them in the first 126 and just less than that in the collection entire' (de Grazia 2000: 97).

While the 'sweet boy' (v. 5) in Sonnet 108, the 'lovely Boy' (v. 1) in Sonnet 126 and even the 'tender churl' (v. 12) in Sonnet 1 define the addressee as being male, some sonnets do not reveal the gender at all (e.g. sonnets 2, 7, 12). Others are more subtle about revealing the gender of the addressee, such as Sonnet 11, in which the speaker argues in the final couplet, 'She [nature] carved thee for her seal, and meant thereby/ Thou shouldst print more [images of yourself], not let that copy die' (vv. 13-14). The words 'seal' and 'print' in early modern reproductive discourse referred to fathering and not to mothering a child. The same can be said about the group of sonnets 127–152. While some of them clearly refer to a 'mistress' (127.9, 130.1), a 'she' or 'her' (138.1, 2) or '[h]er pretty looks' (139.10), others are less concrete (cf. sonnets 131, 132; cf. also Tetzeli von Rosador 2000: 582).

E/W (2013: 30–1) differentiate between five groups: (a) 'Sonnets which suggest a male addressee', (b) 'Sonnets which might imply a male addressee' because of their context but which could also imply 'a female if read independently', (c) 'Sonnets which suggest a female addressee', (d) sonnets where the context implies a female but also suggest a male 'if read independently', and (e) four 'Sonnets which

THE SEQUENCE, DRAMATIS PERSONAE, AND FORM   47

refer to male and female subjects'. In another publication, E/W provide a helpful overview of possible addressees in the sonnets which lists 121 sonnets as being addressed to people, six sonnets as being directed to abstract concepts (such as Love, Time, or the Muse), twenty-five as general meditations and two as translations of the same Greek epigram (cf. 2020: 28–9).

In the end, however, the authors can list only ten sonnets in which the addressee's gender is not stated or suggested by context. The other 144 would in fact 'suggest' or 'imply' (ibid., 30) a specific gender. As de Grazia concedes, Malone was not entirely wrong: 'clearly no sonnets are addressed to a female in the first 126 and none to a male (except Cupid) in the subsequent twenty-eight. [. . .] Some kind of binary division appears to be at work' (2000: 97–8).

What we can also say in support of the theory that the *Sonnets* can be divided into two groups addressed to or about a male and female character is the fact that sonnets 1–126 seem to be arranged more 'carefully in order' (Burrow 2002: 118) and that sonnets 127– 154 form a 'very disparate group' (ibid., 132) and are 'much less carefully ordered than the preceding group' (ibid.). Also, the fact that many of the addressees in each of the two groups share a number of features and 'context, or subject matter' (E/W 2013: 31) supports a division into two different groups: young, beautiful, and childless in the case of the addressee in sonnets 1–126; dark appearance, morally corrupt, older, and experienced in the case of the addressee in sonnets 127–152. In this introduction I will therefore, like all the scholarly editions of the *Sonnets* consulted for this *Guide*, operate with, and refer to, this division (for an overview of the addressee's identity or addressees' identities for each sonnet cf. Appendix 3 below).

Apart from the youth and mistress sequences, other, smaller groups and mini-narratives within and across the youth and mistress groups have been identified (cf. Appendix 1 below). The first seventeen sonnets in the sequence, for example, are referred to as the procreation sonnets. They have in common that the speaker urges the young man to produce children so that his beauty and memory will be preserved. They approach this theme, however, from various angles and will be discussed in greater detail in Chapter 4.

Another mini-sequence to be found in the sonnets deals with rival poets (sonnets 78–80, 82–86). In some of these sonnets, the speaker refers to just one rival (sonnets 79, 80, 86), in others to more than one (sonnets 78, 82–85). In all these sonnets, the speaker identifies or refers to rival poets who have also praised the young man's beauty and are therefore for the speaker not only rivals in poetry but also rivals in love. As in the procreation sonnets, we find different expressions and variations of the main argument. While the speaker in Sonnet 78 argues that the young man should prefer the speaker's sonnets over the sonnets of rival poets because he, the speaker, is so dependent on the young man's love, he claims in Sonnet 80 that, although the poems of the rival poet may be aesthetically superior to his own poems, his love exceeds that of the other poet. In sonnets 82 and 83, the speaker states on the other hand that his style, although plainer and less elaborate than that of the rival poets, is more sincere and appropriate in praising the young man. Sonnet 84 argues that the rival poets exaggerate in their praise of the young man and accuses the latter of enjoying this kind of flattery. Sonnet 81, in the middle of this sequence, does not include any reference at all to rival poets. It returns instead to the notion of immortalizing the young man through writing, thematized earlier in the sequence (cf. Booth 2000: 546; for a detailed discussion of the rival poet sequence, see Chapter 5).

Throughout the *Sonnets*, Shakespeare keeps changing between and returning to narratives, themes and motifs, as becomes evident, for example, in Sonnet 59. This sonnet, which follows a number of sonnets dealing with the speaker's separation from the young man, rather suddenly introduces the theme of previous poets writing about subjects less worthy than the young man, thereby anticipating the rival-poets sequence referred to above.

Critics have also drawn attention to other mini-sequences, such as the love-triangle sonnets about the relationship between speaker, young man and the woman (sonnets 40–42, 133–134 and 144; cf. E/W 2020: 28; KDJ 2010: 190; Paterson 2010: 120), the sonnets thematizing the speaker's separation from the young man (sonnets 27–31, 43–45, 48, 50–52, 56–58, 61, 87–93, 97–99, 109, 110, 113, 114), sonnets 71–74 on the speaker's 'proximity to death' (Cousins 2011: 128), or a large group of 'jealousy sonnets' (Pequigney 1985: 102), which are scattered across the entire sequence.

Thematic pairing is another linking device in the sequence in which two sonnets are connected by thematic correspondences or

THE SEQUENCE, DRAMATIS PERSONAE, AND FORM 49

by a continuation of the story. These are either neighbouring pairs, like sonnets 44–45, 46–47, 50–51, 56–57, 113–114, 135–136, 153–154 (cf. also Tetzeli von Rosador 2000: 582), or pairs separated by other sonnets such as sonnets 8 + 128, 34 + 120, and 77 + 122.

The neighbouring sonnets 44 and 45, for example, thematize the speaker's separation from the young man and employ concepts and ideas from medieval humoral pathology, according to which the world, including human beings, consists of the four elements earth, water, air and fire, which correspond to the four humours (and character traits) black bile (melancholic), phlegm (phlegmatic), blood (sanguine) and yellow bile (choleric). While the first two, heavier, elements earth and water dominate Sonnet 44, the 'quicker elements' (45.5) prevail in the second. In the first of the two sonnets, we can detect once again the typical syllogistic 'When'/'Then' strategy referred to in the first chapter: the speaker's proposition or rather wish to travel like thoughts across 'sea and land' (44.7) to be with his beloved (first and second quatrain) is followed by the realization that this is impossible (44.9-10) and the conclusion that this impossible desire can leave him only with 'heavy tears' and 'woe' (44.14). The heavy elements, earth and water, characterize the entire poem. References to the 'dull substance' of the speaker's 'flesh' (44.1), his 'foot' (44.5), 'earth' (44.6, 11), 'sea and land' (44.7), 'water' (44.11), the 'elements so slow' (44.13) and the 'heavy tears' (44.14) emphasize the material nature of the speaker and its detrimental effect on the relationship with the youth.

Sonnet 45, on the other hand, focuses on the speaker's thoughts and desire which are related to 'slight air, and purging fire' (45.1). Because the speaker acknowledges in the earlier sonnet that he cannot 'jump both sea and land' (44.7), he can only send his 'thought' (45.3) and 'desire' (ibid.) in 'tender embassy of love' (45.6) to the youth. This, however, leaves him even more depressed since once the 'quicker elements' (45.5) air and fire (i.e. thought and desire) have departed, he is left with the two heavy elements which make him sink 'down to death, oppressed with melancholy' (45.8). The sonnet is characterized by a sophisticated reciprocal relationship between the slower and quicker elements: the speaker's thoughts return to him with news from the beloved which gives him joy, but only for a moment, as this only increases his desire to be with him. So, he sends the thoughts back to the young man, leaving him 'sad' (45.14) and oppressed again. As long as he is separated from the young man, the speaker therefore finds himself in a state of constant restlessness and unfulfilled desire. Expressions like 'slight' (45.1), 'with swift motion slide' (45.4), 'quicker' (45.5) and 'swift' (45.10) contrast with the respective antonyms in the previous sonnet. Although each sonnet can stand on its own, the two together create a unity that exceeds their own. E/W (2020: 18–19) find altogether nineteen pairs of this kind and fourteen mini-sequences covering 100 sonnets in the collection (cf. also the table 'Groups of sonnets' in ibid., 2013: 33).

Yet another organizing principle in the *Sonnets* are numbers. In her introduction to the Arden edition, KDJ comments on some of the numerological readings of the *Sonnets*. She argues, for example, that if one dismisses from the sequence the unfinished 'non-sonnet' (KDJ 2010: 99) number 126, one can identify two groups in the young-man sequence: the procreation sonnets 1–17 and the remaining ones 18–125, 'in which the speaker for the first time expresses his own devotion to the youth, and determination to immortalize his beauty in "eternal lines"' (ibid., 100). This second group consists of 108 sonnets, the same number we find in Sidney's highly influential sonnet sequence *Astrophil and Stella* briefly discussed above. Shakespeare is not the only poet to use that number. Sidney's close friend Fulke Greville also included 108 sonnets in his lyric sequence *Caelica*, published posthumously in 1633. Shakespeare's Sonnet 108 also seems to nod to Sidney's sequence with the speaker taking 'stock of his achievements' (KDJ 2010: 326) and complaining that he can find no new way of expressing his love, a sentiment that we also find in many of Sidney's sonnets, especially the first of the sequence (see the discussion in Chapter 5).

As regards the twenty-eight sonnets addressed to or about the mistress, KDJ (2010: 99) suggests that the number corresponds to the lunar month and menstrual cycle and that the sequence thereby draws attention to the physical and corrupted relationship between the speaker and the woman. Individual sonnets have also been read in a numerological way: Sonnet 12 in which the speaker 'count[s] the clock that tells the time' (v. 1; cf. Burrow 2002: 404), the 'embarrassingly anatomical' (KDJ 2010: 101) Sonnet 20, whose number corresponds to the twenty fingers and toes of the human body, sonnets 49 and 63, which have been understood to refer to the minor and grand climacteric respectively, the ages at which 'a

THE SEQUENCE, DRAMATIS PERSONAE, AND FORM 51

person was considered to be particularly liable to change in health or fortune' (*OED*, 'climacteric, n., 2.a'; cf. Burrow 2002: 108; for numerological interpretations of sonnets 52, 60, 70, 71, 126 and 144 cf. KDJ 2010: 100; Booth 2000: 545–46).

Shakespeare's *Sonnets*, then, do not tell a straightforward story, and too 'often the reader is left with large gaps in the story' (Matz 2008: 6), a quality that Emma Smith calls 'gappiness' (2020: 2) and identifies as the defining feature of Shakespeare's works. The aesthetic value of the *Sonnets* lies precisely in the way they frustrate our narrative expectations, with their 'jolts and sudden shifts of tack between groups' (Burrow 2002: 109). In view of this lack of narrativity and the 'patterned' (ibid., 111) quality of the *Sonnets*, I will propose to organize the collection by identifying five thematic clusters (see Chapter 4).

Dramatis personae

When addressing the relationships between the figures in the collection we should keep in mind to treat them as fictional constructs, as 'literary sign[s]' (Hunt 2000: 370), as Marvin Hunt advises us in his discussion of the mistress. Secondly, even treating the figures as fictional constructs does not automatically imply that they always have to be the same fictional character. As E/W argue, the poems' 'addressees may not remain constant throughout the collection' (2013: 40) and their 'characteristics may not inhere in any single individual, whether real or imaginary' (ibid.). The fact that the speaker repeatedly contradicts himself and suggests different strategies in negotiating his relationships with the youth and the mistress (cf. the chapters on the theme clusters below), makes the idea that we are maybe dealing with different youths and mistresses not entirely implausible.

Therefore, rather than to think of speaker, youth, mistress and rival poet as fully rounded individual characters in the collection, I would suggest to follow E/W who conceive of them as 'at least four *kinds* of persons' (ibid., 39; my emphasis) whose relationships with and attitudes towards each other are acted out as on a stage: a poetic voice, a male desired other, a female desired other and another person who is involved with both objects of desire (cf. ibid.).

The speaker

Although it is possible that the speaker 'may be reimagined as female' (E/W 2013: 39), much of the evidence points to him being a man. For example, in many sonnets the speaker is either explicitly or implicitly characterized as a man in his sexual relationship with the mistress described in sonnets 127–152 or his sexual incompatibility with the youth in Sonnet 20. We also find sexual puns on male genitalia, for example in Sonnet 151, and references to a male Christian name in sonnets 135 and 136. Furthermore, and as we will see in Chapter 5, in many sonnets, especially in the sequence to and about the youth, the speaker describes himself as a poet, a public role in Shakespeare's time which was almost exclusively associated with and performed by men rather than women.

The speaker is also not young anymore: in Sonnet 138 he says his 'days are past the best' (v. 6) and refers to himself as being 'old' (v. 10; cf. also 62.10), and he is certainly older than the young man addressed in the first group (cf. e.g. sonnets 12 and 73). He has an intimate relationship with both the young man and the woman, but he never says that he is married (E/W 2013: 40), although it can be inferred that the married state of the speaker is maybe one of the possible reasons for the temporary separation from the youth (cf. the discussion of the separation sonnets in Chapters 6 and 8). In sonnets 135, 136 and 145, the speaker reveals that his (but also the youth's) name might be 'Will'. While the predominantly physical relationship with the woman is mostly associated with corruption, disease and lust, the love and desire for the young man is generally expressed in more 'loving terms' (E/W 2013: 41; for a detailed discussion see Chapter 6 below).

The youth

The young man is alternatively addressed or referred to as 'youth', 'sweet boy', 'friend', 'thou', 'you' and 'he' (see Burrow 2002: 123). As we will see, by using these different terms and alternating between the respectful and polite 'you' and the more intimate 'thou' the speaker highlights different and contradictory qualities of his relationship with the youth (for the difference between 'you' and 'thou' see Hope 1999: 246–8) which can be intimate, respectful,

THE SEQUENCE, DRAMATIS PERSONAE, AND FORM 53

erotic and even contemptuous. Burrow suggests using the term 'friend' for the male addressee in the first group as it encompasses all these possible meanings and does not restrict this figure to one particular role (cf. also E/W (2013: 68) and Garber (2004: 293) on the semantic overlap of 'friend' and 'lover'). I will, however, use the terms 'youth' and 'young man' instead to refer to the male addressee since 'friend' seems to downplay the intimate physical relationship that exists between the two men.

We do not learn a lot about the youth as the sonnets reveal 'very little by way of portraiture' (Schalkwyk 2002: 8). Although the speaker keeps praising the young man's beauty, he 'remains relatively colourless' (Salkeld 2023: 338). We do not really find out anything specific about his looks, apart from the fact that he resembles his mother (3.9). He is younger than the speaker, unmarried (E/W 2013: 41) and, much to the speaker's disappointment and frustration, childless. Poets other than the speaker have also celebrated his beauty and his name might also be Will (sonnets 135, 136). He has been unfaithful to the speaker (sonnets 33–35, 40–42, 48), has a relationship with the speaker's loved one(s) (sonnets 40–42, 133, 134 and 144) and we learn – rather unusual for the sequence in its specificity – that the speaker has known him for three years ('Three beauteous springs to yellow autumn turned', 104.5; cf. also Tetzeli von Rosador 2000: 582).

The mistress

Unlike the 'colourless' youth, the mistress is given greater depth in that we receive more information about her personality and appearance: 'She appears to have been musical ([Sonnet] 128), real (130), controlling (131), compellingly attractive (132), dominating (133), sexually available to other men (135), given to lying (138), cruel or proud (140) and likely to pass on a venereal infection (144)' (Salkeld 2023: 338).

She is also described as sexually insatiable (sonnets 135 and 136), depraved (Sonnet 137), unfaithful (sonnets 139, 142, 152) and deceitful (Sonnet 152). By endowing her with these attributes the mistress becomes a foil for both the youth and the speaker. The mistress's experience and the physical relationship she has with the speaker are juxtaposed with the young man's beauty, his youth and the admiration the speaker has for the young man. At the same time, the speaker recognizes some of the mistress's traits in the youth and himself as the speaker also accuses the young man (sonnets 69 and 70) and himself (sonnets 109 and 110, 117–121) of betrayal, deception and depravity. As I will show in the following chapters, just as the figure of the mistress is necessary to comprehend the nature of the relationship between speaker and youth, so the youth is necessary to understand the speaker's relationship with the mistress (cf. also Chapter 6 below).

The mistress was also often referred to as the 'dark lady' although this title is used nowhere in the sequence. Only once is she explicitly referred to 'as dark as night' (147.14; cf. Pequigney 1985: 144 and Gray 2011: 31). The idea of a 'dark lady' mostly stems from the fact that in five of the sonnets about the mistress the word 'black' occurs in various contexts. In sonnets 127, 130 and 132, the term has a positive connotation: the mistress's 'raven black' (127.9) eyes are considered beautiful (127.13–14, 132.4), referred to as 'loving mourners' (132.3), and express pity for the speaker's 'pain' (132.4). Her black hair, although described as 'black wires' (130.4), is considered as 'rare/ As any she belied with false compare' (130.13-14), and her dark 'complexion' (132.14) is praised as beautiful. In the other two sonnets, however, the speaker refers to her 'black [. . .] deeds' (131.13) and concludes that although he has praised her fairness, she, i.e. her character, is in fact as 'black as hell' (147.14). Furthermore, the speaker also describes her as 'a woman coloured ill' (144.4) with breasts that are 'dun' (130.3), i.e. of a 'a dull greyish-brown colour, typical of the coats of donkeys, mice, and numerous other animals' (*OED*, 'dun, adj., 1.a').

Describing the mistress's exterior and interior as dark and black raises several important questions. Which aspects of the mistress do these signifiers exactly refer to? What is the connection between her external and internal 'blackness'? Where do the positive and negative connotations of blackness and darkness come from and what can they tell us about an understanding of race at Shakespeare's time?

Let us approach those questions by looking at the first sonnet of the mistress sequence, Sonnet 127. Here the speaker argues that the mistress with her 'raven black' (v. 9) eyes and, by implication, a dark complexion conforms to a new ideal of beauty. While '[i]n the old age black was not counted fair' (v. 1), the fashion has now

THE SEQUENCE, DRAMATIS PERSONAE, AND FORM   55

changed and black is 'beauty's successive heir' (v. 3). But while fair women feel impelled to darken their appearance with the use of cosmetics ('with art's false borrowed face', v. 6) and thereby 'profaned' (v. 8) true beauty, the mistress does not need to do that since her 'raven black' (v. 9) eyes are a sign of natural black beauty.

Scholars have drawn attention to the critical attitude towards women's cosmetic practices in general and blackening practices in particular at Shakespeare's time. Cosmetics were believed to have a contagious effect (cf. Loomba 2016: 240), to 'rub off' on a woman's inner being:

> Literature of the period associated femininity with artifice on the grounds that women were given to cosmetic practices that distort the 'raw matter' of the body in its natural simplicity. Worse yet, painting was not merely a surface-level intervention, a temporary adornment that could be removed to restore the subject to her unadulterated state. The shockingly toxic ingredients conscripted into early modern beauty routines could permanently alter the skin, hair and neurological systems of those who used them. (Gordon 2020: 272)

The speaker in Sonnet 127 even introduces an element of mockery in his description of the mistress's superior natural black beauty by suggesting that his mistress's black eyes mourn for and pity those unfortunate women who require cosmetics to create a false dark complexion: 'Her eyes so suited, and they mourners seem/ At such who, not born fair, no beauty lack,/ Sland'ring creation with a false esteem' (vv. 10-12). These lines are difficult to understand because they hinge on a central paradox. 'Fair' in this poem is used in a double sense, meaning both 'of a light complexion' and 'beautiful'. In that sense, 'black' is turned into 'white' and 'foul' (v. 6) into 'fair'. The couplet concludes that the fact that the mistress pities those rivals who are 'not born fair' (v. 11) only increases her attractiveness for everyone.

The volta in verse 9 ('Therefore') adds an interesting twist to the argument of the poem. Is the speaker saying in this line that he chose a dark woman as his mistress *because* now 'is black beauty's successive heir' (v. 3) or is he saying that 'his mistress has chosen her own fashionable eye-colour' (KDJ 2010: 368)? The former reading would undermine the uniqueness of the mistress, since it would mean that the speaker has chosen her not because she is so different from but because she is so much like the other 'fair' women. The latter interpretation could refer to the practice of using the plant *atropa belladonna*, also known as deadly nightshade, to dilate the pupils and thereby simulate darker eyes (cf. Stuart 2004; Schneckenburger 2023: 168, 173). Paul Innes offers a third interpretation by suggesting that the word 'Therefore' draws attention to the fact that the mistress is not real but a poetic construct (cf. 1997: 179–81), a reading that is in line with viewing Sonnet 130, discussed in greater detail in Chapter 5, as an anti- or meta-Petrarchan statement debunking or deconstructing the conventions and beauty conceptions of an outdated literary discourse. This could also explain why the speaker argues that while in 'the old age black was not counted fair' (127.1) it is now regarded as 'beauty's successive heir' (127.3): the beauty ideal once championed by Petrarchan poets (fair skin, golden hair, bright eyes) along with its hyperbolic tropes has now been replaced by a counter model and a more sincere type of poetry.

For a long time, this was in fact the traditional view of the mistress's 'black' features: to see them primarily in the context of a vague early modern aesthetics (according to which anything dark or black represents the opposite of purity, innocence and beauty) and as denoting her 'moral blackness' (Innes 1997: 185). But as Ania Loomba (and other scholars) have shown, one needs to also consider the specific socio-cultural contexts of Shakespeare's time and to acknowledge that 'seventeenth-century English ideas about blackness and slavery [. . .] rework medieval notions of skin colour, labour, and religious difference' (2016: 235). The recognition that blackness has, since biblical times, been associated with faithlessness, sin, stubbornness of faith, and ingratitude (cf. ibid., 238–40) has come to challenge 'literary criticism's traditional (and almost pathological) insistence that blackness means nothing beyond its antithesis to "whiteness"' (Hall 1996: 69; cf. also Hall [1998] 2008).

Also, seminal studies like Shyllon (1977), Hall (1996), Habib (2000; 2008) and more recent work by Olusoga (2016), Kaufmann (2017), Nubia (2019) and Sanghera (2021) has shown that the idea of a 'pure white London' (Karim-Cooper 2021: 22) in Shakespeare's age is 'a false narrative' (ibid.). Contrary to earlier claims that Black people in sixteenth-century London were 'rare enough to have stimulated Shakespeare's and Southampton's interest' (Fleissner 1973: 315) and that there was 'little or no hostility toward members of a different race' (ibid. 2005: 76), these studies have shown that the second half of the sixteenth century saw 'a radical increase in the numbers of black people in England' (Habib 2008: 65).

Many scholars have therefore called for a greater awareness of a racialized ideology emerging in Shakespeare's time and for an acknowledgment of the fact that early modern racism and xenophobia did in fact exist (cf. Dadabhoy 2021: 30; Espinosa 2016: 63; Little 2016: 93; Loomba 2002: 52; Park 2023: 269). Not only has it been argued that 'the concept of race existed for Shakespeare and his contemporaries' (Thompson 2021a: 2), but that early modern plays also give 'evidence of the ways race was being constructed in the period [. . .] by a social process that one might call race-making or "racecraft"' (ibid., 7) at a time of 'intensified English interest in colonial travel and African trade' (Hall 1996: 3). Therefore, when in the sixteenth century, because of intensifying trade relations and early forms of slavery (cf. Shyllon 1977: 6; Loomba 2002: 13), the English, Londoners in particular, witnessed an increase in Black population, 'Blackness was a staple (although not static) ingredient in images of wildness, of evil, of class difference, and of female disorderliness' (Loomba 2000: 207; cf. also Loomba 2002: 36, 47). It is therefore very possible that the majority of people in early modern England would 'have reacted with racist fear, judgement, and even wonder' (Karim-Cooper 2021: 22) when encountering people of colour and that this attitude would have been reflected in the literary works of the time.

Imtiaz Habib, however, has drawn attention to the contrast between the increasing presence of Black people in England on the one hand and the few acknowledgements of them 'as a distinct, considerable population' (2008: 4) on the other. He conceives of them as a 'secret black population' (ibid., 101), not perceived in public and 'imperceptible in the cultural acknowledgements of the age' (ibid., 7). He argues that even when they become visible in popular representations of the time, such as in the works of Kyd, Marlowe, Jonson and Shakespeare – Thompson (2021a: 6) refers to between fifty and seventy plays between 1579 and 1642 that include racialized figures – 'their historical reality fades under the deformative force of cultural metaphor and becomes exotic fiction' (Habib 2008: 7), just as the contours of the mistress remain diffuse through the general and vague references to black and dark attributes.

Some scholars had in fact no doubts that the mistress is of African or Caribbean origin. The first to do so was the German poet and novelist Wilhelm Jordan in 1861, on account of her curly black hair ('black wires', 130.4) and 'hot-blooded coquetry' (qtd. in Schoenbaum 1980: 231). G. B. Harrison followed in 1933, suggesting that the mistress is a Black prostitute from London's brothels, an idea on which Anthony Burgess based his 1964 historical novel, *Nothing Like the Sun*. While these approaches are more concerned with the real-life identity of the mistress (see also Chapter 2), later scholars have been more interested in how her fictional Black identity is constructed. Robert F. Fleissner bases his argument for an African or West Indian origin of the mistress predominantly on evidence from sonnets 127, 130 and 132: her 'lips were less red than those of a Caucasian' (1973: 316), her 'black wires' (130.4) and her 'dun' (130.3) skin would show that Shakespeare did not have a Caucasian but 'a mixture of different bloods or West Indian' (Fleissner 1973: 316) in mind, suggested also by evidence from Sonnet 131, and, most conclusively for Fleissner, the couplet of Sonnet 132, which 'point[s] to a woman who is black in more than the color of her hair' (ibid., 317).

Marvin Hunt (2000), Margreta de Grazia (2000), and Abdulla Al-Dabbagh (2012) also argue that 'black' refers to the mistress's skin colour. While Hunt has supported his argument by showing how widespread the literary practice of 'praising the beauty of black women' (Hunt 2000: 379) was at the time, de Grazia has drawn attention to the subversive power of an interracial union between the 'fair', white men and the Black mistress (cf. 2000: 105–6). Al-Dabbagh even boldly claims (without, however, providing specific evidence) that Shakespeare, in staging the relationship between a Black mistress and white speaker, 'defiantly rejected conventions and racist stereotyping' (2012: 27) and prevailed over 'social prejudices' (ibid.).

After all, we do not have conclusive evidence as to the ethnic identity of the fictional mistress. Unlike in so many other English poems of the sixteenth and seventeenth centuries, such as William Dunbar's 'Ane Blak Moir', Eldred Revett's 'One Enamour'd on a Black-Moor' and George Herbert's 'A Negress Courts Cestus, a Man of a Different Colour' (cf. Hunt 2000: 378–83, Fleissner 2005:

48–57, and the twenty-six poems in the appendix of Hall 1996), in which the African origin of the woman is unmistakably referred to, we do not find similarly concrete markers in Shakespeare's *Sonnets*.

However, in the end, it does not really matter that Shakespeare leaves us in doubt as to the precise nature of the mistress's 'black' features. As Roland Greene has noted about early modern colonial discourse, colour itself is 'one of the most semantically weighted categories in European writing about the New World' (1995: 148); so when the speaker refers to the colour black to describe the mistress's negative attributes ('a woman coloured ill', 144.4; 'black as hell', 147.14) and also feels the need to 'rehabilitate' this blackness by redefining it as a new type of authentic beauty, it alerts us to the forms and context of 'premodern race-making and racecraft' (Park 2023: 269) outlined above.

The rival poet

While speaker, youth, and mistress to varying degrees are given at least some contour, not a lot can be said about the character and appearance of the rival poet. In the sonnets in which he appears (sonnets 78–80, 82–86), he remains even more indeterminate and vague than the other actors in the sequence, 'a shadowy player in the drama' (E/W 2013: 45). Sometimes the speaker's rival is referred to as being a part of a group of poets, as in sonnets 78, 82–85, at other times he is mentioned only in the singular but remains nameless and faceless. He is 'thy poet' (79.7), a 'better spirit' (80.2), 'another' (79.4) or merely a 'He' (79.8) whose poetry is superior but also less sincere than that of the speaker. But as is the case with the youth and mistress, we cannot be entirely sure that he is always the same character. Moreover, as far as the content of the poems in question goes, the rival poet could also be a woman. The context, however, in which the poems are placed, the fact that the speaker in Sonnet 79 uses the pronoun 'He' (v. 8) and the predominantly male literary scene at Shakespeare's time, suggest a male rival. E/W also draw attention to the fact that based on sonnets 78 and 86 the rival poet 'appears to be regarded as learned' (2013: 45). As the discussion of sonnets 78–80 and 82–86 will reveal in Chapter 5, the rival poet competes with the speaker not only for the favour of the young man and the mistress, but also for recognition

60   A COMPREHENSIVE GUIDE TO SHAKESPEARE'S SONNETS

and fame in the 'marketplace for patronage' (Hyland 2003: 25) which was characterized by 'fierce competition' (ibid., 29) in the trading of favours and payments between poets and patrons.

The Shakespearean sonnet

Having already addressed some features of the Shakespearean sonnet in previous chapters, I will offer a more comprehensive summary of its most salient attributes in this section. With only a few exceptions, Shakespeare's sonnets consist of fourteen lines written in iambic pentameter, each line consisting of five disyllabic feet with an accent on the second syllable. This is one of the most often used metres in English poetry and 'can be recognised involuntarily, as a dancer will recognise the rhythms of a waltz, a foxtrot, or a tango' (Evans 1998: 13). The metre, however, should be understood as something *underlying* the poem, an organizing grid which provides the poem with a general pattern, through but also against which the poem realizes its unique rhythmic dimension. Compared to a piece of music, a poem's metre is like the beat, while the realization of this metre is its melody or rhythm. Reciting Sonnet 73, for example, by strictly adhering to the iambic pattern would make this a very disappointing experience. Only by making pauses between 'leaves' and 'or' and between 'none' and 'or' in verse 2, by not making any pauses between the end of verse 2 and the beginning of verse 3 (and between the end of verse 5 and the beginning of verse 6), and by recognizing and speaking the trochaic inversions in the first two metric feet in verse 11 ('As the deathbed') can one (re-)create the 'directness of colloquial speech that a strictly regular metre would distort' (Evans 1998: 13) and that Shakespeare intended.

Sonnet 73
That time of year thou mayst in me behold,
When yellow leaves, or none, or few do hang
Upon those boughs which shake against the cold,
Bare ruined choirs where late the sweet birds sang;
In me thou seest the twilight of such day
As after sunset fadeth in the west,
Which by and by black night doth take away,
Death's second self that seals up all in rest;

THE SEQUENCE, DRAMATIS PERSONAE, AND FORM   61

In me thou seest the glowing of such fire
That on the ashes of his youth doth lie,
As the deathbed, whereon it must expire,
Consumed with that which it was nourished by;
   This thou perceiv'st, which makes thy love more strong,
   To love that well, which thou must leave ere long.

As Sonnet 73 shows, the rhyme scheme of the Shakespearean sonnet follows Henry Howard's sonnet form: three quatrains in alternating rhymes are followed by a couplet. The volta, the turn of argument or mood, does not take place after the second quatrain, as in the Italian sonnet, but between the third quatrain and the couplet. Sonnet 73 has only one volta, but many other sonnets, like sonnets 63 and 127, retain the dramatic shift or change of mood between the second and the third quatrain (for a brief survey of the different attempts to find a common structural principle for Shakespeare's sonnets cf. Booth 1969: 15–28).

Sonnet 73 not only features the standard metrical pattern, rhyme scheme and volta position of the Shakespearean sonnet, it also perfectly illustrates how Shakespeare uses the sonnet form to develop his argument. In this sonnet, the speaker acknowledges that the young man is aware of the former's mortality and ageing. Each quatrain employs a metaphor for the process of decay: autumn ushering in the end of the year (quatrain 1), twilight announcing the end of the day (quatrain 2), and the dying fire signalling end of life (quatrain 3). All three quatrains deal with the speaker's (and the youth's) awareness of his gradually approaching death, but as we go through the quatrains, the speaker increases the urgency of this idea. While the first quatrain merely states that the trees only have a few (or no) leaves left and that the sweet singing birds have gone, the concept of death is explicitly stated in the second quatrain when night is called 'Death's second self' (v. 8). The third quatrain becomes even more explicit, when the speaker talks about 'the ashes of his youth' (v. 10) and introduces the notion of the 'death-bed' (v. 11). What we can observe in the three quatrains is a gradual movement from abstract and general to more concrete signifiers, a zooming in that brings the notion of death temporally ever closer to the speaker: from the end of the year (quatrain 1), to the end of the day (quatrain 2), to the final stages of a dying fire (quatrain 3; for selected interpretations of the sonnet cf. Schwanitz (1985), Standop's (1986:

62   A COMPREHENSIVE GUIDE TO SHAKESPEARE'S SONNETS

228) harsh critique of Schwanitz's analysis, and Berensmeyer's (2020) more recent hermeneutical reading). In the couplet, the speaker concludes that he is confident that the youth's awareness of the speaker's approaching decrepitude and the transience of existence make his love for the speaker even stronger.

Paterson, however, suggests a different conclusion by paraphrasing the couplet as follows: 'you see all this; and that must mean your love is pretty strong, if you can love this decrepit thing as well as you do, especially when you know death will take it from you soon' (2010: 212). In the first reading, the youth loves the speaker *because* of this awareness of decline, in Paterson's interpretation he loves the speaker *although* he is aware of this decline. Another reading emerges if we understand the 'that' in the last line as not to refer to the poet but to the young man. In that case, the speaker advises the youth, because of his decline, *not* to love the poet anymore and to make the most of his own life while he is still young.

Many regard Sonnet 73 as one of Shakespeare's most accomplished sonnets (cf. Paterson 2010: 210), and this has not only to do with the way the metaphors in the quatrains develop and enforce the main argument but also with the particular metaphor in verse 4 ('Bare ruined choirs where late the sweet birds sang') which the critic William Empson in his book *Seven Types of Ambiguity* uses, with somewhat too much interpretative fervour, to illustrate his understanding of the first type of ambiguity where 'a word or a grammatical structure is effective in several ways at once' ([1930] 1995: 20–1):

> the comparison [of 'Bare ruined choirs' with 'boughs'] holds for many reasons; because ruined monastery choirs are places in which to sing, because they involve sitting in a row, because they are made of wood, are carved into knots and so forth, because they used to be surrounded by a sheltering building crystallized out of the likeness of a forest, and coloured with stained glass and painting like flowers and leaves, because they are now abandoned by all but the grey walls coloured like the skies of winter [. . .]. (ibid., 21)

For Empson, the single line 'Bare ruined choirs where late the sweet birds sang' (73.4) simultaneously activates a wide range of semantic

THE SEQUENCE, DRAMATIS PERSONAE, AND FORM   63

fields, materials, senses and activities: different locations (monastery, tree); the senses of seeing and hearing; activities such as singing and sitting; the materials of wood and glass; and so forth. This production of different and conflicting meanings by way of ambiguity is another of the central features of the *Sonnets*.

Although the fourteen-line sonnet in iambic pentameter and arranged in three quatrains with alternating rhymes followed by a concluding couplet is the standard form Shakespeare uses, there are a few exceptions. As shown above, Sonnet 145 (the 'hate away'-Sonnet) is written in iambic tetrameter. Sonnet 99, on the other hand, has fifteen instead of fourteen lines, and Sonnet 135, also referred to as the 'Will Sonnet', has six end rhymes on 'Will', 'still' and 'kill'. The most interesting, and to many scholars also most puzzling deviation from the norm is Sonnet 126, which ends the young man sequence, which I reproduce here as printed in the 1609 Quarto (see Figure 3.1).

This sonnet's structure is striking on two accounts. First, it consists only of couplets, second, it lacks the final two lines, or, to be more precise, the final two lines only include two sets of empty parentheses. To find a possible explanation for the empty couplet, let us take a closer look at the three quatrains.

In the first quatrain, the speaker addresses the 'lovely Boy' and argues that he is in control of time by imagining him holding an hourglass in his hands (vv. 1-2) and referring to the 'sickle' (v. 2), both symbols for man's transient existence in medieval and early modern depictions of death. With the passing of time, so the argument continues, the lover, the 'lovely Boy', has matured and grown (in age? beauty? wisdom? in his love for the poet?) while the poet himself has withered (v. 4).

The second quatrain argues that nature, which rules everything, will slow down or even arrest the young man's decay (vv. 5-6) with one purpose in mind: to 'put time to shame by eclipsing or outdoing' (KDJ 2010: 365) and eventually killing it (vv. 7-8). The 'Yet' at the beginning of line 9 introduces the volta: in spite of what the speaker said in the first two quatrains, the youth should fear time because 'She may detain, but not still keep, her treasure!' (vv. 9-10), and to settle her account, she has to send the young man eventually to his death (vv. 11-12). After this bleak statement one would expect another turn or at least a conciliatory conclusion, such as turning the inevitability of death for the young man into something positive.

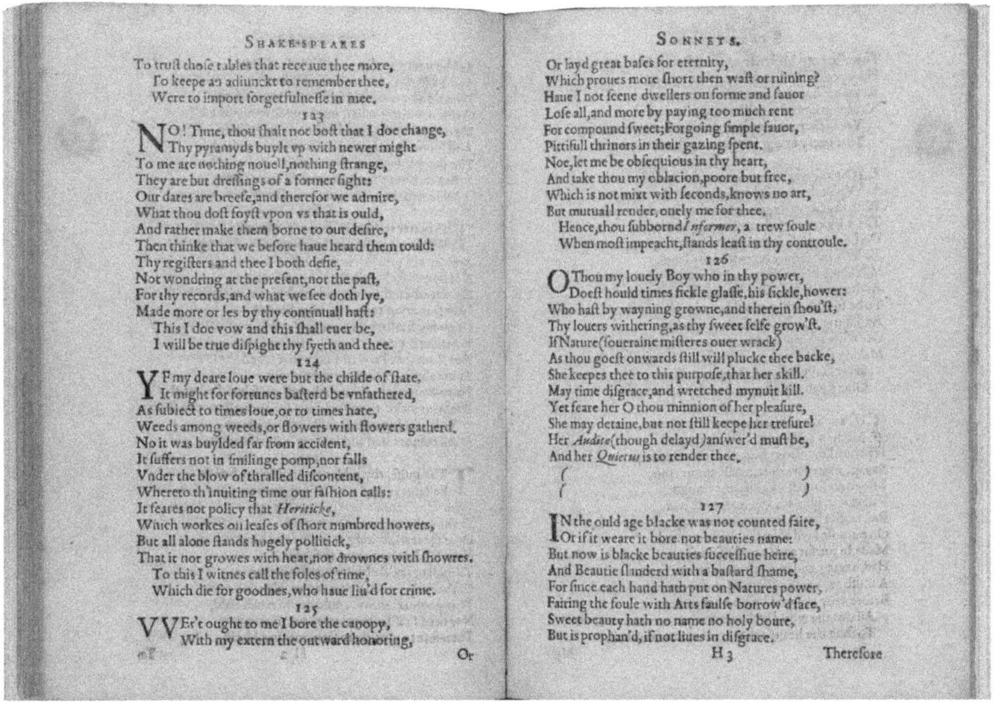

To trust those tables that receaue thee more,
To keepe an adiunckt to remember thee,
Were to import forgetfulnesse in mee.

123

NO! Time, thou shalt not bost that I doe change,
Thy pyramyds buylt vp with newer might
To me are nothing nouell,nothing strange,
They are but dressings of a former sight:
Our dates are breefe,and therefor we admire,
What thou dost foyst vpon vs that is ould,
And rather make them borne to our desire,
Then thinke that we before haue heard them tould:
Thy registers and thee I both defie,
Not wondring at the present,nor the past,
For thy records,and what we see doth lye,
Made more or les by thy continuall hast:
  This I doe vow and this shall euer be,
  I will be true dispight thy syeth and thee.

124

YF my deare loue were but the childe of state,
It might for fortunes basterd be vnfathered,
As subiect to times loue,or to times hate,
Weeds among weeds,or flowers with flowers gatherd.
No it was buylded far from accident,
It suffers not in smilinge pomp,nor falls
Vnder the blow of thralled discontent,
Whereto th'inuiting time our fashion calls:
It feares not policy that Heriticke,
Which workes on leases of short numbred howers,
But all alone stands hugely pollitick,
That it nor growes with heat,nor drownes with showres.
  To this I witnes call the foles of time,
  Which die for goodnes,who haue liu'd for crime.

125

WEr't ought to me I bore the canopy,
With my extern the outward honoring,

n   Or

Or layd great bases for eternity,
Which proues more short then wast or ruining?
Haue I not seene dwellers on forme and fauor
Lose all,and more by paying too much rent
For compound sweet;Forgoing simple fauor,
Pittifull thrinors in their gazing spent.
Noe,let me be obsequious in thy heart,
And take thou my oblacion,poore but free,
Which is not mixt with seconds,knows no art,
But mutuall render,onely me for thee.
  Hence,thou subborned Informer, a trew soule
  When most impeacht,stands least in thy controule.

126

OThou my louely Boy who in thy power,
Doest hould times fickle glasse,his sickle,howers:
Who hast by wayning growne,and therein shou'st,
Thy louers withering,as thy sweet selfe grow'st.
If Nature(soueraine misteres ouer wrack)
As thou goest onwards still will plucke thee backe,
She keepes thee to this purpose,that her skill.
May time disgrace,and wretched mynuit kill.
Yet feare her O thou minnion of her pleasure,
She may detaine,but not still keepe her tresure!
  Her Audite(though delayd)answer'd must be,
  And her Quietus is to render thee.
(   )
(   )

127

IN the ould age blacke was not counted faire,
Or if it weare it bore not beauties name:
But now is blacke beauties successiue heire,
And Beautie slanderd with a bastard shame,
For since each hand hath put on Natures power,
Fairing the foule with Arts faulse borrow'd face,
Sweet beauty hath no name no holy boure,
But is prophan'd,if not liues in disgrace.

H 3   Therefore

FIGURE 3.1 *Shakespeare, William. [Sonnets] Shake-speares sonnets. Neuer before imprinted. (London: G. Eld for T[homas]. T[horpe]. and are to be solde by William Aspley, 1609), leaf H2 verso || leaf H3 recto.*

THE SEQUENCE, DRAMATIS PERSONAE, AND FORM 65

But the missing lines withhold this conclusion from us. There is no closure to the sonnet and on a larger scale also no closure to the 126 sonnets addressed to the young man.

One way to interpret these empty lines is to see the two pairs of parentheses as additions made by the printer who thought that two lines were missing. In that case, the poem would in fact be incomplete. This is the reading that Stephen Booth favours in his edition although he concedes that the 'poem's sudden *quietus* after twelve lines is – probably accidentally – an illustrative analogy that demonstrates the justice of the warning the poem offers' (2000: 430).

But one could also view the empty parentheses as intentional. In that case, the blank space between the parentheses become part of the poem, *they* are the conclusion. Various suggestions have been made to this effect: that the parentheses represent the 'emptiness which will ensue' (KDJ 2010: 366) after the young man's death, that they represent the shape of an empty hourglass (cf. Graziani 1984: 81), or that they are meant to symbolize little crescents, representing a repeated waxing and waning of the moon. The latter reading is suggested by John Lennard (cf. 1991: 41–3), who also sees the last two lines representing 'either the silence (quiet) of the grave, or the empty grave which the corpse of the "louely Boy" must sooner or later fill' (ibid., 43; cf. also KDJ 2010: 366 and Burrow 2002: 632). Another possibility is suggested by Evans who argues 'that [the publisher] Thorpe intentionally omitted a final couplet, perhaps, because it gave too obvious a clue to the identity of the "lovely boy"' (1998: 241).

In view of the patchwork character and gappiness of the sequence discussed above I strongly support the reading that the final two lines of the sonnets (and the youth sequence) are not missing but intentionally left empty. The empty parentheses invite the reader, just like the other gaps and moments of ambiguity in the sonnets, to take part in the production of meaning. Moreover, by frustrating our expectation and withholding a solution to the conflict staged in the quatrains, we are placed in a similar position like the speaker who must acknowledge in the end that there is no strategy that can prevent the young man's beauty from passing and the youth from dying.

Apart from these irregular sonnets in terms of metre, rhyme and number of lines, there are also sonnets with less striking irregularities.

For example, Sonnet 66 consists of only one sentence and contains ten lines beginning with 'And', and Sonnet 96 repeats the couplet of Sonnet 36. These deviations from the norm only show that the *Sonnets*, although clearly anchored in the sonnet tradition, do not shy away from exploring and stretching the boundaries of the genre and thereby give testimony of the genre's high self-reflexive quality.

Further reading

Structure of collection: Burrow 2002: 103–11, 118–38; Dubrow 1996: 2007; Edmondson 2013; E/W 2013: 28–46; E/W 2020: 28–9; Hyland 2003: 148–87; Jackson 1999a; Monte 2021; Pequigney 1985; Rudenstine 2015; Schiffer 2007; Schoenfeldt 2010: 60–4. *Sonnets* **and 'A Lover's Complaint':** Burrow 2002: 138–46; Dubrow 2007; E/W 2013: 105–13; Healy 2007; Healy 2011; Hyland 2003: 187–93; Kerrigan [1986] 1999: 12–18; KDJ 2010: 88–95; Sanchez 2013. **Division into youth and mistress sequence:** Booth 2000: 434; Burrow 2002: 123; Burto [1964] 1999: xl–liii; KDJ 2010: 47–50; Evans 1998: 243; Ingram and Redpath [1964] 1978: 290; Kerrigan [1986] 1999; Vendler 1999: 14–15; Proudfoot et al. 2021: 17. **Early modern notions of 'race' and Blackness; xenophobia:** Alexander and Wells 2000; Espinosa 2016; Greene 1995; Habib 2000; Habib 2008; Hall 1996; Hall [1998] 2008; Kaufmann 2017; Little 2016; Loomba 2002; Loomba 2016; Nubia 2019; Olusoga 2016; Park 2023; Sanghera 2021; Shyllon 1977; Thompson 2021b. **Black mistress:** Akhimie 2018; Al-Dabbagh 2012; Crewe 1995; de Grazia 2000; Franssen 2010; Harvey 2007; Hunt 2000; Pequigney 1985; Richmond 1986; Salkeld 2023; Schalkwyk 2004; Scheil 2021. **Rival poet:** Jackson 2005; Monte 2021. **Shakespearean Sonnet:** Booth 1969; Booth 2007; Cousins 2011; E/W 2013: 47–62; Paterson 2010: 485–500; Vendler 1999: 4–10, 17–37; Vendler 2007.

PART TWO

Themes

4

Preservation

Before discussing the theme of preservation in the *Sonnets*, I should like to say a few more words about my thematic approach and explain the idea of the theme clusters. As has been established in the previous chapters, it is difficult (and also not very productive) to identify in the sequence a chronological narrative with clearly identifiable characters, addressees and voices. As Heather Dubrow reminds us, referring to C. S. Lewis, 'focusing on these sections of narrative is rather like appreciating a Mozart opera mainly because of its plot' (1987: 183). One encounters similar problems when trying to identify the main themes in the *Sonnets*. While in some instances it may seem fairly easy to identify the prominent theme, it proves to be rather difficult in others. For example, while many would agree that Sonnet 116 ('Let me not to the marriage of true minds') is primarily about the notion of perfect love, Sonnet 49 deals with a variety of subjects. While it seems to be primarily about the speaker's fears of being forsaken by the youth, it also touches on a number of themes that we encounter in other sonnets, such as the fickleness of love and desire, when love is 'converted from the thing it was' (v. 7). But the poem also deals self-reflexively with the writing of poetry. By writing poetry, i.e. this very sonnet, the speaker defends the youth's abandoning of the speaker ('And this my hand against myself uprear,/ To guard the lawful reasons on thy part', vv. 11-12). Moreover, the sonnet also deals with betrayal and deception. The speaker's 'defects' (v. 2) imply that the youth may be justified in abandoning and to 'strangely pass,/ And scarcely greet' (vv. 5-6) him in the future.

The problem of identifying *the* main theme may have something to do with Sonnet 49 being such a 'dense little number' (Paterson

2010: 143) and the fact that the main verb does not appear until verse 9 ('ensconce'). The anaphora in verses 1, 5 and 9 ('Against that time') at the beginning of each quatrain serves to increase our expectation as to what the speaker will actually do to guard himself 'against that time' when the young man will turn away from him. This constant deferral of the sentence's as well as the speaker's conclusion is maintained until the volta in line 9 when the speaker finally discloses what it is that he will do in expectation of that moment: he will write this sonnet and reflect on his own unworthiness.

Another dense example with multiple themes is Sonnet 137. It begins with the speaker accusing the blind love god Cupid of clouding his clear vision so that he, the speaker, is not able to see the world and its people as they really are ('Thou blind fool love, what dost thou to mine eyes,/ That they behold, and see not what they see?', vv. 1-2). Although his eyes can see, they cannot recognize true beauty (vv. 3-4). The speaker then claims that he views his mistress too favourably, with 'over-partial looks' (v. 5), and complains to Cupid that his clouded, deluded vision has affected 'the judgement of my heart' (v. 8). In the next quatrain, the speaker takes a step back and reflects on this divide between his eyes and his heart, showing us that he is well aware of his self-deception. In doing so, he adopts an insulting and misogynistic tone. He accuses the mistress of promiscuity (referring to her as 'the bay where all men ride', v. 6), argues that she sleeps with many men ('the wide world's common place', v. 10) and that she has 'so foul a face' (v. 12). He concludes by cursing both his perception ('eyes', v. 11) and feelings ('heart', v. 13) which have been compromised by his self-delusion and desire for the mistress, once again charging her with promiscuity and corruption by associating her with the 'plague' in the last line. While the main theme of this sonnet is the speaker's self-deception, which he also addresses in sonnets 138–141 and 147–151, the sonnet also addresses other topics, such as corruption, uncontrollable desire, misogyny and inconstancy.

As shown in the previous chapter, numerous attempts have been made to organize the sonnets according to addressees and voices (youth, woman, rival poet), structural aspects (pairs, numerological references) and, to some extent, themes (sonnets on procreation, love triangle, separation etc.). E/W suggest a list of smaller 'groups of sonnets and sequences within Shakespeare's collection' (2013: 33), which they, however, do not view as exhaustive and admit as

PRESERVATION

being 'subjectively inflected' (ibid.). Their table of groups and pairs lists more than thirty sequences, with names like 'Writing for eternity', 'Groaning Sonnets', 'Seasons' and 'Lies, dishonesty' (cf. ibid.), to name but a few (for a detailed summary see Appendix 1 below).

In a more recent publication the authors provide a table with an overview of the 'Direction' (E/W 2020: 289) of the sonnets suggesting further groupings like sonnet letters (sonnets 26, 77), sonnets on or addressed to abstract concepts such as Love, Time, the Muse and the poet's soul (sonnets 137, 56, 19, 123, 100, 146), meditations (twenty-five sonnets) and translations (sonnets 153, 154).

As becomes evident from Appendix 1 below, such a detailed classification is only partially helpful when it comes to identifying the collection's main themes, and begs the question how useful it is, for example, to discriminate between sonnets on 'falsity' (E/W 2013: 33), '[c]ontradiction of constancy and falsity' (ibid.), and '[l]ies, dishonesty' (ibid.) or to combine structural correspondences (pairs, keywords) with thematic ones. What are we to do with the more than fifty sonnets left unaccounted for in E/W's first list (although some of those poems can be found in groups suggested in the table on direction in the more recent publication)? How do these groups relate to the 'themes and concerns' (ibid., 63) the authors identify in the sequence? Lastly, as many sonnets in the more recent table appear in more than one group (for example, sonnets 5, 6, 9, 10, 15–17, 57, 58, 67, 68, 109, 131–133, 140–142), the usefulness of such a differentiated classification in identifying the themes in the entire sequence remains uncertain. As Stephen Booth has argued, in the *Sonnets* one can find 'a confusing number of different factors in which relationships among the sonnets are perceptible' (1969: 117; cf. also ibid., 1–14; Boyd 2012: 5–6; Dubrow 1987: 183).

This is not to suggest that such groupings cannot be helpful in throwing light on the structural composition of the sequence and on how individual sonnets are linked to others. In the absence of a clear unifying narrative, however, it might be more helpful to focus on broader thematic clusters when dealing with the heterogeneous quality of the sequence. I have in mind what Booth calls 'frames of reference' (1969: 14) and what E/W refer to as 'connecting interpretative threads' (2013: 63) through which the sonnets are connected in the collection.

72   A COMPREHENSIVE GUIDE TO SHAKESPEARE'S SONNETS

Naturally, identifying frames and threads increases the risk of neglecting others that are equally possible: '[t]o point out or construct a group usually requires that a grouper arbitrarily dictate his chosen focus as paramount and determinate' (Booth 2000: 546). The following groups are therefore meant to be understood as *one* of many possible ways to organize and group the sonnets, the main purpose being to break down the collection of 154 heterogeneous poems into accessible (thematic) units, a procedure which I hope will also allow a more systematic introduction to the collection.

Following E/W in their identification of six 'themes and concerns' (2013: 63) in the *Sonnets* (time, image, verse, desire, sexuality, and 'Black Beauty'), I argue that the *Sonnets* deal mainly with five theme clusters and that each poem is dominated by one of these. These thematic clusters are preservation, writing, desire, deception and imagination. Once again, I am not suggesting that these groups are definite or exclusive. For example, while Sonnet 49 discussed above primarily deals with the speaker's desire for the youth, it also deals with writing as an act of preservation and deception. Similarly, Sonnet 137 – as we have seen – foregrounds the speaker's self-deception while at the same time thematizing his desire for the young man. However, by identifying one main theme for each sonnet (which naturally is also influenced by one's perspective and experience), I hope to show by careful analysis of selected sonnets that in the end there is always one theme that dominates over others.

I suggest the following thematic clustering of the sonnets:

Preservation	1–17, 126, 146
Writing	18, 19, 21, 23, 26, 32, 38, 54, 55, 59, 60, 63, 65, 71, 72, 74, 76–86, 100–108, 122, 152
Desire	20, 22, 24, 25, 36, 37, 39–42, 50–53, 56–58, 62, 64, 66–70, 73, 75, 87–99, 109–17, 123–125, 127–136, 144, 145, 147–151, 153, 154
Deception	33–35, 48, 49, 118–121, 137–143
Imagination	27–31, 43–47, 61

This chapter and the subsequent four will examine each of these theme clusters in greater detail and at the same time investigate how they relate to the other main themes in the sonnets. In doing so, sonnets from the other four clusters will also be referred to, thereby underlining the patchwork quality of the sequence's structure. Beginning with the first theme cluster of preservation I will, after preliminary remarks on the connection between death and preservation in the *Sonnets*, address the strategy of procreation as a means of preservation and conclude with a section on those poems in which the speaker reflects on the limitations of the preservation strategy.

The desire to preserve manifests itself most prominently in the first seventeen sonnets of the collection, the so-called procreation sonnets, in which the speaker urges the youth to father children so that he may be preserved after his death. Most often this desire is directed at preserving the youth's beauty, but it also refers to other aspects, such as his youth or entire personality. The wish to preserve, however, also features prominently in many sonnets from the theme cluster 'writing', in which the speaker wants his poetry to be saved so that he can keep the memory of either the youth or himself for future generations.

The longing to preserve can also play a significant role in those sonnets dealing primarily with love and desire, such as when the speaker struggles to keep his feelings for the youth alive in the face of separation. It can also express itself in the sense of wanting to outlive time and to preserve one's life when confronted with decay and death. Ultimately, in the *Sonnets* the desire to preserve, to commemorate and to maintain always has to be understood in the context of death, ageing and decay. Every sonnet that expresses the speaker's wish to preserve is also always about the presence and inevitability of death.

Sonnet 2 is the first sonnet in which the speaker explicitly expresses his wish that something should be preserved, in this case the young man's beauty. In the first verse, the speaker confronts the addressee with what age has in store for him. When he is forty his face will be marked by lines and wrinkles ('trenches', v. 2), his appearance will be one of 'tattered weed' (v. 4) as opposed to his 'youth's proud livery' (v. 3) and his former beauty will be buried in his old 'deep-sunken eyes' (v. 7). In the third quatrain, the speaker changes his tactic by telling him that there is a way of preserving his youth and beauty, namely by fathering a child in which his beauty can live on.

Although the sonnet is primarily about the addressee's youth and beauty, it draws our attention to the opposite ideas of old age, decay

74   A COMPREHENSIVE GUIDE TO SHAKESPEARE'S SONNETS

and death. The speaker does not convey an idea of the young man's present youthful and beautiful appearance but takes great pains to visualize for the young man, and for us, the time when the young man's beauty will be gone. Even in the couplet, the speaker does not turn to the youth's present youthful state but looks forward to the time when he is 'old' (v. 13) and his blood is 'cold' (v. 14).

Death as a theme also figures in the sonnets of the other clusters. It appears in sonnets which thematize writing as a means to outlive death (sonnets 18, 71, 74), it figures in sonnets about desire (when the speaker is removed from the object of desire by death, either his own or that of the young man; cf. sonnets 63, 64, 73), and it surfaces in poems about deception and imagination, for example when the youth's betrayal (Sonnet 92) or the limits of his imagination are experienced as a kind of death by the speaker (Sonnet 44).

In sonnets 126 and 146, however, death is strongly linked to the theme of preservation. While Sonnet 126 (discussed above in Chapter 3) addresses the impossibility of preserving the youth against 'time's fickle glass, his sickle hour' (126.2), Sonnet 146 is a more general reflection on the passing of time and death. E/W call it the '[m]ost detached of all' (2013: 35) sonnets, since it is not addressed to a person but to the speaker's '[p]oor soul' (v. 1). As KDJ has noted about this sonnet, 'the absence of any explicit allusion to a love-object is unusual' (2010: 408). It is one of the few, if not the only explicitly religious sonnet in the sequence, in which the speaker asks the soul (and himself) to repudiate earthly riches and prepare for life after death (for a discussion of the sonnet's religious quality, cf. Booth 2000: 501–17). The central idea of the poem can be found immediately after the volta in verses 9-10: 'Then soul, live thou upon thy servant's loss,/ And let that pine to aggravate thy store'. Only by neglecting the body, which is subject to decay (here referred to as the 'servant' and 'that'), can the soul 'live' and grow.

Sonnet 146 is also interesting in that the desire to preserve does not relate to the very 'earthly' concerns of preserving the youth's beauty or memory, or the speaker's reputation as a writer, but to the speaker's soul. The speaker casts the material and physical side of his existence in a negative light: the body is a 'sinful earth' (v. 1), a short-lived 'fading mansion' (v. 6) and perceived as 'rebel powers' (v. 2) which cover and hide ('array', v. 2) the precious soul under 'costly gay' (v. 4) and hence unnecessary clothes.

PRESERVATION 75

The poem employs conceits and metaphors to express its general idea. A conceit is a 'complex and arresting metaphor, in context usually part of a larger pattern of imagery, which stimulates understanding by combining objects and concepts in unconventional ways' (Preminger and Brogan 1993: 231). While describing the body as 'sinful earth', a 'fading mansion' and as something which covers the soul may not be highly 'unconventional', the imagery in the third quatrain and the concluding couplet is more sophisticated. The speaker in the volta literally 'turns' the argument around. Whereas the poem suggests at the beginning that the body, the 'rebel powers' (v. 2), feed on the soul in a parasitical manner, it is now the soul which feeds on and grows through the decaying, dying body. The body changes from a 'rebel' into a 'servant' (v. 9) in the service of the soul. KDJ suggests paraphrasing verses 9-10 as follows: the soul should live on 'the (impending) loss of the body, which should properly be subordinate to the soul' (2010: 408) and 'allow the body to languish or waste away [. . .] in order to increase [. . . its] own abundance of possessions' (ibid.). However, the relationship between soul and body is understood not only in organic but also in financial terms: the more 'dross' (v. 11) of the body the soul sells, the more it gains in 'divine' (v. 11) riches. What is lost in material existence is gained in spiritual life.

Procreation

The main argument in the procreation sonnets is that the best means of preservation is procreation. The speaker calls upon the youth to preserve his youth and beauty, and also other aspects of his personality, for future generations by producing children.

A look at the first sonnet of the sequence will illustrate how the speaker unfolds his argument in accordance with the general logical structure of the Shakespearean sonnet outlined in Chapter 3. The first quatrain contains the proposition: 'fairest creatures' (1.1) are under the obligation to reproduce so that their beauty can be passed on to the next generation ('That thereby beauty's rose might never die', v. 2) and the parent's beauty be remembered (v. 4). The second quatrain features the second proposition, which states that the addressee violates this natural law by being 'contracted to [. . . his] own bright eyes' (v. 5) and by squandering his beauty (vv. 6-7). The third quatrain elaborates on this violation by highlighting the self-destructive quality of such selfish behaviour.

But what is the precise nature of this violation? The speaker accuses the youth of not sharing his beauty with the world and of keeping it only for himself, thereby denying the world, i.e. other lovers, (sexual) pleasure. Even more so, by keeping his beauty to himself, he kills that beauty by carrying it with him into the 'grave' (v. 14). This is the third part of the sonnet's syllogism, the conclusion expressed in the couplet. Not only does the speaker harm himself with his decision against 'increase' (v. 1), he also does not fulfil his obligation to society. He 'eat[s] the world's due' (v. 14).

The imagery and tropes employed by the speaker to express his charges are worth noting: 'contracted to thine own bright eyes' (v. 5), 'Feed'st thy light's flame with self-substantial fuel' (v. 6), and 'mak'st waste in niggarding' (v. 12). These are all examples of the type of ambiguity discussed earlier, which define Shakespeare's sonnets. They make the reader pause in order to figure out some of the potential layers of meaning. For example, 'contracted' points to the fact that the speaker is 'pledged to himself, as in a contract of marriage' (KDJ 2010: 112), but he is also contracted in the sense of being diminished 'to the self-reflexive scope of his *own bright eyes*' (ibid.). As the linguist Roman Jakobson (1960) has argued in his influential essay on the poetic function of language, poetic language is characterized by the fact that it activates several meanings at the same time, and it is this paradigmatic quality of language which accounts for the richness and complexity of the *Sonnets*.

In Sonnet 3, the speaker urges the youth to look into the mirror ('Look in thy glass', 3.1) and to realize that this beauty must be renewed (cf. v. 3) through procreation ('that face should form another', v. 2). The imagery employed in this sonnet is interesting in many respects. The 'face' in verse 2 is a metonymy representing the young man *pars pro toto* who is called upon to form another copy of himself. A few verses later the youth who is unwilling to beget children is compared to a 'tomb' (v. 7), which is both a metonymy and a metaphor. On the one hand, the relationship between vehicle ('tomb') and tenor ('youth['s body]') is one of contiguity in that the speaker's body is the container for the wasted seeds not used in creating children. On the other hand, 'tomb' functions also as a metaphor for the 'youth', since both are also linked by a relationship of similarity, sharing lifelessness, coldness and darkness.

Comparing the young man to his 'mother's glass' (v. 9) and the 'April of her prime' (v. 10) were already in Shakespeare's time conventional metaphors for likeness and youth. Similarly, 'golden time' (v. 12) is anything but an original trope for youth and happier days. On the other hand, the expression 'windows of thine age' (v. 11) for the youth's 'age-dimmed eyes' (Booth 2000: 139) is more original: through the windows of his eyes the addressee will behold his child as a reminder and preserver of his beauty in his youth. This refers back to the 'glass' in the first line of the sonnet into which the youth is asked to look, and joins the literal to the metaphorical meaning of the mirror: the actual mirror through which the addressee beholds his beauty will or should be replaced by the metaphorical mirror through which he will see his (former) beauty, i.e. his child.

The most prominent metaphor, however, can be found in the first half of the second quatrain: 'For where is she so fair whose uneared womb/ Disdains the tillage of thy husbandry?' (vv. 5-6). As KDJ notes, '[h]uman procreation was often described in terms of agriculture' (2010: 116). Terms like 'uneared', 'tillage' and 'husbandry' foreground the physical and even 'bawdy' quality of marriage and procreation: the speaker essentially asks which virgin ('uneared womb') would not want to be impregnated ('tillage') by such a farmer and husband ('husbandry') as the young man.

As pointed out earlier in the third chapter, although we learn that the youth is beautiful, the speaker is not specific about this beauty, neither in this nor the other sonnets. All we learn in this sonnet about the young man's appearance, for example, is that he does not have old eyes and wrinkles *yet* (vv. 11-12) and that he resembles his mother (3.9-10). Other sonnets are equally vague: Sonnet 5 mentions the addressee's 'lovely gaze where every eye doth dwell' (5.2), Sonnet 6 describes him as 'much too fair' (6.13) – which could mean both 'too beautiful' and 'too white' – and Sonnet 11 states that nature gave the youth her best gifts, among them beauty (11.11-12).

It should be kept in mind, however, that the speaker not only desires (and wants to preserve) the young man's beauty but also his entire being, his 'inward worth' (16.11) as well as his faults and weaknesses, even including those acts of betrayal and deception which will be discussed in Chapter 7. Perceiving the young man therefore only as the 'fair youth' unduly reduces the complexity of the relationship between addressee and speaker.

78 A COMPREHENSIVE GUIDE TO SHAKESPEARE'S SONNETS

For the speaker has a pronounced interest in preserving the young man's entire identity, as becomes evident in Sonnet 13. The central idea in this poem is expressed through a remarkable conceit. The speaker argues that only by fathering a child can the youth remain the same after death. Over the course of the poem he stresses the importance of the addressee preserving his identity three times: at the very beginning of the sonnet ('O that you were yourself!', v. 1), in verses 1-2 ('you are/ No longer yours, than you yourself here live', which E/W paraphrase as 'you are yourself for no longer than you are alive' (2020: 261)), and in the second quatrain when he argues that the youth, if he fathers a child, 'were/ Yourself again after yourself's decease' (vv. 6-7). By paradoxically arguing that the dead addressee will have preserved his identity through having produced a child and that by having given his 'semblance to some other' (v. 4) he will remain himself, the speaker suspends the difference between life and death, between self and other, and adds a quasi-religious, spiritual quality to his argument.

Sonnet 13 is also the first poem in the collection which 'marks the momentous instant in which the speaker first uses vocatives of love: he addresses the young man as *love* and *dear my love*' (Vendler 1999: 102) – although, as shown below, already in Sonnet 10 the speaker 'indicates his own devotion to the young man' (KDJ 2010: 130) by invoking the youth's 'love of me' (10.13). In Sonnet 13, the speaker addresses the young man twice as 'love' (13.1) or even 'dear my love' (v. 13; cf. also Sonnet 15 in which the speaker declares his 'love of you', v. 13).

In Sonnet 13, the agricultural metaphor identified in Sonnet 3 above extends to the sphere of the *oikos*, the household. The young man's beauty is only 'lease[d]' (13.5) from nature and has to be returned, his beautiful appearance is compared to a 'house' (v. 9) which needs to be maintained through good 'husbandry' (v. 10) – the same term is used in Sonnet 3 – and if he fails to meet his obligation as responsible husband and farmer and squanders his assets like an 'unthrift' (v. 13), his legacy will be 'barren' (v. 12).

Apart from describing the aspects that will be preserved by fathering children, the speaker also explains why the youth should have a strong interest in procreation. First, his beauty is, like existence itself, transient. It is subject to time, decay and death. This is stated throughout the entire sequence. Hours will 'play

PRESERVATION

the tyrants' (5.3) and 'deface' (6.1) the addressee and 'nothing 'gainst time's scythe can make defence' (12.13). If the youth does not procreate, the speaker argues, he will kill his beauty: 'Within thine own bud buriest thy content' (1.11), 'Thy unused beauty must be tombed with thee' (4.13), beauty 'unused the user so destroys it' (9.12), 'Thy end is truth's and beauty's doom and date' (14.14).

This transient quality of beauty (and life) is connected to another reason why the addressee should have children. As has already become evident, it is actually his obligation to share this beauty with the world and especially women: '[f]rom fairest creatures we [the public] desire increase' (1.1), he should have '[p]ity [on] the world' (1.13) and not 'beguile' (3.4) it by keeping his beauty, or more specifically his semen, to himself. Since his beauty was only given to him as a 'loan' (6.6), it is his duty to return the 'bounteous largesse' (4.6) given to him by nature.

The notion that procreation is an obligation is referred to in Plato's *Symposium*, in which the prophetess Diotima explains to Socrates the object of love:

Its object is to procreate and bring forth in beauty [...] procreation is the nearest thing to perpetuity and immortality that a mortal being can attain. If, as we agreed, the aim of love is the perpetual possession of the good, it necessarily follows that it must desire immortality together with the good, and the argument leads us to the inevitable conclusion that love is love of immortality as well as of the good. (Plato, *Symposium* 205e–207b, 87)

According to Diotima, procreation, although only the lowest 'of the forms which Eros can take' (Hamilton 1951: 22), is a way of achieving 'anything like perpetuity' (ibid.), clearly an objective the speaker in the *Sonnets* also has in mind.

Shakespeare must have also been familiar with Erasmus' epistle on marriage, *Encomium Matrimonii*, from 1518, an English translation of which was published in Thomas Wilson's *The Arte of Rhetorique* (1553). In the *Praise of Marriage*, Erasmus, like the speaker in the *Sonnets*, urges a young gentleman to marry. The reasons he gives bear a striking similarity to some of the arguments the speaker mentions in the *Sonnets*. Erasmus reminds the gentleman

80 A COMPREHENSIVE GUIDE TO SHAKESPEARE'S SONNETS

to 'give that unto the posterity the which we have received of our ancestors' (1518, fol. 22v), to not let his posterity 'decay forever through your willful single life' (fol. 33v), that 'there is no building of pillars, no erecting of arches, no blazing of arms, that doth more set forth a man's name than doth the increase of children' (fols 24v-25), that it is a man's obligation 'to make the whole kind immortal' (fol. 25v), which 'can never be done without wedlock and carnal copulation' (ibid.), and 'that we should wax young again in our children. . . . For what man can be grieved that he is old when he seeth his own countenance which he had being a child to appear lively in his son?' (fol. 31; cf. also Burrow's (2002: 111, 128, 382) discussion of Erasmus' influence).

This human obligation to procreate becomes particularly apparent when the speaker's pleas to the youth extend to the preservation of beauty in general, and the survival of mankind. It is not only the duty of the speaker but also of all 'fairest creatures' to procreate, so that 'beauty's rose might never die' (1.2) and that, even more importantly, humanity will not 'make the world away' (11.8).

But the young man also has a personal obligation to the speaker to procreate, as Sonnet 10 shows. Picking up the cue 'shame' from the last line of the preceding sonnet (a linking device which one can observe regularly in the collection), the speaker begins by first arguing that, as long as the youth neglects to father children (is 'so unprovident' (10.2) of himself), he cannot really love others, and second, that while he may be loved or desired by many, he does not or cannot love others himself. In the second quatrain, the tone becomes more aggressive. The youth is 'possessed with murd'rous hate' (v. 5) against himself and by refusing to beget children he destroys his own 'roof' (v. 7), i.e. his family line, whose maintenance should be his (and every man's) purpose in life. In the third quatrain, the speaker's voice acquires a more imploring character, now urging the young man to 'change thy thought' (v. 9) and to be 'gracious and kind' (v. 11). In the concluding couplet, the speaker for the first time in the *Sonnets* explicitly expresses his *own* devotion to the young man and uses it as an argument to make the addressee change his mind: 'Make thee another self for love of *me*,/ That beauty still may live in thine or thee' (vv. 13-14; my emphasis). If the young man is not willing to fulfil his duty to the world (by producing children), he should at least do so for the sake of the speaker.

PRESERVATION

In imploring the youth to procreate, the speaker not only appeals to his duty but also to his vanity and the personal benefits he might have from producing and having children. One such benefit is the admiration of others. In Sonnet 7, the sun's course during the day serves as a metaphor for the various stages in the addressee's life. Just like the people who will turn away from the sun in the afternoon, so the youth's admirers will turn away from him once he is older, past 'strong youth in his middle age' (7.6), if he does not father a child. Unlike in the procreation sonnets discussed so far, the speaker in this poem appeals to the young man's vanity to convince him to father children, the main argument not being that in doing so he would fulfil the obligation to pass on his beauty to future generations, but that he would still be admired in his old age and even after death.

The central subject in the first three quatrains of the sonnet is the sun, referred to as the 'gracious light' (7.1), 'his' (vv. 2-4, 7-8, 12) and 'he' (v. 10). The first two quatrains describe the sun's ascent in the morning to its climax at midday when it has 'climbed the steep-up heavenly hill' (v. 5) during which it is admired by everyone. But once it has eclipsed the zenith and like 'feeble age he reeleth from the day' (v. 10), people turn away.

Until the concluding couplet, in which the youth appears, the sonnet has a very general character. The first twelve verses read like a general allegory on the passing of youth and time, and only in the last two lines does the speaker address the young man by relating the allegory to the latter's situation: 'So thou, thyself out-going in thy noon,/ Unlooked on diest, unless thou get a son' (vv. 13-14). This allegorical quality places the sonnet in a group of poems with a similar impersonal quality: Sonnet 116, which deals with the idea of perfect love ('Let me not to the marriage of true minds', v. 1), Sonnet 121, which is about false reputation (''Tis better to be vile than vile esteemed', v. 1), Sonnet 123, which addresses personified Time ('No! Time, thou shalt not boast that I do change', v. 1), Sonnet 129, which thematizes the corrupting effects of 'lust in action' (v. 2), and Sonnet 146, which, as shown at the beginning of this chapter, addresses the relationship between material body and immaterial soul.

Another argument the speaker puts forward to convince the youth to beget children invokes the time when he will be old. His (beautiful) children will then be able to remind him of and allow him to appreciate his former beauty (3.11-12). Moreover, by producing children, the youth will avoid accusations and 'all-eating shame' (2.8) for not having fulfilled his natural obligation.

The speaker also implies that the addressee might become a happier and kinder person once he has children. In Sonnet 10, the speaker calls upon him to be kinder towards himself ('to thyself at least kind-hearted prove', v. 12), and in Sonnet 8 the youth's unhappiness as a consequence of remaining childless becomes the central theme. The speaker points out that the young man cannot enjoy music ('why hear'st thou music sadly?', v. 1) and even takes delight in that which troubles him ('receiv'st with pleasure thine annoy', v. 4). The second quatrain attempts to give an explanation for the addressee's inability to delight in music: 'the true concord of well-tuned sounds' (v. 5) rebuke him because he 'confounds/ In singleness the parts that thou shouldst bear' (vv. 7-8), which E/W paraphrase as 'because you, being single, ruin the music by not playing all the notes you should' (2020: 259). The youth cannot take delight in the harmony and finely tuned notes of music because they show him what he so far neglected to do, which is further explained in the final quatrain. Just as one string (of a lute or viola da gamba) sustains and forms a union with another to produce musical harmony ('how one string, sweet husband to another,/ Strikes each in each by mutual ordering', vv. 9-10), the young man should also establish harmony by founding a family of 'sire, and child, and happy mother' (v. 11). Strings, in order to produce music and harmony, need other strings, the speaker concludes. Staying single, the young man is simply 'none' (v. 14), nothing.

However, the speaker also has ulterior motives for wanting the young man to procreate. By producing beautiful children, he would also confirm the speaker's repeated claims about his beauty made in the sonnets and thereby prove the speaker right. Interestingly, and maybe not coincidentally, this ulterior reason is introduced in the last of the procreation sonnets, Sonnet 17. While the main idea of the sonnet seems at first sight pretty straightforward ('Produce children and then you will prove my poems true'), the argument is in fact more complex and even self-defeating. After saying in the first two verses that even if his poetry were able to give expression to the youth's 'high deserts' (v. 2) (which it cannot), no one would believe that such a person could really exist ('Who will believe my verse', v. 1). The speaker goes on to explain that the reason his poems fail to adequately voice the young man's qualities, are his own insufficiencies as a poet: his poetry is 'as a tomb' (v. 3) hiding instead of exposing the young man's beautiful 'parts' (v. 4). By using the conditional tense ('If I *could* write the beauty of your eyes,/ And [. . .] number all your graces', vv. 5-6; my emphasis), the speaker admits to the fact that his poetry is inadequate in preserving the youth's 'parts' (v. 4), 'the beauty' (v. 5) of his eyes and 'all [. . . his] graces' (v. 6). And even *if* the speaker could give adequate expression to the young man, his poems would only be perceived as 'lies' (v. 7), they would be 'scorned' (v. 10) and 'termed a poet's rage' (v. 11).

The couplet provides the solution to this dilemma: 'But were some child of yours alive that time,/ You should live twice: in it, and in my rhyme' (vv. 13-14). Only if the young man produces children, can he and his beauty live on in them and in doing so, will he also continue to exist in the speaker's poems. On closer inspection, however, the sonnet does not really make sense. If, as the speaker has argued throughout the entire poem, his poetry fails to capture the youth's beauty, how can living proof of the children improve the poems' quality? Does bad poetry become good poetry the moment the poem's subject answers the poet's pleas?

After having discussed the speaker's side of this argument, it is also interesting to look more closely at the youth's objections to procreation. Why does he not want to have children? This question is difficult to answer as the young man is not given a voice. One can infer, however, possible reasons from the speaker's demands, expectations and charges.

The charge mentioned most often is the youth's self-centredness. He is 'contracted to [. . . his] own bright eyes' (1.5), instead of loving and marrying others, he is married to himself and seems too much in love with himself and his beauty. Elsewhere the speaker is more direct and accuses him of 'self-love' (3.8) and irresponsibility.

In Sonnet 4, the speaker argues that by squandering and wasting his resources the young man becomes, paradoxically, both a spendthrift and a miser. The main argument of the sonnet is that instead of saving his beauty for future generations by passing it on to children, the youth spends that beauty on himself ('Unthrifty loveliness, why dost thou spend/ Upon thyself thy beauty's legacy?', vv. 1-2). The word 'spend' and the accusation that the youth has 'traffic with thyself alone' (v. 9) have a clear sexual meaning and invoke the wasting of semen in unreproductive sexual congress.

Instead of moderately using the resources nature has lent him, he wastes them and at the same time withholds them from the world. He is both '[u]nthrifty' (v. 1) and a 'niggard' (v. 5), both a 'use[r]' (v. 7) and a 'usurer' (ibid.). The poem underscores this ambiguity when it refers to beauty and sexuality in terms of financial transactions resulting in gains and losses by using terms such as 'spend' (v. 1), 'bequest' (v. 3), 'lend' (v. 3), 'profitless' (v. 7), 'usurer' (v. 7), 'sum of sums' (v. 8) and 'executor' (v. 14). Manfred Pfister refers to this quality as the 'erotic economy of Shakespeare's sonnets' (2018: 64). Although the charges directed at him are explicit, the youth's motives for his actions remain blurry. Apart from the fact that he enjoys life and sexual pleasures and prefers to remain independent, the sonnets only tell us that he is rather self-centred and 'self-willed' (6.13) and that he is unhappy or discontented from time to time (cf. Sonnet 8 discussed above). Occasionally these traits in the youth turn into self-loathing, self-hate, and the desire to harm and destroy himself (as shown in the discussion of Sonnet 10 above). At the end of the day, the youth, just like the desired female in Petrarchan poetry, remains voiceless and is not given the chance to speak for himself.

The limits of procreation

The impressionistic quality of the *Sonnets* referred to earlier is enhanced by the fact that the speaker at various times expresses his doubts as to the effectiveness of his persuasion strategies. The speaker seems to realize that '[t]ime, transience, and awareness of mortality gradually undermine any attempts to create defenses against their power' (Tetzeli von Rosador 2000: 597; my translation). Although the speaker keeps protesting that producing children is an effective means to preserve the young man's beauty and memory, there are moments in the sequence when he seems to doubt his own claim.

For example, in Sonnet 12 the 'poetic evocation of time's all-inclusive operation is so persuasive' (KDJ 2010: 134) that the sonnet's conclusion in the couplet leaves 'the remedy [of producing children] in doubt' (ibid.). The first line introduces time by referring to a clock, and it is striking how slavishly the verse adheres to the iambic pentameter and thereby emulates the sound of a clock. It is as if the syllables, each of them consisting of one word, announce the relentless ticking away of life: 'When I do count the clock that tells the time' (v. 1; cf. also Innes 1997: 100). What follows in the remaining lines of the first quatrain and in the second quatrain is a description of decay in different spheres of life: the day sinks into 'hideous night' (v. 2), the violet turns 'past prime' (v. 3), black hair turns grey (v. 4), trees lose their leaves, and corn turns from green to grey (vv. 7-8). In the light of this omnipresent decay, the speaker realizes that the youth too will have to succumb to 'the wastes of time' (v. 10) and eventually 'die' (v. 12). The solution to counter this decay is offered only in the very last verse, almost hidden, after the speaker reiterates once more that 'nothing 'gainst time's scythe can make defence' (v. 13) except producing children: 'Save breed to brave him, when he takes thee hence' (v. 14). Considering, however, the strong emphasis on death and decay in the first twelve verses of the poem, this solution does not appear to be very convincing.

A similar self-cancelling effect occurs in Sonnet 15 which is also the first sonnet in the sequence which introduces the theme of writing. As in Sonnet 12, the speaker in this sonnet gives a lot of room to the description of the 'instability of all mortal things' (KDJ 2010: 140). He argues that 'everything that grows' (15.1) – and this would also include the idea of children – is perfect for only a short time; that the universe ('this huge stage', v. 3) is nothing but a play (v. 3), which is by definition temporary; that 'man as [well as] plants' (v. 5) begin to 'decrease' (v. 7) the moment they reach perfection and that they will eventually be forgotten ('wear their brave state out of memory', v. 8). This insight makes the speaker realize that even the youth's beauty will fade (vv. 9-12). Against this overwhelming evidence of the power of time, death and deterioration, the speaker introduces a new idea to immortalize the youth. Instead of preserving his beauty through producing children (who as we learnt in the first two quatrains are also subject to decay), the speaker suggests that he will 'engraft [him . . .] new' (v. 14) by way of writing poems about him. Although this seems at first to be a plausible argument (paper and ink being able to outlive human beings), the main argument of the poem undermines this sincerity. If everything will in the end be forgotten, then even poems will be powerless against 'time's scythe' (12.13).

It almost seems as if the speaker at this stage, fifteen sonnets into the sequence, begins to have doubts about the effectiveness of his

86   A COMPREHENSIVE GUIDE TO SHAKESPEARE'S SONNETS

strategies of persuasion. Not only does he seem to have 'forgotten' (Paterson 2010: 49) the argument of the previous fourteen sonnets (the youth should produce children to outlive death), also the tone in which he introduces his new strategy (immortalizing the youth by writing about him) seems to be less confident.

The next poem, Sonnet 16, confirms this impression by setting the two strategies against each other. Unlike Paterson, who finds some of the lines 'muddy, involuted and ambiguous' (2010: 50), I think this is a rather clever poem. After the speaker in the previous sonnet reflected on writing poems about the youth as being a possible alternative strategy of preservation, he now returns to his initial strategy of procreation, but compares its efficacy to that of writing poetry.

As if the speaker senses that his conclusion in the earlier sonnet (immortalization through writing poetry) is not really satisfactory, he begins by asking the question whether there is not a more powerful, a 'mightier way' (v. 1) of preservation than his 'barren rhyme' (v. 4). The second quatrain provides the answer: 'many maiden gardens, yet unset' (v. 6) would gladly bear his child and thus create a much more convincing copy of the youth than the 'painted counterfeit' (v. 8) of the poet's sonnets. The third quatrain ('So should the lines of life that life repair,/ Which this, time's pencil or my pupil pen,/ Neither in inward worth nor outward fair,/ Can make you live yourself in eyes of men', vv. 9-12) has caused a few problems – Booth calls it a 'devil's puzzle' (2000, xii) – but I think Paterson offers a conclusive translation: 'Thus should the bloodlines of life renew that very life of yours – that life, which neither time's pencil (which created lovely you), nor my student-of-time's pen (which attempts to depict lovely you) has the power to make you live again in the eyes of future men – whether in terms of your inner virtue or outward beauty' (2010: 50; for a detailed analysis of the third quatrain, see Booth 2000, xi–xvii.).

Children can renew the youth's beauty and 'inward worth' (v. 11) in a much better way than the ageing addressee or the poet's sonnets. Only by giving himself in marriage to a woman, the couplet concludes, will the young man be able to keep his identity and life. Therefore, after suggesting in the previous sonnet that writing poetry might be a more efficient way to preserve the youth, the speaker discards the idea again in this and the following sonnet in favour of the strategy of procreation. Writing, however, remains a prominent and constant theme in the *Sonnets*, as will be shown in the next chapter.

Further reading

Themes and concerns of the *Sonnets*: Booth 1969; Dubrow 1987; E/W 2013: 63–81; Hyland 2003: 154–67, 175–87; Leishman 1963; Schoenfeldt 2010: 69–111. **Memory, preservation, procreation:** Crosman 1990; Guy-Bray 2020; Herman 2000; Knecht 2021; Sullivan Jr. 2007; Sutphen 2000; Watson 2007.

5

Writing

For Stephen Guy-Bray, Shakespeare's *Sonnets*, and indeed all sonnet sequences, are 'forms of metarepresentation' (2020: 127), that is, they are concerned with the writing of poetry. Although this seems to apply to a vast number of sonnets in the sequence, there are some poems in which the speaker, when referring to writing, seems to have something other than poetry in mind. When the speaker mentions 'tables' (v. 1) in Sonnet 122 and 'table' (v. 2) in Sonnet 24 (discussed in Chapter 6), he refers to 'either "A small portable tablet for writing upon, especially for notes or memoranda" (*OED* table 2b) or, more probably, synonymous here with "table-book", a pocket notebook' (KDJ 2010: 354). Shakespeare uses the term in this sense frequently (cf. e.g. *TGV* 2.7.3, *KJ* 2.1.503, *1H6* 2.4.101, *R3* 1.4.196), probably most famously in *Hamlet* when the protagonist, after meeting the ghost of his murdered father, exclaims: 'Yea, from the table of my memory/ I'll wipe away all trivial fond records' (*Ham* [Q2] 1.5.98-99). Only a few lines later he may even produce an actual writing tablet on stage: 'My tables! Meet it is I set it down' (107).

The argument of Sonnet 122 is that the notebook the youth gave to the speaker to record a memory of the former is not really needed by the speaker, as the young man's attributes are firmly lodged within the speaker's 'brain' (v. 1). The meaning of the first quatrain is ambiguous. Either the speaker argues that everything he wrote about the youth in his notebook he has now memorized, or he claims that that which he *could* have written in the notebook is written in his memory and ranks above all other memories 'to eternity' (v. 4). The second quatrain qualifies this statement by saying that 'at the least' (v. 5) the speaker will remember the young man as long as he lives (which is quite different from 'to eternity'!): as long as his 'brain and heart' (v. 5) exist. The third quatrain then

90   A COMPREHENSIVE GUIDE TO SHAKESPEARE'S SONNETS

returns to the idea of the notebook from the opening line. Realizing that it is a very inadequate means 'to score' (v. 10) the youth's 'dear love' (v. 10), the speaker concedes that he gave the notebook away preferring to trust his tables of memory (vv. 11-12). Not only is memory a more reliable means of remembering the youth than a notebook, but needing the latter to tally the young man's love would also imply forgetfulness on the speaker's part.

A notebook is also the subject of Sonnet 77. Although built on the rather simple classical rhetorical figure of *correlatio*, 'in which lines or stanzas exhibit two (or more) series of elements, each element in the first corresponding to one in the same position in the second, respectively' (Preminger and Brogan 1993: 242), the sonnet is in fact more complex than it appears.

In the first quatrain the speaker gives the youth three *memento mori*, symbolic objects to remind the addressee of his mortality: a mirror ('glass', v. 1), a clock ('dial', v. 2) and a notebook ('vacant leaves', v. 3). The second and third quatrains explain and elaborate upon the functions and meanings of these gifts. The mirror will remind the youth of his physical decay (vv. 5-6) and the clock will keep reminding him that his time on earth is limited (vv. 7-8). The notebook, however, will give him the opportunity to reflect on his condition and to obtain some 'learning' (v. 4) from this reflection, as announced at the end of the first quatrain. Consequently, the entire third quatrain is devoted to the uses of the notebook. The speaker encourages the addressee to write down his thoughts because then he will find 'Those children nursed, delivered from thy brain,/ To take a new acquaintance of thy mind' (vv. 11-12). This is an ingenious way of saying that writing down our thoughts will enable us to confront and to reflect on them as well as learn from them. The more often we engage in this process of self-reflection, the more we and the notebook will benefit from it, because these reflections will enrich our 'memory' (v. 9) which will conversely 'enrich [... the] book' (v. 14). Writing is here understood as a means of rationalization and self-inspection leading to greater self-awareness.

Imitatio vs. *inventio*

Apart from sonnets 77 and 122, all the other sonnets in the writing group focus on the writing of poetry. This does not come as a surprise as the speaker is in fact a poet, as can be seen not only from the references to his 'pupil pen' (16.10), his 'verse' (17.1), his 'papers' (17.9), 'metre' (17.12) and 'rhyme' (17.14) and, of course, from the fact that he calls himself a poet (17.7, 17.11).

The idea that the speaker in love poems is a poet was well established at Shakespeare's time. Petrarch's speaker is also a poet, and the fact that his unattainable object of desire is called Laura highlights the fact that the speaker in wanting her also desires to be recognized for his poetry. The name 'Laura' goes back to the laurel wreath received by the poet laureate (see Chapter 1 above) and points to the ephemeral quality of fame since *l'aura* also means a 'puff of air' (Bates 2011: 116). Petrarch himself was crowned 'poet laureate' in 1341.

Similarly, when Sidney's 'lover of stars' (Astrophil), desires the 'star' (Stella), he is not only expressing his love in well-wrought poems, but also trying to secure his reputation by virtually reaching for the stars. In this sense, not 'winning the Lady, not winning the argument, not winning the bays . . . it's all one' (ibid., 117).

Consequently, many of the sonnets focus on the speaker being a poet and on his awareness of the literary traditions and conventions he is indebted to but from which he also tries to free himself. For example, in Sonnet 76 the speaker-poet struggles with old and new poetic forms of expression. In the first quatrain, the speaker points out the deficits in his poetry. His verse is lacking in 'new pride' (v. 1) which, according to the *Oxford English Dictionary*, translates as 'ostentatious adornment or ornamentation' (*OED*, 'pride, n., II.7.c'), in 'variation' (v. 2) and 'quick change' (ibid.), the last term implying that his poems are lacking in life and vividness. He further complains that his language is unoriginal (he has not been looking to 'new-found methods', v. 4) and that he has not tried to come up with 'compounds strange' (v. 4). Both KDJ and Burrow in their notes to this line refer to the entry on 'compound' in the *Oxford English Dictionary* and the meaning 'A compound word, a verbal compound' (*OED,* 'compound, n., 2.c') which also cites this sonnet as one of its sources. In this narrow sense, a compound is simply understood as a verb 'with a prefix' as opposed to a simple verb without one (cf. Booth 2000: 264). The speaker is here exhorting himself for not having produced new ('strange', v. 4) word creations, but compounds also must be understood in a wider sense as 'compositions, literary compositions' (Booth 2000: 264). It is

92 A COMPREHENSIVE GUIDE TO SHAKESPEARE'S SONNETS

somehow ironic, that Shakespeare, who is credited 'with coining more new words than any other author' (Dickson 2009: 521) has a speaker complaining that he is not original.

The speaker continues to reproach himself for this lack of 'invention' (v. 6) in the second quatrain, arguing that his inability to come up with new forms of expression may have resulted in a clearly identifiable style, 'a noted weed' (v. 6) in which 'every word almost doth tell my name,/ Showing their birth, and where they did proceed' (v. 7-8). The speaker is not only concerned about his mediocre style, he also fears that he might be recognized as the author of these highly erotic poems.

In the third quatrain, the speaker suggests an answer to his own charges. The reason why his style has not changed and why he has not tried out 'new-found methods' and 'compounds strange' is simply that his 'stylistically monotonous verse is really a reflection of – a tribute *to*, indeed – the unchanging constancy of [his] love' (Paterson 2010: 219). According to this logic, using the same words again and again is an appropriate means to express a love for the young man that is unchanging and constant. The final couplet summarizes this logic by using the sun metaphor: 'For as the sun is daily new and old,/ So is my love still telling what is told' (vv. 13-14).

Sonnet 76 continues and reflects on the general theme from Sonnet 38. While the poet-speaker in Sonnet 76 explains his conventional style by saying that in order to express his constant love he does not need 'new-found methods' (76.4) and 'compounds strange' (ibid.), the speaker in Sonnet 38 turns the argument around by stating that it is the youth who provides the speaker (and every other poet) with the inspiration to write '[e]ternal numbers' (v. 12), i.e. immortal verses.

The meaning of the first two quatrains is ambiguous because on the one hand, the speaker implies that as his lines are inspired by and about the youth, they are different from 'every vulgar paper' (v. 4). The 'excellent' (v. 3) and 'sweet argument' (v. 3) of the youth finds '[w]orthy' (v. 6) expression in the speaker's poems, implying that they are also sweet and excellent. On the other hand, the speaker suggests that basically any poet who writes about the youth, even those who may be less gifted than the speaker, will be inspired by the subject and able to capture his beauty and excellence ('For who's so dumb, that cannot write to thee,/ When thou thyself dost give invention light?', vv. 7-8). The youth is then perceived as the tenth Muse, who like the nine Greek goddesses of literature, science and the arts, is considered a source of knowledge and inspiration (vv. 9-10).

Both poems, Sonnet 38 and Sonnet 76, are characterized by the speaker's modest assessment of his skill. But while he concludes in Sonnet 38 that his poems may have some quality (even though this is only due to its subject-matter of the youth), the speaker in Sonnet 76 denies any such quality (and excuses this lack with the worth and quality of his love for the young man).

As mentioned before, this self-reflexive quality was common in early modern poetry. Poems, and sonnets in particular, served poets and their speakers as sites to explore their craft and as platforms to express (and stage) the self. The speaker in Philip Sidney's sonnet sequence *Astrophil and Stella* is also a poet who, like Shakespeare's speaker, reflects on the poet's dilemma to conform to conventions while at the same time trying to create something new:

Philip Sidney, 'Sonnet 1'

Loving in truth, and fain in verse my love to show,
That she (dear she) might take some pleasure of my pain;
Pleasure might cause her read, reading might make her know;
Knowledge might pity win, and pity grace obtain;
   I sought fit words to paint the blackest face of woe,
Studying inventions fine, her wits to entertain;
Oft turning others' leaves, to see if thence would flow
Some fresh and fruitful showers upon my sunburnt brain.
   But words came halting forth, wanting invention's stay;
Invention, nature's child, fled step-dame study's blows:
And others' feet still seemed but strangers in my way.
Thus great with child to speak, and helpless in my throes,
   Biting my truant pen, beating myself for spite,
   'Fool,' said my muse to me; 'look in thy heart, and write.'
     (Sidney 2008: 153)

Like the speaker in Shakespeare's sonnets 38 and 76, the speaker in Sidney's sonnet makes it very clear at the beginning that he is a poet. While Shakespeare's speaker refers to his Muse in Sonnet 38 and to his verse in Sonnet 76, Sidney's poet also admits in the first line that he unsuccessfully tried to express his love in verse ('and fain in verse my love to show', v. 1). In the second quatrain, he explains that he

94 A COMPREHENSIVE GUIDE TO SHAKESPEARE'S SONNETS

first tried to find the right words by studying 'inventions fine' (v. 6), a term that we also find in Shakespeare's sonnets. However, where Shakespeare's speaker means it to refer to 'the finding out or selection of topics to be treated, or arguments to be used' (*OED*, 'invention, n., I.1.d') in 38.8 and 76.6, Sidney's use of the term is more ambiguous. He uses it three times in his sonnet with at least two different, even contradictory meanings. The first use in the sixth verse ('Studying inventions fine') refers to ideas and devices used and created by earlier poets. In looking for 'fit words' (v. 5), the speaker decided to read poems and texts by previous authors, hoping that by turning 'others' leaves' (v. 7), i.e. the pages of their books, he would find inspiration, described here as 'fresh and fruitful showers' (v. 8). But consulting the works and 'inventions' of other poets did not prove successful; on the contrary, words only 'came halting forth' (v. 9) lacking 'invention'. This is the second time the speaker refers to invention, but this time he is not referring to the ideas of other authors but to invention in the sense in which Shakespeare's speaker in sonnets 38 and 76 employs it, invention as 'the faculty of inventing or devising; power of mental creation or construction; inventiveness' (*OED*, 'invention, n., I.4'). This faculty is here personified as 'nature's child' (v. 10), who escaped from 'step-dame study's blows' (v. 10). The speaker understands invention and studying as being antonymous to each other. Trying to find ideas by reading other authors is counterproductive and stands in the poet's way to originality. The 'feet' referred to in verse 11 are not only a metonymy for the other authors, but also for their creations written in metrical feet.

Like the speaker in Shakespeare's *Sonnets*, Sidney's poet also feels the weight of the literary tradition on his shoulders and tries to establish his own poetic identity by negotiating between *imitatio* and *inventio*. *Imitatio*, as defined by Roger Ascham in his textbook *The Schoolmaster* in 1570, is 'to follow, for learning of tongues and sciences, the best authors' (2004: 143). *Inventio*, on the other hand, is the first of five stages in ancient rhetoric and describes the invention of the argument. This is the second use of invention in Sidney's poem which, as the speaker concludes in the final line, can be achieved by simply looking 'in thy heart'. But the relationship between *imitatio* and *inventio* is more complex than Sidney's speaker wants us to believe and as the poems discussed up to now show: the 'idea that the average sonneteer looked in his heart and wrote, as Philip Sidney declares, [. . .] could not be further from the truth' (E/W 2013: 19).

Early modern poets were very much aware of the reciprocal relationship between tradition and invention. For example, even those sonnets which invert Petrarchan ideals and conventions (such as sonnets 127 and 130 discussed above and below) are, to some extent, still Petrarchan sonnets. In the sense of Heinrich Plett's dictum that 'the type of imitation determines the character of innovation' (1994: 15; my translation), both the speaker and the poet, in order to set themselves apart from tradition, have to invoke that tradition first in order to transcend it.

The importance of invention is further explored in the sonnets with a primary focus on the theme of imagination which I discuss in Chapter 8 below. As we will see, imagination as a mental power to invent objects and situations that are not present becomes a central concern in those sonnets in which the speaker attempts to come to terms with the state of being separated from the young man.

Uses of poetry

Apart from the two sonnets 77 and 122, which refer to writing in a notebook, the sonnets in the writing group are all concerned with the writing of poetry. They either deal with poetry as

- a means to preserve the youth, particularly his beauty (18, 19, 54, 55, 60, 63, 65, 81, 100, 101, 103, 104, 106, 107)
- an (in-)adequate or deliberately falsifying means of expression (21, 76, 152)
- an expression of love (23, 26, 32, 38, 102, 105, 108)
- a means to make the youth forget or remember the speaker (71, 72, 74)
- or as a means by which poets compete for fame and favours (sonnets 59, 78–80, 82–86)

Sonnet 18, discussed in Chapter 1, is about writing as a means to preserve the youth's beauty. Sonnet 19 also belongs to this mini-group and is a particularly interesting example, since it is addressed to personified Time and not the young man. The sonnet is characterized by an outspokenness and brazenness one usually finds in the poetry of George Herbert or John Donne. After describing the power of '[d]evouring time' (19.1) the speaker bids Time to 'carve not with thy hours my love's fair brow' (v. 9). Employing the writing metaphor, the speaker asks Time not to write wrinkles ('lines', v. 10) with its 'antique pen' (ibid.) in the youth's face and to spare the latter from ageing (vv. 11-12). However, the second volta after verse 12 introduces a second turn of argument. After changing from submitting to the powers of Time to taking command over it in line 9, the speaker now adapts his argument once again: Time may after all subject the youth to decay and ageing because in the end it will be up to the speaker's 'verse' to preserve his beauty for ever.

One of the most famous sonnets dealing with the speaker's attempts to defy the 'inevitable process of maturity and decay in the natural world' (KDJ 2010: 230) by way of writing poetry is Sonnet 60. What makes this sonnet stand out is the way it employs and realizes the English sonnet form of three quatrains and a final couplet. For Helen Vendler, 'sonnet 60 is one of the "perfect" examples of the 4-4-4-2 Shakespearean sonnet form' (1999: 284). In her reading of the sonnet, she has drawn attention to its very logical structure. In highlighting the destructive power of Time, Shakespeare introduces three different 'models of what life is like' (ibid.) in the three quatrains: life as a predictable and orderly state of continuous change (first quatrain), life as a fall of princes tragedy (second quatrain), and life as a sequence of catastrophes (third quatrain).

While the first quatrain describes the effect of time on life as a continuous and gradual erosion, comparable to the effect waves have on the 'pebbled shore' (v. 1), the second quatrain uses a more dramatic picture. It features a 'single changing protagonist' (Vendler 1999: 284), 'Nativity' (v. 5), personified life, which, reaching maturity, is crowned only to be felled by powerful time. While the first quatrain views change and decay as a gradual process, the second quatrain focuses on the suddenness with which 'time, that gave, doth now his gift confound' (v. 8). The third quatrain, however, introduces an even more malign view of Time: 'Time doth transfix the flourish set on youth,/ And delves the parallels in beauty's brow;/ Feeds on the rarities of nature's truth,/ And nothing stands but for his scythe to mow' (vv. 9-12). Now 'existential disaster is, temporally speaking, incessant. Time is now unrelentingly rapid in its destructiveness. Whereas the waves took a full quatrain to change places, and nativity took three lines to be confounded, the catastrophic events in Q3 take place one per line' (Vendler 1999: 285). The verbs in the quatrain denote violent actions: Time transfixes (impales) beauty, delves (digs) wrinkles in the forehead, eats 'nature's truth' (v. 11), and mows everything down.

After describing Time's relentless effects on life in increasingly drastic imagery, the final couplet suggests a solution. Although 'nothing stands' (v. 12) that will not be erased by Time, the speaker argues that his verse will be able to outlive and 'stand' (v. 13) against time. This solution is introduced and formally linked to the problem presented in the previous quatrains by what Vendler calls the 'Couplet Tie – the words appearing in the body of the sonnet (ll. 1-12) which are repeated in the couplet (ll. 13-14)' (1999: xiv), an element she detects in every sonnet with a couplet and identifies here in the word 'stand' in lines 12 and 13. The speaker's faith in his verse, however, is coloured by doubt since he can only '*hope* my verse shall stand' (v. 13; my emphasis) against Time.

In some sonnets, the writing of poetry is understood as a kind of betrayal in which the speaker behaves in a disingenuous way. This can be seen, for example, in Sonnet 152 in which the speaker not only reproaches the mistress but also himself for unfaithfulness on multiple levels. The poem begins with the speaker reproaching himself for having broken his vows by loving (and probably having slept with) the woman. To be 'forsworn' (v. 1) refers to the breaking of a vow, so presumably the speaker has broken his marriage vow. In the next verse, however, the speaker accuses the mistress who is 'twice forsworn' (v. 2) because she has (a) betrayed him by sleeping with someone else – the youth? – ('In act thy bed-vow broke', v. 3) and (b) expresses disdain for either her husband, himself or a third person, since the meaning of verses 3-4 ('In act thy bed-vow broke and new faith torn,/ In vowing new hate after new love bearing') is ambiguous. KDJ suggests the following possible readings: 'the woman [. . .] is recently married, and already expressing *new hate* for her husband, in favour of love for the speaker; or [. . .] she has betrayed both her husband and the speaker in favour of some third party, either, as in 133-4, the speaker's *friend*, or yet another' (2010: 420).

98   A COMPREHENSIVE GUIDE TO SHAKESPEARE'S SONNETS

In the second quatrain, the speaker changes the perspective once again and criticizes himself by arguing that he has broken even more oaths than the mistress, namely 'twenty' (v. 6). On closer inspection, however, it becomes clear that this self-criticism is in fact criticism of the mistress: although the speaker says that he is 'perjured most' (v. 6) for misusing her, he argues that he has lost his 'honest faith' (v. 8) in her. The third quatrain, however, reveals that it is he who has been unfaithful, not in love, but in his verse. In his poems, he portrayed the mistress's 'kindness' (v. 9) – did he really? –, her 'truth' and 'constancy' (v. 10) against his better knowledge. He has deluded himself ('gave eyes to blindness,/ Or made them swear against the thing they see' (vv. 11-12) and 'sworn thee [the mistress] fair' (v. 13). So, the speaker's fault is at least as grave as the mistress's as both colluded in the (self-)deception of the speaker or, as KDJ concludes, 'the poet's self-betrayal through false language is treated as worse even than sexual betrayal' (2010: 420).

Of the seven sonnets I have placed in the mini-group of sonnets reflecting on writing as a means to express the speaker's love for the youth, Sonnet 108 is one of the most explicit treatments of the speaker's attempts (and struggles) to express his feelings. In the first quatrain, the speaker asks himself which of his feelings for the young man he has not expressed yet: 'What's new to speak, what new to register,/ That may express my love' (vv. 3-4). In the next quatrain, he gives the answer himself: 'Nothing' (v. 5). All that can be said has been said, and he can only repeat 'the very same' (v. 6) words like 'prayers divine' (v. 5). He thereby, in a way reminiscent of Petrarch's speaker, glorifies the love object and endows it with godlike qualities: words about and addressed to the youth are like prayers which 'hallow' (v. 8) his 'fair name' (ibid.), a phrase which is almost a direct quotation from the Lord's Prayer's 'hallowed be thy name'.

The final six verses are a bit tricky and their meaning can probably be best paraphrased as: our eternal love is new every day, neither cares about the 'injuries done by age to the body' (KDJ 2010: 326) nor 'yields to the wrinkles which are inevitable [. . . and] makes the object of love, though aged, for ever his boy *page* or attendant' (ibid.). The sonnet questions two great myths of the sequence, i.e. that the beauty of the young man is the main reason for the speaker's love and that true love needs to be expressed in words. Ultimately, this sonnet suggests, 'eternal love' (v. 9) exists independently of 'outward form' (v. 14) and well-wrought verse.

In Sonnet 23, the speaker professes a greater faith in his verses to express his feelings for the youth. The main argument is that the speaker, because of his intense passion, cannot express his love in speech and therefore relies on his poetry to communicate his feelings to the youth. This is a 'very sweet poem' (Paterson 2010: 71) which juxtaposes 'speaking' with 'silent' love. In the first quatrain, the speaker uses two similes to describe his inability to express his love in spoken words. Like an 'unperfect actor on the stage' (v. 1) who is troubled by stage fright or 'some fierce thing' (v. 3), he is so overwhelmed by his emotions that he cannot act according to the 'ceremony of love's right' (v. 6). Verse 7 contains an oxymoron which encapsulates the speaker's problem: his feelings are so strong that this makes him weak. He seems to 'decay' in his own 'love's strength' (v. 7). As is often the case, the third quatrain suggests a solution: the speaker wants his 'books' (v. 9) to speak for him. Some scholars, like Paterson, change 'books' to 'looks'. Burrow, however, argues that Shakespeare deliberately wanted to avoid the cliché of opposing 'looks' with 'tongue-tied addresses' (2002: 426).

The 'books' are usually understood as referring to the *Sonnets* themselves, but, as noted earlier, they could also refer to notebooks, 'loose sheets of writing, single paged documents' (ibid.). The speaker's poems then plead for a 'silent love' (v. 13) where his speech fails (note the opposition between sound and silence that is supported throughout the entire poem by juxtaposing the semantic fields of hearing vs. seeing, tongues vs. books, and speaking vs. reading).

Another function that the writing of poetry fulfils in the sequence can be identified in sonnets 71, 72 and 74. Instead of protecting the youth from Time's 'cruel hand' (60.14), the speaker in these poems reverses the perspective and wants to preserve himself in his verse, and not the youth. In Sonnet 74, the speaker argues that once he is dead ('when that fell arrest/ Without all bail shall carry me away', v. 1-2), his verse ('this line', v. 3) will preserve him for the youth ('for memorial still with thee shall stay', 4). While his body will be taken from him and made a 'conquest' (v. 11) of death, his 'spirit' (v. 8) will live on in his poetry, in 'this [which] with thee remains' (v. 14).

Two sonnets in this group provide a slightly different perspective on the speaker's idea of outliving his death through his poetry. In

Sonnet 71, instead of wanting the youth to remember the speaker after his death, the latter urges the young man to do exactly the opposite, namely to '[n]o longer mourn for me when I am dead' (71.1) and to 'remember not/ The hand that writ' (71.5-6) the poem. When the speaker is 'compounded [. . .] with clay' (71.10), the youth should 'not so much as my poor name rehearse' (71.11). Similarly, in the following Sonnet 72, the young man is asked to 'forget' (72.3) the speaker and not to speak well of him since that would amount to lying ('That you for love speak well of me untrue', 72.10). While the speaker in Sonnet 72 gives as a reason for his concern the poor quality of his verse which would 'shame' (72.12) the youth, in Sonnet 71 he is worried that the 'world' (71.13) might 'mock' (71.14) the young man for speaking well of the speaker.

These sonnets, although they appear to be a plea to make the youth forget the speaker, achieve in fact the opposite. By repeatedly drawing attention to the speaker and the poems themselves ('line', 71.5; 'verse', 71.9; 'that which I bring forth', 72.13; 'things nothing worth', 72.14), they, like Sonnet 74, create a 'memorial' (74.4) of the poet-speaker by following a self-deprecating strategy similar to that employed in the sonnets which deal with the speaker's relationship with rival poets and which will be discussed in the next section.

The rival poet and the marketplace

The rival-poet sonnets approach the theme of writing from a more pragmatic angle. These poems are not only about expressing one's desire in verse, wanting to preserve someone else or leaving a legacy, they are also, and mainly, about vying with rivals for the favour of others and about survival in the 'literary marketplace' (Hyland 2003: 21) of the patronage system. Writing love poems about the young man and mistress is also a way for the speaker to define himself as an accomplished poet in court circles.

In Shakespeare's time, being an author was not yet a profession from which one could make a living. Unlike playwrights, who by the end of the sixteenth century were able to make a good deal of money from box office earnings and holding shares in theatrical companies, poets did not write to publish their poems and finance their existence for several reasons:

When Shakespeare was writing, the book trade was still in the very early stages of its development. The first printing press in England had been established by William Caxton in 1477, hardly more than a century before Shakespeare began his literary career. Even in London the writer's market was limited. Books were very expensive and the percentage of the population that was literate was still small, though increasing. The demand for printed books was likewise small. (Hyland 2003: 21)

Instead, poets had their manuscripts circulated in aristocratic circles to show off their skill and to impress potential supporters and patrons, hoping they would find employment at court. 'In return for some degree (usually not large) of financial or material support (such as board and lodging) writers provided their patrons with poems or dedicated writings to them' (ibid., 20–1). In this patronage system

> [g]ifts and rewards flowed not only from the monarch, but also from major and minor nobility and gentry, royal favorites, government civilian and military officers, virtually anyone who was positioned advantageously to offer, sell, or bargain over those tangible and intangible benefits ambitious men sought. The prizes of patronage included cash, titles and honors, lands, leases, grants, licenses, monopolies, pensions, educational and ecclesiastical positions, parliamentary seats, and places in the employ of the nobility, government officials, and the monarch. (Marotti 2014: 209)

In return, poets were expected to be loyal to and to flatter their patrons, which led to an interesting conflict described in the 'rival poet' sequence (sonnets 78–80, 82–86). On the one hand, the poet speaker is expected to flatter and pay homage to the patron, on the other, he also strives to find his own authentic voice and style in competition with other rival poets who also seek the patron's favour and support.

For example, in Sonnet 78 the first quatrain describes the young man's impact on the speaker. He has served as the poet-speaker's muse and provided him with inspiration ('found [thee] such fair assistance in my verse', v. 2), so much so, that 'alien pen[s]' (v. 3), other writers, have emulated him, the speaker, and also tried to

102 A COMPREHENSIVE GUIDE TO SHAKESPEARE'S SONNETS

acquire the youth as a patron ('under thee their poesy disperse', v. 4). In the second quatrain, the speaker elaborates on the effects the youth as muse has had on poets, including himself: the young man has improved the poetry of both amateur and skilled poets by teaching the first ('the dumb', v. 5) to 'sing' (ibid.), and by improving the style of the latter ('added feathers to the learned's wing', v. 7). The youth, however, as the speaker goes on to argue in the third quatrain, should appreciate the poems of the speaker more than those of the others, as they are wholly inspired by him ('Yet be most proud of that which I compile,/ Whose influence is thine, and born of thee', vv. 9-10). While the youth's influence has only (slightly) improved the style of the other poets ('In others' works thou dost but mend the style', v. 11), it has raised '[a]s high as learning' (v. 14) the speaker's 'rude ignorance' (ibid.).

The competitiveness of the patronage market becomes evident in the triangular relationship between youth, speaker and the other poets mentioned in the poem. The young man is coveted not only by rivals in love, but also by rivals desiring artistic inspiration and support. The object of desire is the youth; he is the 'Muse' (v. 1) who inspires poets (vv. 5-8) and, in particular, the speaker-poet (vv. 13-14). The other poets are only referred to as 'alien pen[s]' (v. 3), 'their' (v. 4) and 'others' (v. 11) and remain a nameless group consisting of both 'dumb' (v. 5) and 'learned[...]' (v. 7) writers.

In the next sonnet, Sonnet 79, the rivals have become just one rival poet, whom the speaker refers to as 'a worthier pen' (79.6), 'thy poet' (79.7), and seven times as merely 'he' (79.8-9, 10-11, 13-14). The speaker-poet admits defeat, acknowledging that 'my gracious numbers are decayed' (v. 3) and that the other poet is 'worthier' (v. 6) to write about the youth and to benefit from his patronage. The speaker, however, also explains *why* his rival's poetry is better suited to celebrate the young man. The rival, according to the speaker, merely gives back to the youth what 'he stole' (v. 9) from him. That which seems original and 'invent[ed]' (v. 7) in the poems, the rival in fact took ('rob[bed]', v. 8) from the youth. Since the rival poet only gives expression to that which is already there (in the youth), he should not be paid, neither in words, money, or favours. The language of commerce and unlawful exchange employed in the poem ('robs', 'pays', 'lends', 'stole', 'give', 'afford', 'owes', 'pay') underscores the idea of the other poet merely appropriating the youth and, moreover, highlights the competitive quality of the patronage system.

The rival-poet sonnets cover a range of themes associated with the patronage system: artistic and emotional dependence (78), (literary) criticism (79), envy (79, 86), sincerity and flattery (80, 82, 84, 85), and aspects of literary style (82–85). The uniting feature of this group – apart from the triangular constellation of poet, youth and rival poet(s) – is the speaker's belief that his plainer style is more sincere and authentic than the more elaborate style of his rivals which the speaker refers to as 'rhetoric' (82.10), 'gross painting' (82.13), 'painting' (83.1) or 'polished form of well-refined pen' (85.8).

The speaker's belief in the superiority of his more sincere style over the rival poets' 'rhetoric', however, is problematic and paradoxical in more than one sense, as sonnets 83 and 84 reveal. Sonnet 83 begins with the speaker saying that since the youth's beauty speaks for itself, he, the speaker, saw no need to praise him (vv. 1-4). The speaker continues by saying that the young man is living proof that poetry can never express this beauty adequately (vv. 5-8). In the third quatrain, the speaker addresses the youth directly by defending himself against the latter's accusation that this silence was reproachable (v. 9). The speaker argues that, on the contrary, by not writing about the youth's beauty he did not, like 'others' (v. 12), i.e. other poets, bury him under insufficient praise. In the couplet, he repeats his belief that no poet can do justice to the young man's beauty.

As convincing as the speaker's argument may be (that poetry cannot do justice to the youth's beauty), it is also illogical and self-defeating. Contrary to his claim that he will not write about the young man and remain 'mute' (v. 11), the speaker does exactly the opposite. The whole sonnet (and most of the other poems in the youth sequence) is in fact about the young man and an attempt to give expression to his beauty and his uniqueness by way of poetry.

In Sonnet 84, the speaker continues not only with his criticism of his rivals' more elaborate style ('Who is it that says most? Which can say more,/ Than this rich praise: that you alone are you', 84.1-2), but also with his discussion of the (im)possibility of writing sonnets about the young man in general. Words cannot give expression to that which is hidden and enclosed ('immured', v. 3) inside the youth and who can only be compared to himself ('the

104 A COMPREHENSIVE GUIDE TO SHAKESPEARE'S SONNETS

store/ Which should example where your equal grew', vv. 3-4). The second quatrain elaborates on the idea that any worth and quality poems inspired by the youth might have, should also be credited to the poem's subject ('Lean penury within that pen doth dwell/ That to his subject lends not some small glory', vv. 5-6). The speaker thereby addresses the main conflict poets are faced with in the patronage system: how to be original and at the same time pay justice to the addressee. How can one praise the subject and at the same time remain true to oneself and find one's own style? The speaker concludes that in the end one can only distinguish oneself by not distinguishing oneself: 'Let him but copy what in you is writ,/ Not making worse what nature made so clear' (v. 9-10). Only by presenting the youth as he is, can a poet develop his own 'style' (v. 12) and acquire 'fame' (v. 11).

The speaker therefore finds himself in a position which he describes as 'a curse' (v. 13). Moreover, the paradox of excelling in one's poetry by not being allowed to excel in it, is connected to another paradox: the youth is both a curse and a 'blessing' (v. 13). On the one hand, his worth and beauty require sincere and restrained admiration in poetry, on the other hand, the youth is 'fond on' (v. 14) an exaggerated style. As a result, the speaker-poet finds himself in a no-win situation. If he gives in to the young man's desire for flattery, he betrays his poetic ideals and will falsify the youth in his poetry, and if he tries to represent his worth and beauty truthfully in a more restrained style he will run the risk of losing his favour.

Petrarchism

The main semantic and formal features of Petrarchism have already been described above in the first chapter: how the speaker celebrates his unrequited love for a beautiful, yet unattainable and chaste woman (because she is either dead, a virgin or married), how she is idealized and at the same time demonized, how the speaker suffers from her rejection, constantly oscillates between hope and despair, retreats into some kind of inner exile, and how the relationship between speaker and love object is never consummated. Moreover, the speaker's desire is not only directed at his mistress but also at poetic self-representation. Every sonnet has therefore, as Tetzeli von

Rosador argues, two addressees, the mistress and other lover-poets who can identify with the speaker (cf. 2000: 585).

In this section I will return to sonnets 127 and 130 which I discussed in Chapter 3 in the context of the mistress's 'black' attributes. Even though the theme of writing in these two poems is subordinate to the primary theme of desire and love, a cluster that will be addressed in the next chapter, these sonnets are also about writing in that they self-reflexively engage with the Petrarchan sonnet tradition.

We have seen how the speaker in Sonnet 127 argues that the traditional idea of a beautiful, fair complexion has been replaced by a new one and how his mistress with her 'raven black' (127.9) eyes represents this new ideal of 'black beauty' (127.3). The rejection of whiteness and fairness in Shakespeare's *Sonnets* has been understood as an outright 'criticism of Petrarchan rhetoric' (Tetzeli von Rosador 2000: 589; my translation) and as an expression of the pervasive anti-Petrarchism (cf. Meller 1985: 47) in the late sixteenth century. And although the speaker's denigration of a fair complexion and his celebration of the mistress's dark appearance as the new beauty ideal (cf. 127.3, 14) do in fact corroborate this view, one should not overemphasize Shakespeare's critique of Petrarchism.

As has been pointed out in Chapter 3, praising Black women in poems of the late sixteenth and early seventeenth centuries was fairly common; Marvin Hunt even speaks of a 'full-fledged cult of lyric poetry praising black beauty in explicit terms' (2000: 379). Therefore, celebrating dark women does not necessarily mean that Shakespeare had a decisively anti-Petrarchan agenda. Also, in view of the increase in Black population and the emerging ambivalent attitude of fascination and fear towards what was perceived as the other in sixteenth-century England (cf. Chapter 3), staging the mistress in the *Sonnets* as both 'fair' and 'black' is not that unexpected.

In this regard, the speaker's criticism of face painting expressed in 'each hand hath put on nature's power,/ Fairing the foul with art's false borrowed face' (127.5-6) and 'Sland'ring creation with a false esteem' (127.12) could refer to the belief that since Black women, unlike white women, did not wear make-up, their beauty was considered more authentic (cf. Loomba 2002: 59–60). Moreover, and as shown above, the use of cosmetics was generally criticized since they were believed to lead to 'permanent bodily change' (Loomba 2016: 240), to transform the body into an unnatural

106 A COMPREHENSIVE GUIDE TO SHAKESPEARE'S SONNETS

artefact (cf. Gordon 2020: 273) and were associated with 'luxurious foreign imports and hence symbolic of the decadence of other cultures' (Loomba 2002: 59; cf. also Hall 1996: 85–91; Iyengar 2005; and Harvey 2007).

If anything, Shakespeare's stance towards Petrarchan themes and conceits can be regarded as meta-Petrarchism and not anti-Petrarchism. As becomes clear in Sonnet 130, the speaker's attitude towards the Petrarchan tradition goes beyond its mere refutation. To begin with, this poem almost reads like a parody of Petrarch's 'Rime 90'. Where Laura's hair is golden (Petrarch 90.1), the mistress's is described as 'black wires' (130.4); while Laura's eyes are radiant (Petrarch 90.3-4), the mistress's eyes in Shakespeare 'are nothing like the sun' (v. 1); while Laura's face has the colour of pity, i.e. red (Petrarch 90.5), no 'roses damasked' (v. 5) are seen in the cheeks of Shakespeare's mistress; while Laura moves like an angel (Petrarch 90.9-10), Shakespeare's mistress 'treads on the ground' (v. 12); and while Laura's voice is purer than that of a human being (Petrarch 90.10-11), 'music hath a far more pleasing sound' (v. 10) than Shakespeare's mistress's voice. Shakespeare's speaker stages his mistress as an anti-Laura, who is the exact opposite of the Italian model. Not only does she violate the Petrarchan beauty ideal, but she is also described as anything but angelical. Apart from the earthly qualities of her appearance, voice and gait, we also hear that her breath 'reeks' (v. 8). Although 'the word does not seem to have had quite such unpleasant associations for the Elizabethans as it was later to acquire' (KDJ 2010: 374), stating that there is 'more delight' in 'some perfumes' (v. 7) than in the mistress's breath, does not paint the latter in a very favourable light.

However, on closer inspection one realizes that the sonnet is not only a critique of Petrarchism. Apart from employing a standard feature of Petrarchan poetry, the blazon, in itemizing the mistress's features (her eyes, lips, breasts, hair, cheeks, breath, voice and gait), the poet also comments on the Petrarchan tradition of idealizing the love object. While in Sonnet 127 the mistress was seen as the model for a new kind of beauty, here her blackness/Blackness is not beautiful anymore. She is described as an undesirable person, a fact which – ironically – makes her desirable, as the couplet states: 'And yet, by heaven, I think my love as rare/ As any she belied with false compare' (130.13-14). Although she is not beautiful 'she is more special than any woman who is misrepresented by false comparison'

(E/W 2020: 236). This is not only a poem about the speaker's 'love' (v. 13), but also about the stale and hyperbolic expressions of other poets who misrepresent their beloved. Whereas other poets distort and falsify in their poems, the speaker argues that his lines are honest and implies that his mistress does not require hyperbolic representation to be loved by him; he loves her just the way she is.

There is another way to read this poem, however. For KDJ, the sonnet suggests 'that the traditional forms of beauty celebrated in love poetry are unnecessary to provoke desire: all that is necessary is that the object of desire is female and available' (2010: 374), or, as Eve Kosofsky Sedgwick has argued, the 'dark lady is, for the most part, perceptible only as a pair of eyes and a vagina' (1985: 36). After all, this sonnet follows one which deals with 'lust in action' (129.2), and the misogynistic conception of the mistress supports the reading that this poem may be primarily about the mistress serving the speaker as an object to gratify his sexual desire. Where the mistress in Petrarchan sonnets is desired because of her unavailability, Shakespeare's mistress is desired because of her availability or, as Gordon Braden argues, in the mistress sequence, 'desire is fully capable of surviving the death of admiration' (2000: 166). Sonnets 127 and 130 are, therefore, as much reflections on writing as they are about desire, multi-faceted and self-reflexive engagements with the Petrarchan lyric tradition that employ and at the same time distance themselves from Petrarchan discourse. They celebrate the speaker-poet's prowess to achieve the impossible by turning the fair/beautiful/white into the dark/ugly/Black, and vice versa (cf. Hall 1996: 67; Loomba 2002: 60).

Further reading

Literary marketplace and patronage: Brennan 1988; Hyland 2003: 20–41; Lytle and Orgel 1981; Marotti 2007; Marotti 2014; Marotti and Freiman 2011. **Use of cosmetics in early modern England:** Gordon 2020; Hall 1996: 85–91; Harvey 2007; Iyengar 2005; Loomba 2002; Loomba 2016: 240–1. **Petrarchism and anti-Petrarchism:** Braden 2000; Kennedy 2011, 2016; Levin 2001: xlv–xlvi; Meller 1985: 35–55; Roe 2018; Tetzeli von Rosador 2000: 583–6.

6

Desire

The third primary theme cluster of desire is by far the most prominent and influential in the sequence. In the end, it is probably impossible to find a sonnet that does not in one way or another deal with desire in the context of the love triangle of speaker, youth and mistress. As E/W have argued, the 'Sonnets repeat strands of emotions and ideas, emphasizing a polyphony of attitudes and approaches to love' (2013: 63). Even those sonnets which I have grouped in the clusters of preservation, writing, deception and imagination often revolve around the idea of preserving love or love objects, of writing about desire, of love's deceptive quality, or of the powers of imagination when thinking about the beloved or desired person. It is, however, possible to differentiate between sonnets in which desire only plays a subsidiary role and those in which love and desire are at the centre of attention. The latter cover a wide range of aspects, such as

- the speaker's love and desire for the youth or the intimate, symbiotic love relationship between them (sonnets 22, 24, 25, 37, 53, 62, 73, 75, 115)
- the sinister aspects of the desired youth (36, 69, 70, 93–96)
- the (supposedly) sinister aspects of the speaker (111, 112, 117)
- the separation (also through death) and/or reunion of speaker and youth (39, 50–52, 56–58, 64, 87–92, 97–99, 109, 110, 113, 114)
- love rivals or, more specifically, the love triangle of speaker, youth and mistress (40–42, 133, 134, 144)

110 A COMPREHENSIVE GUIDE TO SHAKESPEARE'S SONNETS

- the mistress's beauty (127, 128)
- the sinister aspects of the mistress (131, 132, 150)
- the speaker's (irrational) desire for the mistress (145, 147–149, 153, 154)
- sexual desire (20, 130, 135, 136, 151)
- and the nature of love and desire in a changing, corrupted, or decadent world (66–68, 116, 123–125, 129)

Sonnet 39 is from the largest of these mini-sequences which thematizes an ongoing concern in the *Sonnets*: the separation of speaker and youth and how this will affect the relationship between the two. The poem is yet another good example of the way the sonnets in the sequence are thematically connected in more than one way. The main concern in this sonnet is the speaker's desire for the youth but it is expressed by invoking the ideas of oneness and separation. The speaker begins by saying that praising the young man in an adequate manner is not possible as long as he is 'the better part' (v. 2) of him. Praising someone who is (felt to be) part of oneself amounts to self-praise: 'What can mine own praise to mine own self bring' (v. 3). After introducing this problem in the first four verses, the speaker proposes in the second quatrain that they should separate: 'let us divided live' (v. 5). For then the speaker could continue to give the youth praise, which only he alone deserves (vv. 7-8).

What began as a proposal for proactive separation to allow the speaker to praise the youth, after the volta turns into a defensive argument, a strategy to cope with the inevitable separation. Addressing absence itself, the speaker now argues that although being separated from the youth is 'a torment' (v. 9), it is made 'sweet' (v. 10) by giving the speaker 'leisure' (v. 10) to think about and praising him (and only him) in the sonnet. The symbiotic relationship, the 'loving amalgamation' (KDJ 2010: 188) between speaker and youth, which is the object in several sonnets (cf. e.g. sonnets 22, 24, 25, 37, 53, 62, 73, 75, 115), is both a blessing and a curse. On the one hand, it constitutes a very strong and close tie between them, on the other, it blurs the boundaries between self and other and can, as we will see later, make it difficult for the speaker to differentiate between his own faults and merits and those of the youth.

Although it is helpful to identify the various aspects of love and desire the sonnets in this cluster engage with, dividing the many sonnets into further mini-clusters and groups is only of limited use when it comes to providing an overview of the relationships and variations of desire in the *Sonnets*. In this chapter, I will therefore, after a section on the irrational quality of desire, deal first with the speaker's desire for the youth, then with the desire for the woman and finally with those poems that address the triangular desire between speaker, youth and mistress.

Unlike the different culturally encoded conceptions of love, desire is generally understood as something that affects the individual in a more direct and physical manner. Citing an example from Thomas More's *History of Richard III*, the *Oxford English Dictionary* defines desire as 'that feeling or emotion which is directed to the attainment or possession of some object from which pleasure or satisfaction is expected; longing, craving; a particular instance of this feeling, a wish' (*OED*, 'desire, n., 1.a'). The second meaning given, supported by an example from Shakespeare's *Cymbeline*, defines desire even as '[p]hysical or sensual appetite, lust' (*OED*, 'desire, n., 2'). Desire as a 'longing, craving', also in the form of 'sensual appetite' which is directed at the 'possession of some object from which pleasure or satisfaction is expected' is in fact the main theme of the sequence. In the following, it will become clear how much power desire can have over those possessed by it and in particular the speaker.

This physiological longing for another object that is given expression in Shakespeare's *Sonnets* is quite different from the desire one finds in typical Petrarchan poetry in which the speaker desires an unattainable beautiful lady who does not reciprocate his love and leads the speaker to express his unfulfilled longing in poetry. As pointed out before, it is absolutely necessary for this Petrarchan idea of love that the desire is not fulfilled. The speaker's longing, which is continually frustrated and whose object is constantly withheld from him, is the basis and precondition for the speaker's project of fashioning himself as a longing and suffering lover-poet:

[W]hat the 'I' misses takes on a distinct shape or form, most commonly (following Petrarch) that of a beloved female – 'the deare She' or 'cruell Faire' of worn sonnet convention. [. . .] Nevertheless, however much the 'I' might fill the frame with

112 A COMPREHENSIVE GUIDE TO SHAKESPEARE'S SONNETS

details of the mistress's beauty, fame or virtue, it is not she who is the prime concern and not she, when all is said and done, whom the sonnet sequence is really about. Ultimately, the focus of interest is not the desired object but the desiring subject. (Bates 2011: 106–7)

Desire in Petrarchan sonnets is therefore, as mentioned above and unlike in Shakespeare's *Sonnets*, 'intransitive' because it lacks an object. The speaker desires the state of desiring and not the Lady, and the latter becomes 'simply a screen for the more important figure' (ibid., 110). This finding confirms the notion that Petrarchan poetry is a patriarchal discourse that 'manages gender relations' (Innes 1997: 26) and 'a means by which the subjection of women is articulated as a female power that freely relinquishes itself' (ibid.).

Irrational and infectious desire

Compared to the speaker's situation in Petrarchan sonnets, the speaker in the *Sonnets* experiences his desire as something more forceful which he cannot control or explain. This instinctive and urgent quality of desire is articulated in sonnets 153 and 154, the last sonnets in the Quarto of 1609. If one accepts E/W's theory that these are the first sonnets written by the 'young Shakespeare' (2020: 25), they can be understood as announcing his continuing preoccupation with the overpowering effects of desire.

Both sonnets are about Cupid, the 'general of hot desire' (154.7), and retell the story from Marianus Scholasticus' six-line epigram from the sixth century about a nymph stealing from the sleeping 'love-god' (154.1) the torch with which he instils desire in humans. But instead of extinguishing desire 'in a cool well by' (154.9), the nymph in Sonnet 154 achieves the opposite: not only does the burning torch turn the water into 'healthful remedy/ For men diseased' (vv. 11-12), but also, by implication, into an eternal source of desire, making the speaker realize that his love-sick condition will not be cured but aggravated by the 'healing' waters.

Apart from the allegorical meaning that desire cannot be extinguished, the poem also has a more literal and specifically sexual meaning. Cupid's 'heart-inflaming brand' (v. 2) also refers to the male sexual organ, which, inflamed by the disease of syphilis, infects a 'cool well by' (v. 9), 'a bawdy metaphor for the female sex organ' (Booth 2000: 536), in which 'the hot desire of the male is quenched' (KDJ 2010: 426). But the well also refers to a healing bath which is meant to cure those affected by venereal disease ('men diseased', v. 12). Venereal diseases were a major problem in Shakespeare's time, and we find frequent references to them in the *Sonnets* and the plays. Some of the most disturbing allusions can be found in *Troilus and Cressida* in the syphilitic character of the procurer Pandarus.

At the end of the play Pandarus addresses the audience and bequeaths his disease to them:

> PANDARUS
> As many as be here of Panders' hall,
> Your eyes, half out, weep out at Pandar's fall;
> Or if you cannot weep, yet give some groans,
> Though not for me, yet for your aching bones.
> Brethren and sisters of the hold-door trade,
> Some two months hence my will shall here be made.
> It should be now, but that my fear is this:
> Some galled goose of Winchester would hiss.
> Till then I'll sweat and seek about for eases,
> And at that time bequeath you my diseases.

Tro. 5.11.47-56

Pandarus describes what at the time were believed to be typical symptoms of syphilis: swollen eyes, bone ache and a 'goose of Winchester'. The latter could refer to both an infected prostitute from the Southwark brothels south of the Thames and to a 'sore from venereal infection' (Palmer [1998] 1994: 303). Pandarus also alludes to the sweating baths ('I'll sweat and seek about for eases', 55) that were believed to cure those affected by the disease and which correspond to the 'bath and healthful remedy' (154.11) in the sonnet.

Sonnet 153 tells the same story, although with a slightly different emphasis. A 'maid of Dian's' (153.2), a virgin, took the torch from the sleeping love-god Cupid and wanted to extinguish it in a spring nearby, thereby turning the 'valley-fountain' (153.4) into 'a seething bath' (153.7) to cure men of 'strange maladies' (153.8), which can be translated as 'foreign diseases'. As in the companionate sonnet,

114 A COMPREHENSIVE GUIDE TO SHAKESPEARE'S SONNETS

the water that is meant to extinguish desire takes on more than curative functions. However, while the speaker in Sonnet 154 says that his desire for the mistress is not abated by the healing waters, in Sonnet 153 the torch, reignited by the eyes of the mistress and applied to the speaker's breast, rekindles his desire. He has to acknowledge that only his mistress can cure him of his desire by providing him with sexual gratification, and by implication venereal disease ('new fire', v. 14). Both poems have in common a strong emphasis on the uncontrollable power of desire. Desiring someone or something is not understood as a conscious and intentional act but as something that one is subjected to and cannot control. Desire is described as an elementary force, an all-consuming and irrational emotion, but which is also quite at odds with the Petrarchan notions of beauty and self-perfection through suffering.

The irrationality of desire is also thematized in several sonnets leading up to the final two on Cupid, namely in sonnets 141–143 (which I discuss in the cluster of deception), 145, and 147–149. While Sonnet 145, the 'Hathaway'-sonnet discussed in Chapter 2, highlights the speaker's absolute dependence on the mistress, her volatile behaviour and how she 'has the power of life and death over him' (KDJ 2010: 406), the other sonnets are much more outspoken in defining the speaker's desire for the mistress as 'love-madness, which has deranged his judgement' (ibid., 410). One such example is Sonnet 147 in which the speaker sees himself as a patient who is afflicted with 'fever' (v. 1) and suffers from a 'disease' (v. 2).

In the first quatrain, the speaker acknowledges that he is aware that that which he desires 'nurseth the disease' (v. 2) and 'preserve[s] the ill' (v. 3). The mistress only makes the fever worse, which the speaker caught by desiring the mistress in the first place. In the second quatrain, the speaker continues with the assessment of his condition when he admits that 'reason' (v. 5) has left him and when he realizes that his desire is a fatal disease. He compares himself to a madman who cannot be cured and who is also 'past care' (v. 9), not minding that he cannot be cured anymore.

As Vendler has noted, the sonnet is characterized by a number of stylistic, semantic and rhythmical variations. She observes a turn from 'self-diagnostic pose' (1999: 618) in the quatrains to a direct 'second-person accusation' (ibid.) of the mistress in the couplet, which provides the concrete reason for the speaker's predicament: the fact that the mistress is 'black as hell, as dark as night' (v. 14).

The speaker's change from 'elaborate Latinity' (Vendler 1999: 618) to an 'Anglo-Saxon lexicon' (ibid.) in the couplet underscores the move from the abstract to the concrete, from the general to the particular. But Vendler also draws attention to another shift in the poem, from madness to knowledge and rational insight. Although the speaker compares his situation to that of a madman, he is in fact not insane, as he shows quite clearly with his acute diagnosis of his situation.

In Sonnet 141, the speaker concedes that ''tis my heart that loves what they [his eyes] despise' (141.3) and that neither his 'five wits' nor his 'five senses' (141.9) can dissuade him from loving the mistress (the five senses referring to common sense, imagination, fantasy, estimation and memory). In Sonnet 142, the speaker admits that because his irrational love for the mistress is sinful, her scorning him makes her rejection of him virtuous. We learn, however, that her '[h]ate' of the speaker is also 'grounded on sinful loving' (142.2). In Sonnet 148, the speaker calls out 'where is my judgement fled,/ That censures falsely what they [his eyes] see aright?' (148.3-4) and concludes that it is his 'cunning love' (148.13) which keeps him 'blind' (148.13). Sonnet 149 shows us a speaker who finds himself so much under the spell of the mistress that he loves and hates those whom she loves and hates although he is aware that he acts against himself (v. 2-4).

In unwillingly longing for what he in fact 'despises', in being blind to what he should 'see aright', and in seeing his desire as irrational and outside his control, the speaker's perception of the mistress mirrors the early modern conflicted attitude to Blackness and darkness pointed out above.

In Sonnet 143, the speaker addresses irrational desire in a slightly different manner. In an allegorical style reminiscent of Sonnet 7, which compares the young man's loss of admiration to the declining sun (cf. Chapter 4), this sonnet compares the mistress's attitude of neglect towards the speaker to a 'housewife' (143.1) who in chasing after her chickens neglects 'her babe' (143.3).

The first two quatrains develop the 'unusually extended simile' (KDJ 2010: 400) of the housewife putting down her infant while chasing after '[o]ne of her 'feathered creatures' (v. 2). The child is 'neglected' (v. 5), '[c]ries' (v. 6) to catch his mother's attention and expresses their 'discontent' (v. 8). The second part of the sonnet spells out, in a detailed fashion, the meaning of the simile. Like the child, the speaker feels neglected by his mistress who chases after another lover ('that which flies from thee', v. 9), who might or might not be the youth, and implores her to come back to him ('turn back to me', v. 11; 'turn back', v. 14), to 'play the mother's part, kiss me, [and] be kind' (v. 12). Stephen Booth has suggested that the term 'feathered creatures' (v. 2) might imply that the other lover is one of the 'dandified rivals – the "popinjays" – of which men in the speaker's situation are traditionally both jealous and scornful' (2000: 494–5).

The 'Will' in verse 13 (capitalized and printed in italics in the 1609 Quarto) refers to the mistress's hope and desire but also puns on the name William. This is a strategy we also find in sonnets 135 and 136 and which has supplied 'evidence' to those critics who believe that Shakespeare is here either pointing to himself or William Herbert, third Earl of Pembroke, as the mistress's object of desire. Anyhow, the interesting conclusion the couplet draws, is that the speaker wants the mistress to have her 'Will' and then come back to him. So rather than 'either him *or* me' it is a matter of 'him *and* me'.

Paterson, in his characteristically irreverent style finds the sonnet '*bizarre*, certainly, and no good' (2010: 437), and jokingly adds that it 'might tell us something very worrying about WS's [Shakespeare's] relationship to his mum' (ibid.). According to Paterson, it is even 'more worrying [. . .] how *pathetic* he's become. "If you mother me, you can go sleep with that other bloke." Oh have some *pride*, man' (ibid., 438).

Desire for the youth

One of the most conspicuous features of the relationship between speaker and youth is its symbiotic quality, the fact that often the speaker 'does not distinguish between himself and the man' (Gray 2011: 34), that he and the youth are often referred to as being inseparable and forming one entity. In Sonnet 22, the speaker reverts to the traditional trope of the exchange of hearts to express this thought: 'For all that beauty that doth cover thee/ Is but the seemly raiment of my heart,/ Which in thy breast doth live, as thine in me' (22.5-7). The speaker's heart is lodged inside the youth, and the latter's heart inside the speaker, which he will not return to the young man, as the couplet informs us: 'Presume not on thy heart when mine is slain;/ Thou gav'st me thine not to give back again' (22.13-14). As Booth has remarked, the 'wit of these lines [vv. 5-14] derives from seeming to take a metonymy literally' (2000: 170). On the one hand, heart stands for 'love', 'affection' or 'devotion', on the other hand, the speaker is also saying or implying that the heart of each man lives and beats in the breast of the other. This overlapping of the metonymical and the literal meaning is responsible for the irritating effect of the couplet. Reading 'heart' here as a metonymy for 'love' implies that the speaker's desire for the youth will never end, not even after the young man's final rejection of him. Understanding 'heart' literally, however, evokes necrophiliac associations and the disquieting image of the dead speaker refusing to give the youth back his heart. For Paterson, the couplet is simply a 'catastrophe' (2010: 69). Responding to Booth's remark about the 'wit' of the blending of metaphorical and literal meanings, Paterson complains:

> I just don't think its *witty*, exactly, and besides – it doesn't actually *mean* anything: is he taking the YM's [young man's] heart with him? Is it dying with him? Why would he be such a bastard anyway, and play keepers when he doesn't need it any more? How will he do any of that when he's dead? Oh, it's too daft. (ibid.)

Paterson is missing the main point here. First, Booth is not suggesting that we should only read these lines in a literal manner. The wit of the lines lies in the space between the literal and the metaphorical; what we are invited to also understand in a literal fashion is still a metonymy. Secondly, by mixing the literal and metaphorical levels, and thereby creating the type of confusion and illogic Paterson criticizes, the poem only heightens and gives expression to the irrationality of the speaker's desire. The questions that Paterson would like to have answered (Is it? Why? How?) are precisely the questions the speaker struggles with in trying to explain his desire for the youth.

The symbiotic relationship between speaker and youth, and the blurring of the line between self and other also becomes apparent in Sonnet 24, another poem that has puzzled many critics and readers. While for Vendler the sonnet has the 'charm of rococo fantasy' (1999: 142), Booth argues that the sonnet is 'carefully designed to

118 A COMPREHENSIVE GUIDE TO SHAKESPEARE'S SONNETS

boggle its reader's mind' (2000: 172). Evans states that it 'is generally considered one of the most mechanically conceited and imitative of the sonnets' (1998: 137), and Paterson feels that one has to hack one's way through the 'mangrove-swamp of the conceit and its syntax' (2010: 74) to make any sense of it.

A step-by-step analysis can explain the reasons for this puzzling quality. The speaker employs a painting metaphor to describe the intimate relationship he has with the youth. Through his eyes the speaker has painted ('steeled', 24.1) the youth in the notebook ('table', v. 2) of his heart. The speaker's body serves as the easel ('frame', v. 3) on which the painting of the young man is mounted. Seen 'from the right angle it [the painting of the youth] is like a great painter's work of art' (E/W 2020: 264) because the young man will be able to view his 'true image' (v. 6) through the eyes of the speaker and thereby also acknowledge the latter's skill as a painter. The speaker compares his breast ('bosom', v. 7) with a painter's studio ('shop', v. 7) whose windows are 'glazed with thine [the youth's] eyes' (v. 8).

This complex image is fleshed out in the third quatrain. Through his eyes the speaker has perceived the youth and stored the true image of him in his heart. The youth, on the other hand, by looking into the speaker's eyes, is able to behold that image. Conversely, the speaker by looking into the youth's eyes can look into his own heart (v. 11) and see the sun shining out of the youth's eyes (vv. 11-12). Moreover, as Burrow remarks, the speaker 'not only looks at himself in his love's eyes; he looks at himself looking' (2002: 428). However, as the speaker realizes in the couplet, his eyes lack the 'cunning' (v. 13) of 'perspective' mentioned in verse four. Etymologically speaking, the word 'perspective' derives from the Latin *perspicere*, which means 'to see through'. Thus, although the speaker can see in the lover's eyes the images that he has created of him and himself looking at the young man, he, ironically, cannot really 'see through' the youth into the youth's heart. While one can grasp the general idea of the sonnet (while the speaker has opened his heart for the youth, the youth has not opened his), the various metaphors employed do in fact conflict with each other and turn the sonnet into quite 'a bumpy ride' (Paterson 2010: 74).

While Sonnet 22 plays with the idea of exchanging hearts and Sonnet 24 with the idea of exchanging perspectives, Sonnet 62 extends the idea of symbiosis between speaker and youth to include the entire being. After talking for two quatrains about his '[s]in of self-love' (v. 1) and boasting about his beauty and merits ('no face so gracious is as mine,/ No shape so true', vv. 5-6; 'I all other in all worths surmount', v. 8), the speaker realizes, when looking into a mirror (v. 9), that these qualities do in fact belong to the youth: ''Tis thee (myself) that for myself I praise,/ Painting my age with beauty of thy days' (v. 13-14). The young man turns out to be the speaker's 'other self' (E/W 2020: 247), whose beauty and vanity he acknowledges as his own.

Apart from the symbiotic nature, the 'oneness' (Evans 1998: 152) which the speaker ascribes to the youth and himself (see also sonnets 36, 37, 39, 40), he also reflects on the absolute quality of his love for the young man, which, paradoxically, does not stop growing. In Sonnet 115, for example, the speaker argues that his love, which he earlier defined as absolute and unchanging ('Kind is my love today, tomorrow kind,/ Still constant in a wondrous excellence', 105.5-6), 'still doth grow' (115.14). In the first quatrain, the speaker gives three reasons why he thought in the past that his love for the youth had reached its peak. He begins by saying that when he claimed 'before' (115.1) that 'I could not love you dearer' (v. 2), he lied since at the time he simply could not imagine that his feelings could become any stronger ('Yet then my judgement knew no reason why/ My most full flame should afterwards burn clearer', vv. 3-4). Secondly, he argues that then he was not fully aware (because of his youth or inexperience?) that time can bring change and '[d]ivert strong minds to th' course of alt'ring things' (v. 8). In the third quatrain, he adds another reason which belies the first two explanations by admitting that not only was he aware that the course of time can change intentions but that it was in fact this awareness of 'time's tyranny' (v. 9) that caused him to make such a claim ('Might I not then say, "Now I love you best"', v. 10). Although the sonnet attempts to explain the contradiction between his earlier and present claim, the inconsistency of the reasons given and the blunt admission in the first line that the speaker lied in his previous poem, raise the question, that if one cannot really believe the speaker in one poem why should one believe him in any of the other sonnets?

The paradox of a constant yet growing, i.e. changing, love is given poignant expression in the next poem, the well-known Sonnet 116, which is part of a group of general reflections on love and desire in a changing or corrupted world, which also includes sonnets

66, 123–125 and 129. The sonnet is a general meditation on what the speaker considers to be 'true' (116.1) love. The first quatrain proposes that love can only be called love if it is constant. This is, however, expressed in contradictory terms since the speaker argues that in a perfect relationship ('the marriage of true minds', v. 1) affection does not shift from one object to another, and at the same time states that love remains constant even if a change in the love object occurs ('alters when it alteration finds', v. 3). So, on the one hand, the speaker is arguing that constant love requires a match of 'true minds', on the other hand, it can exist even if one of the 'true' minds is not true.

In the second and third quatrain, the speaker employs nautical and conventional imagery to elaborate the idea of a true and constant love. It is like a guiding star ('an ever-fixed mark', v. 5) that is fixed ('never shaken', v. 6) and which guides ships through 'tempests' (v. 6) and darkness. It is not subject to time and decay even 'though physical beauty falls within the range of time's sickle' (KDJ 2010: 342); it endures beyond death until the Second Coming: 'Love alters not with his brief hours and weeks,/ But bears it out even to the edge of doom' (vv. 11-12).

After the unconditional celebration of constant love in quatrains two and three, the couplet returns, however, to the reservations suggested in the first quatrain. Admittedly, the lines 'If this be error and upon me proved,/ I never writ, nor no man ever loved' (vv. 13-14) can be understood as simply meaning 'The truth of my argument is as obvious as me having written sonnets'. The fact, however, that, as we have seen, in the previous poem the speaker gives us a different idea of perfect love (one that is growing and changing) *does* prove the argument of the sonnet to 'be error' (v. 13), which would consequently mean that the speaker has not written (true love) poems and never loved. But we do know that he has, or don't we?

So far, I have shown that the speaker's desire for the youth expresses itself in the wish or feeling that the subject and the object of desire are one and that (his) love is perfect either in the sense that it is constant or ever increasing. Sonnets 36 and 96 couple the idea of a symbiotic relationship between speaker and youth with the notion that there are also other, more problematic traits which connect the two. In Sonnet 36, the speaker suggests that in his relationship with the youth the flaws and sins of one can be transferred to the other. Although both are physically separated ('we two must be twain',

36.1), they are still united by love into 'one' (v. 2) being, making the youth take on the speaker's faults and sins ('those blots', v. 3; 'guilt', v. 10; 'shame', ibid.). The speaker concludes that to protect the young man's reputation he will refrain from greeting him in public '[l]est my bewailed guilt should do thee shame' (v. 10) and the young man should not 'with public kindness honour me' (v. 11). Showing this kind of restraint, the youth will not lose his reputation, which at the same time is also the speaker's reputation, since both 'are one' (v. 2). (Cf. sonnets 111, 112 and 117 for a similar argument.)

While Sonnet 36 stresses the speaker's 'blots' that are shared by the youth, Sonnet 96 reverses the perspective. In this poem, the speaker addresses the 'errors' (96.7) he and others identify in the young man: his 'youth' (v. 1; possibly implying irresponsible behaviour), his 'wantonness' (ibid.) and his 'gentle sport' (v. 2), which Burrow translates as 'elegant recreation' (2002: 572). The main argument is that the youth is admired both for his faults and his attractive features ('grace and faults are loved', v. 3), and that his faults have actually enhanced his attractiveness for people, so much so that his 'mistakes are transformed into admired actions' (E/W 2020: 255). However, the speaker warns the youth not to mislead too many people as this could well harm his reputation. The couplet 'But do not so; I love thee in such sort,/ As thou being mine, mine is thy good report' (vv. 13-14) is identical with the one in Sonnet 36, discussed above. However, while in the earlier poem the faults and 'blots' originate in the speaker, it is now the youth who should guard his reputation so as not to damage the speaker's.

A less veiled criticism of the unfavourable aspects of the young man's character can be found in Sonnet 69. Here, the speaker argues that while everyone, including his 'foes' (69.4), praises the young man's appearance ('Thy outward thus with outward praise is crowned', v. 5), they also see beyond his exterior and 'look into the beauty of thy mind' (v. 9), which is in fact not as beautiful as the exterior, and expose 'the rank smell of weeds' (v. 12) and an 'odour' (v. 13) which does not match his beauty. The speaker also provides the reason for the young man's corrupted nature: it is the fact that he does 'common grow' (v. 14), i.e. 'available for public use' (Booth 2000: 255), by mixing with unworthy and low company.

The speaker's judgement of and attitude towards the youth's weakness remain highly ambiguous throughout the entire sequence. Already in the next poem, Sonnet 70, he defends the youth again against the accusations levelled at him in the previous sonnet by arguing that beautiful people easily become the target of envy and slander ('That thou art blamed shall not be thy defect,/ For slander's mark was ever yet the fair', 70.1-2).

Sonnet 93 changes the perspective once again when the speaker becomes aware that the youth has been disloyal to him and when he reflects on his own attempts, against his better judgement, to deceive himself into 'supposing thou art true,/ Like a deceived husband' (93.1). The youth's deception of the speaker and others, and making them believe he is loyal and true are, however, seen as something that can be forgiven: 'there can live no hatred in thine eye' (93.5) and 'heaven in thy creation did decree/ That in thy face sweet love should ever dwell;/ Whate'er thy thoughts or thy heart's workings be' (93.9-11). The youth's lies and acts of deception only make him the more desirable.

Continuing the focus from Sonnet 93, but adding yet another perspective to the main argument, the speaker in the next sonnet argues that shameful behaviour in beautiful people is even more despicable than in those with a less favourable appearance. While merely one sonnet earlier the speaker argued that the 'sweet love' (93.10) dwelling in the youth remains more or less unaffected by his sinful behaviour, he now argues the opposite: 'sweetest things turn sourest by their deeds' (94.13) and are to be condemned much more as shameful acts than 'weeds' (94.10).

Sonnet 95 continues the idea and metaphor of 'shame/ Which like canker in the fragrant rose/ Doth spot [stain] the beauty of thy budding name' (95.1-3). Throughout the poem the speaker stresses the discrepancy between the youth's 'outward fairness and inward faultiness' (KDJ 2010: 300) and concludes with a warning: 'Take heed, dear heart, of this large privilege;/ The hardest knife ill used doth lose his edge' (vv. 13-14). The youth should not rely too much on his beauty to cover up his 'every blot' (v. 11).

Another central aspect in the relationship between speaker and youth that needs to be singled out is the physical separation and reunion of the two lovers, which plays a central role in the speaker's staging of his desire and which is thematized in twenty-one sonnets from the cluster of desire (sonnets 39, 50–52, 56–58, 64, 87–92, 97–99, 109, 110, 113, 114). Although the speaker already reflects on his separation from his lover in the earlier sonnets 27–31 and 43, which centre on the speaker's efforts to evoke the youth in his imagination (see Chapter 8), it is not until sonnets 44 and 45 (discussed above in Chapter 3), that the idea of an actual physical and enduring separation is introduced into the sequence: 'thought kills me, that I am not thought,/ To leap large lengths of miles when thou art gone' (44.9-10). But while the absence in these sonnets is a hypothetical one ('No matter then although my foot *did* stand', 44.5; '*when* thou art gone', 44.10; my emphasis) and subordinate to the main theme of imagination, the separation becomes very real in Sonnet 50. It describes the speaker's journey on horseback away from a meeting with the youth. The horse is as reluctant as he to leave the lover. While the speaker is 'heavy' (50.1), his travel 'weary' (v. 2), he feels 'woe' (v. 5) and the thought of increasing the distance between him and his 'joy' (v. 14) fills him with 'grief' (ibid.), the horse 'tired with my woe,/ Plods dully on' (vv. 5-6) and the speaker's 'spur cannot provoke him on' (v. 9). Both speaker and horse bewail the departure from the youth and realize that 'grief lies onward and [. . .] joy behind' (v. 14).

In the following Sonnet 51, however, the speaker already imagines the journey back to the youth. He will ride so fast that he will appear not to move at all ('Then should I spur, though mounted on the wind;/ In winged speed no motion shall I know', 51.7-8). Then no horse will be as fast as his desire to be back with the young man (v. 9). The lines 'Therefore desire, of perfect'st love being made,/ Shall neigh no dull flesh in his fiery race,/ But love, for love, thus shall excuse my jade' (vv. 10-12) require some explanation. '[D]esire, of perfect'st love being made' refers to the concept mentioned in Sonnet 45 about the two lighter elements. The speaker's desire is made of 'slight air' (45.1) and 'purging fire' (ibid.), thereby referring to perfect love. Air relates to thought and imagination, and fire refers to burning desire. In E/W's paraphrase, the three lines read as follows: 'so desire, being composed of nothing but love, shall curb no lethargic flesh in its impassioned speed, but love shall find excuses for my horse for love's sake' (2020: 273). The conclusion is almost comical: as his horse will not be able to keep up with his desire the speaker will run home to his lover and allow the horse to return at its own speed.

The sonnets focusing on separation, absence and reunion are the most direct and passionate expressions of love and longing. Desire in this mini-group is not only seen as a markedly physical longing but also as something that increases through separation (cf. also

124 A COMPREHENSIVE GUIDE TO SHAKESPEARE'S SONNETS

sonnets 97–99). This quality reveals itself in different forms. Some sonnets explore separation as a means to maintain or even renew desire (56, 109, 110, 113, 114), others deal with the speaker's suspicion and jealousy during the youth's absence (57, 58), others are about the speaker fearing that the youth might leave him for ever (87–92), and Sonnet 64 anticipates the final separation of speaker and youth with the latter's death.

Finally, one needs to address the question whether or rather to what extent the relationship between speaker and youth is of a physical and sexual nature. This is not an easy question to answer since, as Eve Kosofsky Sedgwick (1985), Bruce R. Smith (1991), Paul Hammond (2002) and E/W (2013) have shown, no clear distinction was made in Shakespeare's time between homosocial and homoerotic relationships, and male-male relationships were characterized by an 'unbrokenness of a continuum between homosocial and homosexual' (Kosofsky Sedgwick 1985: 1). The discussion of the speaker's intense desire and passion for the youth, of the unconditional, forgiving and symbiotic nature of his love, and of the pain that the speaker experiences during the young man's absence has already given evidence of such a continuum. And while most of the sexually explicit sonnets are those about the mistress, there is, however, one poem from the youth sequence that comes closest to expressing a sexual relationship with the young man.

Sonnet 20 begins with the speaker telling the young man that he is superior to a woman both in beauty and constancy: the youth has a 'woman's gentle heart' (v. 3), but is not 'acquainted/ With shifting change, as is false women's fashion' (v. 3-4), his eyes are 'more bright than theirs, less false in rolling' (v. 5), and he attracts the attention of both genders ('steals men's eyes and women's souls amazeth', v. 8). In the third quatrain, we learn that the young man was originally intended to be a woman ('for [i.e. as] a woman wert thou first created', v. 9) but then nature fell in love with her creation 'And by addition me of thee defeated,/ By adding one thing to my purpose nothing' (vv. 11-12), the 'addition' referring to a penis, which is 'nothing' (v. 12) to the speaker.

This can be understood in diverse ways. It could either mean that because the young man is a man and not a woman the speaker cannot have sexual intercourse with him, for KDJ a conclusion 'too simple to be believed' (2010: 150). Or it could mean the exact opposite, as Paul Hammond argues, i.e. that the 'addition' given to the young man serves the speaker as a 'no thing', the early modern colloquial short term for female genitalia (cf. 2002: 16). In that case, the line could be paraphrased as meaning 'the one thing that nature added is, for my purposes, equivalent to a woman's sexual parts' (KDJ 2010: 151).

Although the couplet ('But since she pricked thee out for women's pleasure,/ Mine by thy love, and thy love's use their treasure') undermines the homoerotic content by saying that only women are enjoying the young man's sexual pleasures, the sonnet's argument is couched in slippery and equivocal language about the true nature of the speaker's relationship with 'the master mistress of [his . . .] passion' (v. 2; cf. also Pequigney 1985: 161–5 and Loughlin 2014: 6).

In the wake of the readings that acknowledge the ambiguous nature of the sexual relationship between speaker and youth, more radical interpretations of the youth's sex and gender have emerged in recent years. While Traub argues that the master mistress's sexuality might be 'sometimes distinguished from modern identity categories, and sometimes conflated with them' (2016: 232), Goran Stanivukovic has identified the youth as a 'cross-gendered subject' (2020: 184). Similarly, Colby Gordon suggests that the youth in Sonnet 20 illustrates early modern gender fluidity in that his gender is shown to be crafted and thereby transitional. For Gordon, the 'prick' referred to in verse thirteen does not refer to the natural male sexual organ the youth was born with, but has to be understood in the context of '*pricking*, an activity that opens onto yet another scene of technical fabrication: the aristocratic closet, where women of a certain rank would engage in the prick-work of embroidery' (2020: 277). He concludes,

> the prick-bearing body does not occupy the place of honour as the singular image of God the Creator, with bodily contours fixed for all time according to divine fiat. Instead, the master-mistress is merely a cambric cradled in Nature's lap, a derivative form copied out of a pattern book and then pricked out, one stitch at a time, by Nature's thrusting and penetrative needle [. . .] gender is handmade, it is transitional [. . .] the pricked body is itself a pure fabrication, a technical creation that has been transitional and contingent from the moment of its inception. (ibid. 278)

FIGURE 6.1 *John de Critz (attr.) Henry Wriothesley, 3rd Earl of Southampton in his youth, c. 1592.*

To convey an impression of what such a 'master mistress' with his 'woman's face' and 'woman's gentle heart' might have looked like in Shakespeare's time, E/W refer to the portrait of the young Henry Wriothesley, third Earl of Southampton, one of the candidates for the dedicatee and the young man (cf. Chapter 2 above), which until

2002 was believed to depict a woman (cf. 2013: 76). Reproducing the portrait (Figure 6.1) is in no way intended to fuel biographical speculation, but to help place the gender transgressive desire in the *Sonnets* in its specific historical context and to – literally – lend an exemplary face to the androgynous figure of the youth.

While in 2003 Valerie Traub still complained that 'anxiety about the homoeroticism of the sonnets and, by extension, of Shakespeare, has not disappeared' (279), she was able to attest only thirteen years later 'that the homoeroticism of Shakespeare's sonnets is now routinely acknowledged, not only in literary criticism, but in most editorial introductions and introductory companions including those marketed to undergraduates and the general public' (2016: 232). As we will see in the next section, however, the sexual relationship between speaker and mistress is at least as, if not more transgressive than that between speaker and youth.

Desire for the mistress

Although the mistress sequence begins with a sonnet which refers to her beauty, comparatively few poems in this group continue to do so. Sonnet 127, already discussed in Chapters 3 and 5, describes her appearance in unspecific and indirect terms. We learn that she embodies new, 'black' (127.3) beauty. While others try to imitate this beauty by artificial means ('with art's false borrowed face', 127.6) and thereby slander 'creation with a false esteem' (127.12), the mistress who was 'born fair' (127.11) with her 'raven black' (127.9) eyes represents true beauty. But that is as much as we get to know about the mistress in this poem. It is also interesting to note that the speaker does not address the mistress directly but talks about her in the third person: 'my mistress' eyes are raven black' (127.9) and 'they [her eyes] mourn' (127.13). The speaker addresses someone else (the public, rival poets and lovers, the reader?), he boasts about his mistress's superior authentic dark beauty and – like the mistress herself (cf. 127.11-14) – pities those women who require 'art's false borrowed face' (127.6) to imitate that beauty. The speaker is more interested in boasting about and defending his mistress's superiority and 'darkness' than expressing his feelings for her. Introducing the mistress in the sequence in such a manner suggests that the speaker competes with the rival not only in style but also in desire.

128 A COMPREHENSIVE GUIDE TO SHAKESPEARE'S SONNETS

Although the next poem, Sonnet 128, primarily expresses the speaker's desire to be near and to touch the mistress, it also returns to the idea of rivalry between the speaker and other suitors. The underlying conceit of this sonnet is 'of the traditional type in which a lover wishes he could be transformed into some object or creature used familiarly by the beloved' (Booth 2000: 437–8). The speaker imagines the mistress playing the harpsichord and envies the keys of the instrument for being touched by the mistress's fingers. While the 'blessed wood' (v. 2) refers to the instrument and the 'wiry concord' (v. 4) to its strings, the term 'jacks' (vv. 5, 13) poses a problem. Critics and editors have pointed out that Shakespeare uses the term wrongly here (cf. Booth 2000: 437–9; Burrow 2002: 636; Evans 1998: 245; KDJ 2010: 370). A jack in a harpsichord actually refers not to a key but to 'any of a set of small upright blocks, typically of wood, one of which rests on the back of each key lever, and is fitted with a quill or plectrum which plucks the string as the block rises when the key is pressed down' (*OED*, 'jack, n.2. II.8').

It has been suggested that the speaker may envision the mistress only tuning and not playing the instrument, which would allow for the 'dark lady cupping her hand over the striking mechanism of her instrument' (Kerrigan [1986] 1999: 355) and explain the contradiction. Kerrigan, however, refutes this idea and suggests instead that Shakespeare uses the term 'jack' as a metonymy to 'refer to the whole key mechanism' (ibid.). The jacks can then be understood as an extension of the keys which the mistress touches with her fingers. I am not convinced by either of the two explanations and would argue instead that this is one of the moments in which Shakespeare simply made a mistake. It would not be the only instance: he muddles the time scheme in *Romeo and Juliet* (cf. Weis 2012: 29–30) and the '*Clock strikes*' (2.1.190 SD) anachronistically in *Julius Caesar*. Shakespeare may have also preferred to use this 'incorrect' term here, since 'jacks' (v. 5), and in particular 'saucy' (v. 13) ones, was also 'a standard term of abuse for any worthless fellow and for impudent upstarts in particular' (Booth 2000: 439). Its use here stresses the point once more that the speaker finds himself in a highly competitive marketplace of desires and favours.

In the very first line of Sonnet 131, the mistress is described as 'tyrannous' (v. 1) as she is aware of the speaker's dependence on her: 'For well thou knowst, to my dear doting heart/ Thou art the fairest and most precious jewel' (vv. 3-4). The speaker then goes on to defend the mistress's beauty against the charges of those that 'err' (v. 7) in thinking that she has 'not the power to make love groan' (v. 6), i.e. that she is not sexually attractive. He argues that thinking about her face makes him 'groan [. . .]' with desire (v. 10) and that he considers her dark appearance to be most beautiful (vv. 11-12). Twice does the speaker refer to 'groans', in verses six and ten. In doing so, he activates at least three levels of meaning. First, he alludes to the Petrarchan tradition of the despairing lover who expresses his suffering in groans. KDJ (2010: 376) refers to Sidney's 'Sonnet 54' in which Astrophil lists the traditional signs of love: 'give each speech a full point of a groan' (v. 4). At the beginning of *Romeo and Juliet* Shakespeare's Romeo is also firmly placed in this tradition when we see him unhappily in love with Rosaline:

> BENVOLIO
> Tell me in sadness, who is that you love?
> ROMEO
> What, shall I groan and tell thee?
> BENVOLIO   Groan? Why, no,
> But sadly tell me who.

RJ 1.1.197-99

Secondly, 'groaning' has a clear sexual meaning, invoking expressions of lust and 'erotic delight' (KDJ 2010: 376). Thirdly, and since 'groaning' in Shakespeare's time was 'more frequently associated with "pain or distress" (*OED* groan 1a)' (ibid.), lines 9-10 could also imply that the speaker 'has been venereally infected by her' (ibid.).

While the mistress's availability and her 'black' features, as shown in Chapter 5, were sufficient to turn her into an object of desire for the speaker in Sonnet 130, Sonnet 131 tells us more about her character and its relevance to the speaker's desire. Continuing the oxymoronic play with 'fair' and 'black' with regard to the mistress's dark appearance in Sonnet 127, the speaker now also talks about the mistress's 'black [. . .] deeds' (131.13), thereby establishing a connection between her black appearance and her inner being, 'between somatic and behavioural, moral, or spiritual traits, between outer traits and inner being, between faith and the body' (Loomba 2016: 239). The speaker celebrates the mistress's exterior blackness (or Blackness) and interior 'blackness' but at the same time feels compelled to defend it against the claims of 'some' (v. 5) who argue that her black/Black appearance and character lack the beauty and power to attract lovers.

Booth calls the couplet a 'single graceful razor stroke' (2000: 457) since one 'charge [against the mistress] is disposed of, only to be replaced by a worse one' (KDJ 2010: 376). The speaker argues that the allegation that the mistress is not beautiful is wrong and excuses it by saying that it is *only* her character that is 'black', i.e. corrupted. Moreover, the speaker admits that he is not only attracted to the black or Black appearance of the mistress, but also to her corrupted, 'black' character.

There are two more poems in the sequence in which the speaker focuses on the mistress's corruption, Sonnet 132 and Sonnet 150. In Sonnet 132, the speaker informs us that she has scorned but also pitied him for the fact that she scorned him, thereby tormenting him 'with disdain' (132.2) in her heart and '[l]ooking with pretty ruth upon my pain' (v. 4). The speaker eventually asks the mistress to extend the pity she shows in her eyes to also show in her heart and 'in every part' (v. 12) of her being. If she agrees to do that, the speaker will 'swear beauty herself is black,/ And all they foul that thy complexion lack' (vv. 13-14). As in the previous sonnet, the speaker suggests that as long as the mistress will show (sexual) favours to the speaker, he will claim that her darkness/'darkness' is beautiful.

In Sonnet 150, the speaker continues to reflect on the mistress's 'dark' character and how it controls his desire, a very prominent theme in several sonnets at the end of the sequence. The sonnet is arguably the most explicit criticism of the mistress's 'blackness'. The speaker ascribes to the mistress a number of negative character traits. She is referred to as possessing 'insufficiency' (v. 2) which could refer to either her lack of beauty or her moral deficiencies (or to both). She can make bad things appear pleasing ('this becoming of things ill', v. 5) and the worst of her actions for the speaker still exceeds the 'best' of all others (vv. 6-8). He finds in her 'just cause of hate' (v. 10), aspects which 'others do abhor' (v. 11) and 'unworthiness' (v. 13). But although he sees all these faults in the mistress, her 'powerful might' (v. 1) can 'sway' (v. 2) his heart, make him deny what is obvious to him (v. 3) and disacknowledge reality by swearing that days, as opposed to nights, are not defined by brightness (v. 4). The mistress's blackness/Blackness/'blackness' in both appearance and character exert such a powerful influence over him, that, although he is aware of the mistress's faults, the speaker cannot but desire her (v. 13) and finds in this the more reason for the mistress to love him back.

While the speaker's desire for the youth focuses (albeit not exclusively) on his beauty, expresses itself primarily in his longing to form one being with him, centres on the belief that their relationship is of an absolute nature, and to a certain extent also acknowledges the sinister sides of the young man's character, the speaker's desire for the mistress has different qualities. Although the speaker also praises the mistress's dark/'dark' features, this praise is less directed at her than at the rival lovers and poets as well as the readers whom the speaker seeks to impress. While the youth is praised for his own worth, the praise for the mistress serves ulterior functions in the speaker's self-perception and self-fashioning as lover and poet. The mistress, as it were, becomes for the speaker an exotic trophy whose main worth resides in the fact that she is different from the women desired by others. The speaker almost takes pride in the power the mistress has over him and in the more forceful, irrational and incomprehensible quality of this desire when compared to his longing for the youth.

Triangular desire

A few sonnets thematize the competing and changing constellations of love between speaker, youth and mistress. Sonnets 40 to 42 are the first poems in the sequence in which the speaker reflects on both love objects. In the first of these, Sonnet 40, the notion is introduced that although the youth has taken away the speaker's love, the speaker loves him so much that he forgives him.

The sonnet confuses the reader by its use of the term 'love' in different contexts. The speaker employs it to address the youth ('my love', 40.1, 3), love in general ('true love', v. 3; the first 'my love' in verse 5; 'love knows', v. 11; 'love's wrong', v. 12), and to refer to the other love objects the youth has taken away from the speaker ('all my loves', v. 1; 'No love', v. 3; the second 'my love' in verse 5; 'my love', v. 6). The word 'love' and its inflections appear altogether ten times in the poem. If one adds to these the other terms and phrases that refer to acts of love or loving such as 'hadst' (v. 4), 'receivest' (v.

132 A COMPREHENSIVE GUIDE TO SHAKESPEARE'S SONNETS

5), 'usest' (v. 6), 'wilful taste' (v. 8), 'robb'ry' (v. 9), 'steal' (v. 10), one can see that the sonnet displays an almost obsessive interest in love and (competing) love relationships.

Although the sonnet is characterized by a strong emotional investment and the speaker's intense desire for the young man, the arguments follow a specific logic. In the first quatrain, the speaker argues that in taking his love objects from him, the youth cannot steal his love since he has already given the youth all his love (vv. 1-4). The speaker can therefore not be angry with the youth when he has sexual relations with the one he (the speaker) loves: 'Then if for my love thou my love receivest,/ I cannot blame thee, for my love thou usest' (vv. 5-6). The next argument ('But yet be blamed, if thou thyself deceivest/ By wilful taste of what thyself refusest', vv. 7-8), which Burrow calls 'very obscure' (2002: 460), can be read in two ways. Either the speaker says that the youth can be blamed for 'capriciously engaging in sexual activity' (KDJ 2010: 190) instead of marrying and engaging in procreational sex, or he argues that the youth can be blamed for refusing 'to have sex with your devoted (male) lover [the speaker himself], but wilfully hav[ing] it with a woman (his mistress)' (ibid.). By stressing the fact that the youth 'refuses' to have sex with the speaker, the latter interpretation would not only 'deepen the sonnet's bisexual undercurrents' (KDJ 2010: 190) but also foreground the rivalling desires in the triangular relationship. The final quatrain and couplet include two main arguments: on the one hand, the speaker forgives the youth for his betrayal and concludes that they 'must not be foes' (v. 14), on the other hand, he acknowledges the pain this betrayal has caused him since it is always more difficult to 'bear love's wrong, than hate's known injury' (v. 12).

While the references to the other love object or objects the youth 'stole' from the speaker remain conspicuously ambiguous in this poem, the next two sonnets are more explicit in that respect. Sonnet 41 takes up the theme of excusable betrayal from the earlier poem. Once again, the speaker explains and justifies the youth's transgressions with his 'beauty' (vv. 3, 6, 13, 14), his youth (v. 3), and gentleness (v. 5). This time, however, the third party becomes more clearly identifiable over the course of the poem. While in the beginning the speaker is still referring to '[t]hose pretty wrongs' (v. 1) in an abstract manner, we learn in verse 7 that he is in fact talking about 'a woman' and are eventually informed that it is the speaker's mistress with whom the youth has betrayed the speaker ('thou mightst *my* seat forbear', v. 9; my emphasis) and whom he has made to break '[h]er' (v. 13) pledge. Thus, the speaker stages the youth, the mistress and himself in a triangle of desire, accusing the youth of causing two acts of betrayal, one involving the speaker and another involving the mistress.

So far, only the fact that the speaker is talking *to* the youth and *about* the mistress has revealed a stronger emotional investment in the youth than in the mistress. In Sonnet 42, however, the speaker becomes more outspoken in ranking his affection and desire. The message in the first quatrain is clear: although the speaker admits that he 'loved her dearly' (v. 2), losing the mistress to the young man is not 'all my grief' (v. 1). It is the loss of the youth's love, '[t]hat she hath thee' (v. 3), that touches him 'more nearly' (v. 4). In the second quatrain, the speaker excuses both their betrayals, arguing that the youth only loves the mistress because the speaker loves her and that the mistress in '[s]uff'ring my friend for my sake to approve her' (v. 8) only puts up with the youth's lovemaking because she knows how the speaker feels about him.

In the third quatrain, the speaker first implies that this double betrayal has put him in a win-win situation. The loss of the young man's love is at the same time his 'love's gain' (v. 9), and similarly the mistress's love is not lost because it is now transferred to the youth (vv. 9-10). As long as love is shifted to another recipient within the triangle of desire, it is not lost (cf. Burrow's (2002: 464) note to this verse). As painful as this relocation of love may be for the speaker ('And both for my sake lay on me this cross', v. 12), the speaker concludes that he is still loved by both youth and mistress. Because he and the youth are so intricately connected, being in fact 'one' (v. 13), the mistress in loving the young man at the same time loves the speaker. KDJ has drawn attention to the skewed logic of this conclusion, because 'the argument that love for one person is really love for another is inherently implausible [. . .]; and secondly, the poet has made it quite clear in preceding lines of the sonnet that what he cares about is the young man's defection, not the woman's' (2010: 194).

The speaker's reflections on the triangle of desire continue in sonnets 133 and 134 which, unlike the triangle sonnets discussed up to now, are addressed to the mistress and accuse her of enslaving his youth and himself. Although Sonnet 133 at first seems confusing

134 A COMPREHENSIVE GUIDE TO SHAKESPEARE'S SONNETS

and has led Paterson to the conclusion 'that none of this makes an ounce of sense' (2010: 403), it is in fact a fairly logical poem. The mistress has captured the hearts of youth and speaker in her 'steel bosom's ward' (v. 9) and all that the speaker asks for is that he as the mistress's prisoner may be allowed to 'bail' (v. 10), i.e. to confine the young man's heart in his own heart. The poem makes it quite clear where the speaker's sympathies lie. While the mistress is presented as a cruel jailor who imprisons both men in her breast, who makes the speaker's 'heart to groan' (v. 1), gives a 'deep wound' (v. 2) to both men, 'torture[s]' (v. 3), enslaves (v. 4) and 'torment[s]' (v. 8), the speaker is described as a defenceless prisoner who only wishes to be allowed to be the youth's 'guard' (v. 11).

Sonnet 134 continues the argument and story of the preceding sonnet. After summarizing in the first quatrain the situation at the end of the previous poem, the speaker has to accept that the mistress will not grant him the wish to 'bail' (133.10) the youth. She will not release him but instead will keep him all for herself. Moreover, the youth willingly submits himself to the mistress ('nor he will not be free', 134.5) as he has offered himself to her as 'surety' (v. 7) for the speaker. In doing so, the youth has become (sexually) dependent on and enslaved by the mistress, who greedily claims her right. In the end, the 'covetous' (v. 6) mistress, in possessing the youth also possesses the speaker, and although the youth pays bail for the speaker by satisfying her sexually (cf. KDJ 2010: 382), the speaker still finds himself under the spell of the mistress.

While Sonnet 133 employs metaphors of imprisonment and confinement, Sonnet 134 is couched in legal tropes: the speaker is 'mortgaged' (134.2), legally bound to the mistress's will; he is willing to 'forfeit' (v. 3) his rights to the young man; and by submitting himself to the thrall of the mistress's beauty, the youth has acted 'surety-like' (v. 7) as a guarantor to 'write' (ibid.) for the speaker. Like Antonio in *The Merchant of Venice*, who has signed a bond for his friend Bassanio to Shylock, the youth has become a 'debtor' (v. 11) to the mistress for the speaker's sake and signed a 'bond that him as fast doth bind' (v. 8). Conversely, the mistress, like Shylock, insists on exacting the 'statute' (v. 9), 'a technical term indicating a bond by which a creditor was empowered to seize the property of a defaulting debtor' (Booth 2000: 465). While in *The Merchant of Venice* the debt is a pound of flesh, here it is 'the whole' (v. 14) of the youth and in particular sexual gratification. Although the mistress is described as covetous and associated with sexual voracity, she is also a 'usurer' (v. 10) in the sense that she is very pedantic and miserly in claiming exactly what she thinks is owed to her by the youth.

The sonnets addressed so far (40–42, 133, 134) illustrate and confirm what has become apparent in the discussions of the two groups of sonnets in which the speaker expresses his desire for the youth and for the mistress. Although the speaker feels an intense (physical) desire for both figures, his desire for the mistress is depicted in a less favourable light. While the mistress is perceived as having a corrupting influence on the speaker, and desire for her black/'black'/Black features is presented as an uncontrollable disease – Loomba draws attention to the fact that in theories on interracial conception, 'early modern writers began to understand both virus and sperm in interchangeable ways' (2016: 244) – the fair youth's faults (his egotism, vanity and irresponsible behaviour) are identified by the speaker as being more excusable.

Also, the mistress's desire for the speaker (and other men) is described as being of an altogether more sexual, physical and corrupted nature, resulting in the impression that the sonnets addressed to and about the mistress 'are the frankest in their sexuality' (E/W 2013: 77). The numerous sexual puns on 'groans' (131.10) and 'Will' (135, 136, 143.13) as well as references to and puns on 'the bay where all men ride' (137.6), sexual intercourse ('I lie with her, and she with me', 138.13), 'hell' (144.12), rising, standing and falling (151) and venereal disease (153, 154) testify to this. In this respect, Sonnet 151 is probably Shakespeare's most 'crudely physical' (E/W 2013: 77) and 'most outrageously libidinous sonnet' (Evans 1998: 19), the couplet of which ('No want of conscience hold it that I call/ Her 'love', for whose dear love I rise and fall') might 'almost be spoken by the penis itself' (E/W 2013: 77).

Sonnet 144 illustrates and summarizes some of the findings so far. It compares the speaker's '[t]wo loves' (v. 1) and establishes several dichotomies for both objects of desire. The speaker posits himself between the mistress and the youth. While the latter is associated with 'comfort' (v. 1), 'purity' (v. 8), described as an 'angel' (vv. 3, 6, 9, 12), a 'man right fair' (v. 3) and a 'saint' (v. 7), the mistress denotes the opposite. She is connected with 'despair' (v. 1), 'hell' (vv. 5, 12), 'evil' (v. 5) and 'foul pride' (v. 8), and understood as a 'worser spirit' (v. 4), a 'devil' (v. 7), 'fiend' (v. 9), and 'bad angel'

(v. 14). Moreover, she is also perceived as a black/Black or dark presence, as 'coloured ill' (v. 4), as opposed to the man's white ('fair', v. 3) appearance.

We have already seen how the mistress's association with the colour black not only defines her as violating the norms of Petrarchan discourse, but how it also must be understood in the context of early modern racecraft. However, as critics have pointed out, the mistress's threat to normative sexuality and desire stems not only from the notion of a possible sexual union between 'fair' speaker or youth and Black mistress (cf. also Habib (2008: 95–6) on cross-racial marriages in sixteenth-century London). At least equally, if not more, disruptive was the threat posed to rank and class, the idea that by placing the 'dark' female of dubious social origin in the triangle of desire with the 'fair', white and presumably aristocratic youth and the poet-speaker, heterosexual desire 'imperil[s] social distinction' (de Grazia 2000: 103) much more than the homosocial relationships between speaker and young man: 'For the love of the youth "right fair" which tradition has deemed scandalous promotes a social programme while the love for the mistress "collour'd ill" which tradition has allowed threatens to annihilate it' (ibid.; cf. also Hall [1998] 2008: 73; Sanchez 2019a: 100–1). But male-male love relationships were also considered to be more refined than male-female relationships in Shakespeare's time, a notion that can be traced back to three main influences: biblical texts, the so-called one-sex model and Plato.

One of the origins of the idea that women are more defective and corrupted than men is the Book of Genesis, which states that Eve, who was created as a 'help mete' (Gen. 2.18) for Adam, ate of the Tree of Knowledge and caused mankind's sorrow. As punishment for Eve's transgression, God made conception and childbearing painful and made Eve's desire secondary to Adam's: 'thy desire *shal be subject* to thy housband, and he shal rule over thee' (Gen. 3.16).

In the New Testament, the apostle Paul says in the Epistle to the Ephesians 'the housband is the wives head, eve as Christ is the head of the church' (Eph. 5.23). Correspondingly, Elizabethan and Jacobean society was patriarchal and patrilinear. Title, name and possessions were usually passed on to sons, and women were seen as beings of inferior value and importance.

The alleged superiority of men over women was further justified by the notion that women were an underdeveloped, imperfect version of men. This theory was first conceptualized by the Greek philosopher and physician Galen (129–c. 200), elaborated in early modern medical accounts and described by Thomas W. Laqueur as the 'one-sex model' (1990, viii). According to this theory, 'the woman's organs are an interior version of the man's genitals; they correspond to the man's genitals except that a lack of heat has failed to turn them outside' (Schleiner 2000: 180). It was not until the eighteenth century that males and females were divided into two discrete sexes (cf. de Grazia 2000: 98).

Apart from the religious and anatomical explanations of women's alleged inferiority to men, a third, philosophical source may have influenced Shakespeare and his contemporaries in their perception not only of the difference between men and women but also of the difference between male-male and male-female relationships.

In Plato's *Symposium*, mentioned earlier in the discussion of the procreation sonnets, Aristophanes expounds his theory of the origin of love. For him 'love is simply the name for the desire and pursuit of the whole' (Plato, *Symposium* 192e–193e, 64), 'man's attempt to regain his former happy state by uniting himself to his lost half' (Hamilton 1951: 16). That half was lost when Zeus, as punishment for the proud mortals' rebellion against the gods, divided the three original sexes (male, female and hermaphrodite) into halves (cf. Plato, *Symposium* 188e–190b, 59). Ever since, each of the halves tries to reunite with its lost half.

Aristophanes distinguishes between several types of love that exist between the male and female halves of the three original sexes. Of the formerly hermaphrodite sex, the male halves are lovers of women, and the female halves are lovers of men. While 'most adulterers' (ibid., 191c–192e, 62) come from the male halves, the female halves 'are mad about men and sexually promiscuous' (ibid.). Female halves who on the other hand were parts of the original female being 'direct their affections towards women and pay little attention to men; Lesbians belong to this category' (ibid.). Those male halves however, who strive to reunite with their former other male half 'are the best of their generation, because they are the most manly' (ibid.). Consequently, Aristophanes defends male-male desire against charges of indecency:

> Some people say that they [male lovers of males] are shameless, but they are wrong. It is not shamelessness which inspires their

138 A COMPREHENSIVE GUIDE TO SHAKESPEARE'S SONNETS

behaviour, but high spirit and manliness and virility, which lead them to welcome the society of their own kind. A striking proof of this is that such boys alone, when they reach maturity, engage in public life. When they grow to be men, they become lovers of boys, and it requires the compulsion of convention to overcome their natural disinclination to marriage and procreation; they are quite content to live with one another unwed. (ibid., 62–3)

This critical assessment of male-female desire can also be found in the way sexual relations and desire are perceived and staged in the *Sonnets*, and in particular in the poems about the triangular relationship between speaker, youth and mistress (cf. also Gray 2011).

Sonnet 129, which is one of the few sonnets with a 'universal, impersonal point of view' (Bell 2007: 297; see also sonnets 116, 121, 123, 146) and an 'almost breathless meditation on the feelings and consequences of lust' (E/W 2020: 57), is a case in point. The speaker comments on the three stages of lust: the anticipation, enjoyment, and the aftermath of sexual fulfilment, leading Michael Schoenfeldt to conclude that this is 'one of the first poems in English to depict orgasm' (2007: 4).

All three stages of lust are portrayed in negative terms. Looking forward to sexual intercourse makes us break promises and become violent, untrustworthy, rude and cruel ('lust/ Is perjured, murd'rous, bloody, full of blame,/ Savage, extreme, rude, cruel, not to trust', 129.2-4) and causes us to act in irrational ('past reason hunted', v. 6), '[m]ad' (v. 9) and 'extreme' (v. 10) ways. The next phase, sexual gratification, is described as a 'waste of shame' (v. 1) and 'lust in action' (v. 2). It drives us mad and makes us behave in an 'extreme' (v. 10) manner. Lastly, once having enjoyed sexual pleasure, we 'despise [. . . it] straight' (v. 5), 'hate [. . .] it' (v. 7), behave in an 'extreme' (v. 10) way and feel wretched ('a very woe', v. 11) and look back upon it as a 'dream' (v. 12), as something that has not really happened. The couplet spells out the misogynistic thrust of the poem: although men are aware of the negative effects of heterosexual congress, they cannot resist being drawn to 'the *hell* of shame and hatred [. . .]; the female sex organ' (KDJ 2010: 373). For Valerie Traub, this sonnet 'establishes the illicit and terrifying figure of woman-as-sodomite [and . . .] constructs the female body as the vile repository of the seed and shame of conventional intercourse' (2000:

436; for a discussion of the importance of the different aspectual forms (prospective, imperfective and perfective aspect) for the three stages of lust in the poem cf. Brinton 1985).

Considering the socio-cultural, biblical, Galenic and Platonic influences sketched out above, this overly pessimistic perception of (hetero-)sexual intercourse should not really surprise us then. Unsanctioned sexual relations destabilize the social order, and procreation is viewed as something inherently sinful and only accepted as an unavoidable evil to guarantee the continuation of mankind. As Keenan argues, 'the only acceptable form of sex, according to the Church, was chaste heterosexual sex between married men and women. Heterosexual sex before or outside marriage was frowned on' (2008: 22).

The unreproductive heterosexual relationship between speaker and mistress is in this regard more 'unnatural' than the homoeroticism between speaker and young man, as Valerie Traub argues in her reading of Sonnet 144:

> The defiling sense of profligate consumption that opens this poem constructs erotic encounters as a violation of those recognitions upon which a fantasy of normative sexuality depends. With heteroeroticism rendered penetrative but nonprocreative, with the circle of shame extended to include the man who wastes his semen, the erotic economy of this poem is, *in the terms of Shakespeare's culture*, sodomitical. (2000: 437)

Similarly, Goran Stanivukovic in his analysis of the influence on Lucian of Samosata's *Amores* on the *Sonnets* argues that the 'Lucianian idea of non-procreative heterosexual sex as unsatisfying for man, and lacking pleasure, becomes in Shakespeare's hand a radical rendering of such sex as hard to be sure what it is about and infectious' (2020: 186).

This unnatural and sodomitical desire contrasts with the desire between the male figures in the sequence. Although it is also nonreproductive, the intimate relationship between speaker and young man is somehow excused as it is not (or rather cannot be) productive in the first place. Moreover, since the speaker in a number of sonnets urges the youth to procreate, their relationship is more closely associated with a sanctioned, reproductive sexuality than the relationships the mistress engages in.

Some critics have spoken against the view that the desire for the mistress is more disruptive than the one for the youth and that the 'promiscuous womb threatens social order' (de Grazia 2000: 104). Melissa E. Sanchez, for example, argues that 'the speaker's relationship with the youth is as compromised and faithless as that with the mistress' (2019a: 100) and that Shakespeare in the sequence 'struggles against the assumption that desire finds its *telos*, or perfection, in monogamous coupledom, whether in the form of classical friendship or companionate marriage' (ibid.).

Arguing that the relationship between speaker and youth is more natural than the one between speaker and mistress is by no means implying that sexual relationships between men were accepted at the time. Male-male sexual acts in early modern England were clearly considered a crime and a violation of religious, ethical and state laws — the official terms being 'sodomy' or 'buggery' (Burrow 2002: 125) which were also applied to any 'unnatural' acts between man and woman (cf. Traub 2000: 432). But for the reasons mentioned above, intimate male-male relationships, when discovered, were 'dealt with on the whole with surprising moderation — admonitions, exhortations to abstain. In fact, [...] women are felt to pose the more serious problem: heterosexual fornication was much more energetically prosecuted' (Orgel 1989: 19). Again, this 'selective blindness' (ibid., 20) towards male-male sexual relationships has to be seen in the context of early modern patriarchal power structures and the fact that unsanctioned female sexuality posed a far greater threat to the patriarchal structures of society than sexual relations between men, carried out 'within a structure of institutionalized social relations' (Kosofsky Sedgwick 1985: 35; cf. also Orgel 1989: 26; de Grazia 2000).

Further reading

Homosocial desire and sexuality in early modern England: Bray 1982; Goldberg 1992; Goldberg 1994; Hebron 2008: 106–10; Keenan 2008: 18–23; Smith 1991; Traub 1992. **Early Modern Trans Studies:** Chess, Gordon and Fisher 2019; Joubin 2023a; Joubin 2023b. **One-sex model:** Adelman 1999; Greenblatt 1990: 79–81; King 2013; Laqueur 1990; Orgel 1989; Schiebinger 1989: 160–5; Schleiner 2000. **Desire in Shakespeare's *Sonnets*:** Bates 2011; Clarke 2007: 193–8; E/W 2013: 68–81; Garrison 2023; Hyland 2003: 159–75; Innes 1997: 178–206;

Schoenfeldt 2010: 88–111; Trevor 2007; Wells 2010. **Homosocial desire in Shakespeare's** *Sonnets*: de Grazia 2000; Hammond 2002; Kosofsky Sedgwick 1985; Kullmann 2010; Pequigney 1985: 161–5; Sanchez 2019a; Smith 2000; Stanivukovic 2020; Stapleton 2004; Traub 2000; Traub 2003. **Transgender and Queer desire in the** *Sonnets*: Gordon 2020; Sanchez 2019b; Stanivukovic 2020; Traub 2016. **Love-Triangle in the** *Sonnets*: Eklund 2021; Warley 2005: 123–51. **Shakespeare's** *Sonnets* **and Plato's** *Symposium*: Gray 2011.

7

Deception

As shown in the last chapter, competing ambitions, wishes and desires lead speaker, youth, and mistress to acts of deception, unfaithfulness and betrayal. This has become most evident in the sonnets which address the triangular desire between them. While in sonnets 40–42 the speaker accuses the youth of having betrayed him with his 'love' (40.5), a 'woman' (41.7), 'her' (42.1), in sonnets 133 and 134 the speaker charges the mistress with having deceived him with the youth. In the following, I will first look at those sonnets in which deception, although prominent, is still subordinated to the main theme of desire. Afterwards I will turn to the sonnets in which deception becomes the main subject, dealing first with the sonnets to and about the youth and then with those to and about the mistress. Finally, I will turn to those poems which centre on the connection between poetry and deception.

Deceptive desire

In the sonnets with a primary focus on desire, the theme of deception manifests itself in numerous ways, when, for example, the speaker suspects the youth of betrayal in the sonnets addressing their separation. In one of these separation poems, Sonnet 57, the speaker, although he says in the first two quatrains that he will patiently wait for the young man's return (vv. 1-4) and not complain about this separation ('Nor dare I chide the world-without-end hour/ Whilst I, my sovereign, watch the clock for you', vv. 5-6), nonetheless indicates in the second half of the poem that he fears his lover might deceive him while being away. The speaker admits to his 'jealous

144 A COMPREHENSIVE GUIDE TO SHAKESPEARE'S SONNETS

thought' (v. 9) about the youth's 'affairs' (v. 10), which are very likely 'amorous' (KDJ 2010: 224). The couplet 'So true a fool is love, that in your will,/ Though you do anything, he thinks no ill' (vv. 13-14) nourishes 'the very suspicions which it claims to suppress' (KDJ 2010: 224). Arguing that even though the youth *might* do 'anything' and that the speaker will nevertheless not suspect any 'ill' suggests in fact that the young man *is* doing *something* and that he, the speaker, *does* think ill of him. Vendler defines this sonnet as one of Shakespeare's 'ironic shadow-poems' (274), in which the speaker says one thing and means its opposite, and compares it to 'a double hologram-image, winking on and off as we tilt it in one direction (toward suspicion) or the other (toward abjectness)' (ibid.).

This double perspective of abjectness and suspicion can also be found in the separation sonnets 92 and 93. In Sonnet 92, the speaker becomes more outspoken in his suspicions concerning the youth's unfaithfulness. The young man has done his worst 'to steal thyself away' (v. 1) from the speaker, has an 'inconstant mind' (v. 9) and is very likely 'false' (v. 14) to him now and in the future. At the same time, the speaker declares that his life 'depends upon that love' (v. 4) and 'humour' (v. 8) of the youth and that he is '[h]appy to have thy love' (v. 12). In the conclusion, however, he is less sure of his unconditional devotion to the youth than in Sonnet 57. While in the earlier sonnet the speaker ends by saying that he will think 'no ill' (57.14) of him, he now is not that sure anymore and allows for the possibility that he may 'be false' (92.14).

In the following Sonnet 93, the speaker extends the idea of deception to include the act of self-delusion (a view I have already identified in the speaker's desire for the mistress in Chapter 6, especially in sonnets 147–151), thereby emphasizing that deception and collusion in the *Sonnets* are contagious and self-replicating. The speaker compares himself to a 'deceived husband' (93.2) who tricks himself into thinking that he is not deceived by his wife. Greedily and all too readily he ignores any signs of inconstancy and betrayal in the youth: 'love's face/ May still seem love to me, though altered new' (v. 3). Although the speaker feels the young man's 'heart [to be] in other place' (v. 4) he makes himself believe that 'there can live no hatred in thine eye' (v. 5). Both parties collude in the deception of the speaker who goes on to state that while other people's corrupted character is reflected in their appearance ('In many's looks, the false heart's history/ Is writ in moods and frowns and wrinkles strange', vv. 7-8), this is not the case with the youth: 'heaven in thy creation did decree/ That in thy face sweet love should ever dwell' (vv. 9-10), the implication being that the speaker knows that although the youth, like others, possesses a 'false heart' (v. 7), it does not show in his appearance. Interestingly, the fact that the youth's 'fair' appearance is not compromised by his corrupted character constitutes a telling contrast to the mistress, whose 'black' character shows in her black/Black appearance (cf. the last section and Chapter 3 above for the early modern conviction that a dark appearance 'naturally' mirrors a corrupt character).

The sonnet's conclusion 'How like Eve's apple doth thy beauty grow,/ If thy sweet virtue answer not thy show' (vv. 13-14) reads like a warning to both men: if your character is indeed as flawed as I suspect it to be, then your beauty is like the forbidden fruit, beautiful from the outside but once 'tasted', it will have corrupting effects (see also KDJ 2010: 296).

The speaker not only allows himself to be deceived, however; he is also a deceiver himself, a fact which is addressed in a number of sonnets exploring separation as a means to maintain or renew desire and made even more prominent in those sonnets in which the theme of deception is given even greater room (see below). In sonnets 109 and 110, the speaker looks back on his sins during his separation from the youth. In Sonnet 109, he half-heartedly and not very convincingly denies any wrongdoing during his voluntary 'absence' (109.2) from the youth. He admits that his feelings for the young man *may* have weakened during his absence ('Though absence seemed my flame to qualify', v. 2), that he *may* have strayed ('ranged', v. 5) and stained his own reputation (v. 8), and that in his 'nature reigned/ All frailties that besiege all kinds of blood' (vv. 9-10). But the speaker asserts that these acts do not affect his devotion and that he would 'leave for nothing all thy sum of good' (v. 12) since he holds the youth above anything and anyone else (vv. 13-14).

While in Sonnet 109 the speaker only cautiously implies that he *may* have betrayed the youth in his absence, he clearly acknowledges it in the next sonnet. "[T]is true' (v. 1), he concedes in Sonnet 110, 'I have gone here and there' (ibid.), made a fool of myself, and mixed and engaged with company less worthy than you (vv. 2-3). The speaker admits that he looked at the true love that exists

146 A COMPREHENSIVE GUIDE TO SHAKESPEARE'S SONNETS

between him and the young man '[a]skance and strangely' (v. 6), i.e. that he turned his attention away from him to other objects of desire. He concludes, however, that these 'blenches' (v. 7), these 'sideways glances' (Kerrigan [1986] 1999: 324), only showed him the true value of his love (v. 8). He promises that from now on he will refrain from trying to rejuvenate his 'appetite' (v. 10) by looking and desiring elsewhere and asks to be readmitted to the youth's 'pure and most most loving breast' (v. 14).

In the next sonnet, Sonnet 111, the speaker pursues a slightly different strategy in defending his deception. Instead of arguing, as in the previous poem, that his faults are somehow excusable because they have led him to appreciate and recognize the true value of the youth, he now asks the young man to blame 'Fortune' (111.1) for his 'harmful deeds' (v. 2) and to '[p]ity' (v. 8) him. He is willing to do 'double penance to correct correction' (v. 12) and concludes that the youth's 'pity is enough to cure' (v. 14) him of his deceitful behaviour.

The argument continues in Sonnet 112 when the speaker says that the youth's 'love and pity' (112.1) efface the public 'scandal' (v. 2), the 'ill' (v. 3) and 'shames' (v. 6) of the speaker. Within only four sonnets the speaker has come a long way from demanding 'O never say that I was false of heart' (109.1) to acknowledging his 'bad' (112.4) behaviour.

Sonnet 117 introduces yet another argument to explain and excuse the speaker's unfaithfulness. It begins with the speaker granting the young man the right to hold him to account for all his transgressions of the past: that he did not 'repay' (117.2) and acknowledge the youth's 'dearest love' (v. 3); that he has 'frequent been with unknown minds' (v. 5), i.e. strangers, the implication being that he has done more than merely conversed with them; and that he has 'hoisted sail to all the winds' (v. 7) which transported him 'farthest' (v. 8) from the young man. Paterson points out that the 'wand'ring bark' (116.7) of the previous sonnet on perfect love has become 'much less passive here, and has *hoisted sail*' (2010: 344). Booth has even called this sonnet 'something like a pun on sonnet 116' (2000: 392), playing with and undermining the idea of a (perfect) love that controls our lives.

The speaker then asks the youth to take stock of his 'wilfulness and errors' (117.9) and even to 'heap up suspicion on the basis of what you've found' (Vendler 1999: 495). The speaker admits to

DECEPTION 147

all these transgressions because in the end, he argues, he only committed them to test the 'constancy and virtue' (v. 14) of the young man's love, an argument which, to put it mildly, is less than fully convincing.

So far, we have seen the various ways in which the theme of deception is employed in expressing the speaker's desire for the young man: he suspects the youth of betrayal, he acknowledges his own part in that betrayal by reflecting on his position between abjectness and suspicion, he makes himself believe against his better judgement that the young man is faithful (although he knows he is not), and he produces different and contradictory explanations for his own acts of deception. In the next two sections we will see how deception itself becomes the dominant focus, in the sonnets addressed to the youth as well as to the mistress.

Deception: speaker and youth

While the majority of sonnets in the cluster of deception are addressed to the mistress, a few can also be found in the youth sequence, attesting to the fact, as shown above, that not only the mistress, but also the youth has 'the ability to deceive the speaker' (Kosofsky Sedgwick 1985: 41).

The few sonnets addressed to or about the youth with a primary focus on his betrayal contain arguments already identified in some of the sonnets discussed in the previous section. In sonnets 33 and 34, for example, the speaker compares the young man's betrayals to dark clouds obscuring the face of the sun. In Sonnet 33, the 'morning' in the first verse stands for the sun which flatters those on whom it shines or rather those who see it (cf. 33.2). But at the same time, it also allows dark, 'basest clouds' (v. 5) to obscure it with 'ugly rack' (v. 6), which translates as 'a mass of cloud moving quickly, esp. above lower clouds' (*OED*, 'rack, n.2, 3.a'). In a similar manner, the youth first bestowed favours on the speaker and 'did shine/ With all triumphant splendour' (vv. 9-10) on his brow, but then the 'region cloud' (v. 12), i.e. clouds in the upper air and here referring to other suitors, came between them. But, as in some of the sonnets discussed before, the speaker tries to rationalize the youth's faults and comes up with an excuse: just as the beautiful sun is sometimes disfigured by base clouds and thereby in turn 'may stain' (v. 14) the world, so the young man, a '[s]un [and son] of the world' (v. 14), is at times corrupted and may corrupt.

What at first sight looks like an ordinary sonnet using a very traditional, almost stale conceit (the beloved is compared to the sun), is in fact more complicated. There are two tropes employed here: in the first eight lines the sun is personified and endowed with human attributes. It '[f]latter[s] the mountain tops with sovereign eye' (v. 2), it kisses 'with golden face the meadows green' (v. 3), it permits 'the basest clouds to ride' (v. 5) and steals away 'unseen to the west' (v. 8). In the third quatrain, however, the parts of the metaphor are reversed: now the sun becomes the vehicle and the youth the tenor ('*my* sun', v. 9; my emphasis). Like the sun, the youth shone on the speaker with 'all triumphant splendour' (v. 10) but is now corrupted by the influence of other courtiers. Although the poem is divided into two clearly distinguishable parts with the first two quatrains describing the sun and the third quatrain describing the youth, they are closely tied together through the reversed tenor-vehicle relationship.

Another interesting feature of the sonnet is its peculiar logic, the fact that the 'conceit is starting to creak' (Paterson 2010: 100). The statement about the sun flattering the 'mountain tops' (v. 2) does not make a lot of sense for Paterson since it is usually not the sovereign who flatters the inferiors but the other way around. However, as Booth (2000: 186) has shown, when applying different meanings of 'to flatter' to the speaker-youth relationship, the conceit is plausible, since 'to flatter' in Shakespeare's time could also mean to 'touch or stroke lightly and caressingly' (*OED*, 'flatter, v.1, 1.b') or to 'gratify the vanity or self-esteem of; to make self-complacent; to make (one) feel honoured or distinguished' (ibid., v.1, 4). The first meaning highlights the tender and physical relationship between sovereign youth and subject speaker, the latter emphasizes that the speaker feels honoured by the attention he receives from the sovereign lover.

The conceit also ingeniously deflects the blame away from the youth to those that he has allowed to come between him and the speaker. Although the speaker concludes that sun and youth 'may stain', the underlying assumption is that it is really the 'basest clouds' which must be held accountable for the young man's transgressions and deceptions.

This forgiving attitude towards the youth changes in the following Sonnet 34, which elaborates the previous sun conceit and places more blame on the youth's deceptive behaviour. The speaker begins by accusing the young man of falsely promising a sunny day (34.1), which made the speaker 'travail forth without my cloak' (v. 2) and being consequentially surprised by the rain. He then confronts the youth by saying it is not enough to make amends by shining through the clouds and drying 'the rain on my storm-beaten face' (v. 6) since the speaker still suffers from the wet 'salve' (v. 7) and is still affected by the original 'disgrace' (v. 8), i.e. 'disfigurement' (Paterson 2010: 103) he received from the young man. Neither can the youth's 'shame' (v. 9) and 'repent[ance]' (v. 10) ease the speaker's 'grief' (v. 9) and the 'strong offence's loss' (v. 12) the latter has experienced. After these accusations, the couplet's conciliatory tone comes as a surprise. Although the speaker throughout the three quatrains is adamant that neither the youth's amends nor his sorrow and penitence can offer him any relief, he nevertheless concludes that the tears the youth sheds for him (presumably of remorse and love) *do* in fact 'ransom all ill deeds' (v. 14).

In the next Sonnet 35, the speaker changes his argumentative strategy once again and employs a logic we are already familiar with from earlier sonnets: he emphasizes his own cooperation in the youth's betrayal of him. In the first quatrain, the speaker excuses the young man's faults by referring to the fact that '[r]oses have thorns, and silver fountains mud' (35.2), that the moon and the sun are sometimes darkened by '[c]louds and eclipses' (v. 3) and that 'loathsome canker lives in sweetest bud' (v. 4). At bottom, the speaker argues one should not judge too harshly since '[a]ll men make faults'. Moreover, by '[a]uthorizing' (v. 6), i.e. justifying the youth's transgressions by writing a poem about them, the speaker admits that he too 'morally compromises himself' (KDJ 2010: 180). The meaning of the next two lines is more obscure. 'Excusing these sins more than these sins are' (v. 8) could have two meanings: either the speaker bestows on the sins more excuse than they deserve, meaning that he should not excuse them because they are so grievous that they cannot be excused, or he gives the sins more excuse than they require, meaning that they are too insignificant and need no excuse. The next line is equally ambivalent. 'For to thy sensual fault I bring in sense' (v. 9) could either mean that your 'sensual fault' is so grievous that it cannot be explained and excused with reason, or that your 'sensual fault' cannot and should not be judged by common sense.

150 A COMPREHENSIVE GUIDE TO SHAKESPEARE'S SONNETS

This ambiguity also shows itself in the speaker's legalistic terminology with which he attempts to rationalize the youth's behaviour. He finds himself both 'adverse party' (v. 10) and 'thy advocate' (ibid.), both opponent and defender, experiences a 'civil war' (v. 12) in his 'love and hate' (ibid.) for the youth and feels like an 'accessory' (v. 13) to a 'sweet thief' (v. 14) who 'robs' (ibid.) from him. The self-accusatory and self-deprecating tone in holding himself responsible for the young man's betrayal can also be found in sonnets 48 and 49 on the theme of separation.

Sonnet 48 begins with the speaker blaming himself for the betrayal by the youth: while locking up his earthly possessions, each 'trifle' (v. 2), before leaving on his journey, he neglected to secure his most valuable treasure, the young man. However, other rivals, 'every vulgar thief' (v. 8), who steal the youth from him, are also held responsible for the latter's unfaithfulness, but are ultimately excused since it is only understandable that they would desire the youth, 'a prize so dear' (v. 14).

In Sonnet 49, discussed in Chapter 4 above, the speaker worries that his own 'defects' (v. 2) will make the youth betray and disown him (vv. 5-6). Accordingly, the sonnet ends in typical self-deprecating manner: 'To leave poor me, thou hast the strength of laws,/ Since why to love, I can allege no cause' (vv. 13-14), which Burrow paraphrases as 'You have the strength of law on the side of ceasing to love me, since I can present no legally binding reason why you should love' (2002: 478). The speaker goes to extraordinary lengths to understand, excuse and cope with the youth's betrayal by suggesting that since he is not worthy of his love, it is within the latter's rights to leave him. There is, however, another way to read the last line of the sonnet: 'Why should you love me – but, come to that, why should I love you?' (KDJ 2010: 208). Once again, the speaker's conflicted state between abjectness and suspicion is reflected in the ambiguous language he employs.

In the previous section I discussed a number of sonnets towards the end of the youth sequence in which the speaker explores different strategies to explain and justify his betrayal of the youth, namely sonnets 109 to 112 and Sonnet 117. In sonnets 118 to 121, the speaker continues this exploration, with a greater emphasis, however, on the theme of deception. In these sonnets, he views his own inconstancy either as a bitter medicine or as a cure to revive his love for the youth. He presents his own unfaithfulness as an excusable fault which he hopes may find in the youth similar forgiveness which the speaker extended to the youth for his betrayal, and he declares that it is altogether better to be corrupt than only to be thought corrupt.

In Sonnet 118, for example, the speaker uses a combined food- and medicine-metaphor to explain why he has been unfaithful to the young man. Finding himself sated with the 'ne'er-cloying sweetness' (118.5) of the lover, he felt he needed to make his appetite 'more keen' (v. 1) by turning to other, 'eager compounds' (v. 2) and 'bitter sauces' (v. 6), the idea being that apart from refining his appetite he also wanted to make himself ill to immunize himself against future sickness, thereby calling to mind the early modern 'practice of taking regular "purges" at certain times of year (e.g. spring) to ward off infection' (KDJ 2010: 346). But contrary to the desired effect, infecting the healthy relationship of speaker and youth with the virus of betrayal has not led to immunizing their love against future deception but to the poisoning of the speaker instead: 'But thence I learn, and find the lesson true,/ Drugs poison him that so fell sick of you' (vv. 13-14).

Sonnet 119 is more specific as to the nature of this poisoning. In drinking 'potions [...] from limbecks foul as hell within' (119.1-2), i.e. by engaging with other lovers, the speaker finds himself in a situation of insecurity and self-delusion, '[a]pplying fears to hopes, and hopes to fears,/ Still losing when I saw myself to win' (vv. 3-4). Although he knew himself to be blessed in the youth's love, he committed 'wretched errors' (v. 5) and allowed himself to be deluded by the 'madding fever' (v. 8) brought about by affairs with others. But while the lesson learned in the previous poem was rather disquieting (the medicine proved to be poison), the sestet in this sonnet offers a much more positive conclusion. The speaker realizes that the madness and confusion brought about by the poison has in fact led to a renewal of his love for the young man: 'better is by evils still made better,/ And ruined love when it is built anew/ Grows fairer than at first, more strong, far greater' (vv. 10-12). Therefore, the strategy of applying bitter medicine proves to be successful and the speaker's betrayal has paid off after all.

The speaker continues to discuss and justify his unfaithfulness in the following two poems. In Sonnet 120, he uses the forgiveness he extended towards the youth's betrayal in the past as leverage for the forgiveness he in turn hopes to receive from the young man for his

152 A COMPREHENSIVE GUIDE TO SHAKESPEARE'S SONNETS

own behaviour ('But that your trespass now becomes a fee,/ Mine ransoms yours, and yours must ransom me', 120.13-14).

In the last sonnet in this mini-sequence, Sonnet 121, the speaker's reasoning becomes more aggressive and unapologetic. The main argument is presented in the first two lines (''Tis better to be vile than vile esteemed/ When not to be, receives reproach of being', 121.1-2) and can be paraphrased as 'being sinful and enjoying the sins one commits is preferable to only being thought sinful without the pleasure of committing the sinful acts'. The speaker then turns against those hypocrites who judge his wanton behaviour although they are themselves 'false' (v. 5) and 'adulterate' (ibid.). He self-confidently states 'I am that I am' (v. 9), thereby echoing 'And God answered Moses, I AM THAT I AM' from the Book of Exodus (3.14). However, instead of claiming divinity for himself, as suggested by KDJ (cf. 2010: 352), the speaker seems to say 'rather "I know in my private counsels what kind of man I am (and I am not perfect, but I am better than they say)"' (Burrow 2002: 622; cf. also Evans 1998: 234 and Booth 2000: 410). In asserting his individuality and autonomy he exposes those people who in criticizing his behaviour are merely projecting their own faults onto him: 'they that level/ At my abuses, reckon up their own' (vv. 9-10). While the 'others' (vv. 4, 5) are 'bevel' (v. 11), i.e. crooked, he considers himself 'straight' (v. 11) in his open acknowledgement of his faults.

Deception: speaker and mistress

Looking at the sonnets which focus on acts of deception in the relationship between speaker and mistress (sonnets 137 to 145), we find a less conciliatory attitude towards acts of betrayal and a greater reluctance to rationalize and excuse these transgressions than in the youth sonnets. Moreover, it is far more difficult to distinguish between the love object's deception of the speaker and the latter's self-delusion. The speaker is more conflicted about his own role in the mistress's deception of him than he is about his collusion in the relationship with the youth.

Sonnet 138, an analysis of 'mutually dependent self-deception' (KDJ 2010: 390), is a case in point. It is a poem about two people who not only deceive each other but also themselves by pretending

DECEPTION 153

to believe the other's deceptions. Although the speaker knows that the mistress lies, he believes her ('When my love swears that she is made of truth,/ I do believe her, though I know she lies', 138.1-2), so that she may think he is naive (vv. 3-4). Conversely, the mistress pretends to believe that the speaker is still young, although 'she knows my days are past the best' (v. 6). 'On both sides thus is simple truth suppressed' (v. 8). In the following sestet of this 'rather depressing little poem' (Paterson 2010: 421), the speaker claims that this 'mutual deception and self-deception' (Evans 1998: 25) is not only true for the mistress and himself but also for the way love generally works: 'love's best habit is in *seeming* trust' (v. 11; my emphasis). The role of deception and collusion in defining the relationship between speaker and mistress becomes even more important and pronounced than in the speaker's relationship with the youth. While the speaker 'was in spiritual communion' (Paterson 2010: 421) with the young man, 'there's nothing at all like that here, just a self-flattering dishonesty in which both parties collude' (ibid.). The speaker cannot stop desiring the mistress although he is aware of her depravity. He finds himself helplessly subjected to the mistress's power, a sentiment which is also poignantly expressed in sonnets 143 to 145, discussed above in greater detail. In these poems, the speaker stresses his dependency on the mistress (143), the latter's corrupting influence (144) and her volatile nature (145).

In Sonnet 142, the speaker expresses his (sexual) dependence on the mistress despite (or even because of) being aware of her betrayal. After stating in the first quatrain that his love for the mistress is 'sinful loving' (142.2) and that she should not rebuke him for this, since her loving has been as sinful as his ('O but with mine compare thou thine own state,/ And thou shalt find it merits not reproving', vv. 3-4), the speaker in the second quatrain specifies the mistress's betrayals: her lips 'have profaned their scarlet ornaments,/ And sealed false bonds of love' (vv. 6-7) as often as his, and she has '[r]obbed others' beds' revenues of their rents' (v. 8), i.e. 'by adultery [. . .] stolen the dues of marriage (and robbed others of the children which are the productive yield of their marriage)' (Burrow 2002: 664). Because the mistress's behaviour is just as sinful as his own, the speaker concludes that it is only 'lawful' (v. 9) that he woos her. Moreover, if she wants others to extend 'pity' (v. 12), i.e. sexual favours to her, she should set a good example and grant the same to those who seek 'pity' from her, including the speaker.

154   A COMPREHENSIVE GUIDE TO SHAKESPEARE'S SONNETS

While Sonnet 137, as shown earlier, argues that the speaker's eyes deceived him in misjudging the mistress's true character, Sonnet 141 emphasizes the heart's collusion in the speaker's self-deception: 'But 'tis my heart that loves what they despise,/ Who in despite of view is pleased to dote' (141.3-4). Neither his eyes, nor the other senses, his 'ears' (v. 5), 'tender feeling' (v. 6), 'taste, nor smell' (v. 7) can '[d]issuade one foolish heart from serving thee' (v. 10). The most pronounced admissions of self-deception, however, after Sonnet 138, can be found in sonnets 139 and 140.

Sonnet 139 is another remarkable poem on the speaker's collusion in the mistress's betrayal of him. What at first sight seems to be a plea for more honesty on the mistress's part ('Wound me not with thine eye, but with thy tongue', v. 3) turns out to be another act of self-deception. Although the speaker knows that the mistress has been unfaithful to him and has eyes for other men, he asks her 'in my sight,/ [to . . .] forbear to glance thine eye aside' (vv. 5-6). On the one hand, he wants her to be open with him, on the other, he does not want to see her looking at other lovers. The speaker then goes on to 'excuse' (v. 9) the mistress by arguing that she only looks at other suitors to spare him the 'injuries' (v. 12) her looks (his 'enemies', v. 10; his 'foes', v. 11) might cause him. This, however, she should not do since he is already 'slain' (v. 13) by his desire for her. Instead, he demands that she '[k]ill me outright with looks, and rid my pain', v. 14), thereby revoking his earlier request that the mistress '[w]ound me not with thine eye' (v. 3) and wilfully accepting the mistress's betrayal

In a similar vein, in the following Sonnet 140, the speaker asks the mistress not to show him 'too much disdain' (140.2) and to tell him she loves him, despite her true feelings: 'better it were,/ Though not to love, yet love to tell me so' (vv. 5-6). Like 'testy sick men' (v. 7) who know that death is near and who do not want to hear the news from their doctors, the speaker, against his better knowledge, wants to sustain the illusion that the mistress desires him. In the third quatrain, the speaker's tone becomes more aggressive when he changes his strategy from merely imploring the mistress to deceive him into self-deception to outright threatening and blackmailing her: 'For if I should despair, I should grow mad,/ And in my madness might speak ill of thee' (vv. 9-10). If the mistress does not want him to stain her reputation by spreading (false) rumours about her, she should at least pretend to love him, although they both well know that her 'proud heart go[es] wide' (v. 14), i.e. that she 'carries her affections *wide* of the mark' (KDJ 2010: 394) from him.

Poetry as deception

As demonstrated, in some sonnets the theme of deception is also closely linked to the act of writing and in particular to the writing of poetry. We have seen in Chapter 5 how the speaker in Sonnet 152 accuses himself of having lied in his poetry, and how in Sonnet 21, discussed in the Introduction, he calls upon himself to 'truly write' (v. 9) and not to misrepresent through exaggerated or stale conceits.

Equating poetry with lying has a long tradition. Plato famously banishes poets from his ideal republic and argues, 'imitative poetry is the last thing we should allow' (*Republic* Book 10, 595b, 313) in an ideal state, as it leads human beings further away from the truth. According to the philosopher, all that we see in the natural world are imitations, copies of the original forms or ideas, which are invisible to us. In the tenth book of his *Republic*, Socrates explains poetry's 'destructive influence on the minds' (ibid.), using the example of a painter who paints a couch. A painting of a couch is a copy of the couch that served the painter as a model, but this 'real' couch is itself a copy of the eternal form of a couch. While God is the 'true creator of the true couch' (ibid., 597d, 316), the carpenter makes a couch at one remove from the original, and the painter makes a couch 'two removes from nature' (ibid., 597e, 316). Plato therefore differentiates between a creator, a maker and a mere imitator of things in descending order of importance and ranks the painter, 'the writer of tragedies' (ibid., 597e, 316), and 'all other imitators' (ibid., 597e, 317) in the last group.

Philip Sidney, however, defends poets and poetry against these charges, since 'the poet, [. . .] nothing affirms, and therefore never lieth. [. . .] The poet never maketh any circles about your imagination, to conjure you to believe for true what he writes' (2008: 235). While Plato sees in poetry a distortion of truth, Sidney argues that truthfulness does not really matter when it comes to poetry.

The speaker in Shakespeare's *Sonnets* can be placed somewhere between these two positions. On the one hand, he shares Plato's concern about the falsifying effect of mimesis when he acknowledges that his sonnets cannot do justice to youth and mistress, on the other hand, he, like Sidney, sees in poetry a way to find an original voice in expressing his thoughts and desires.

Sonnet 103 can serve as a poignant example of a poem, in which the speaker struggles with the deceptive and inadequate nature of poetry in celebrating the young man. Unlike many of the other sonnets from the writing cluster, this poem features a speaker-poet who shows little confidence in the power of his verse to truthfully preserve the youth's beauty. His muse only 'poverty [...] brings forth' (103.1), the 'argument all bare is of more worth' (v. 3), he 'no more can write' (v. 5), his invention is 'blunt' (v. 7), the young man's beauty is 'dulling [... his] lines' (v. 8), i.e. 'showing up [... his] verse as dreary and inadequate' (KDJ 2010: 316) and doing him 'disgrace' (v. 8). In short, by 'striving to mend' (v. 9), to improve his verses in praising the youth in his poetry, the poet-speaker only 'mar[s] the subject' (v. 10).

The main argument of the sonnet is that the speaker's verse can never do as much justice to the young man's 'graces and [...] gifts' (v. 12) as when the latter simply looks into the mirror (vv. 6, 14). Although the mirror, according to Plato, can only show the youth a copy of his appearance (which is itself only a copy of the youth's soul), the speaker's verse is removed even one step further from the youth's essence. But not only is the youth 'of more worth' (v. 3) than the speaker's poetry, the latter also distorts the love object and 'mar[s]' (v. 10) it, brings the speaker to shame and is even considered 'sinful' (v. 9).

At the same time, however, by expressing his lack of faith in his poetic skills and describing them as inadequate compared to the young man's graces and gifts, the poet in the end does in fact manage to find an original way of conveying an idea of the young man's beauty. While Sonnet 103 is a poem about the inadequacy of poetry, it paradoxically manages to do precisely that which the speaker thinks his verses fail to do, namely 'of [... the friend's] graces and [...] gifts to tell' (v. 12).

Further reading

Desire and deception in the *Sonnets*: Andrews 1982; Gardner 1974.
Poetry as deception: Faas 1986; Plett 1994; Vickers [1999] 2004.

8

Imagination

As in the case of the other clusters, the theme of imagination in the *Sonnets* is also closely connected to the other primary themes, for example, when the speaker imagines the youth as an older man in the procreation sonnets, when he reflects on the limitations of his skill as a writer, when the desire for the youth is understood as nourishment for the speaker, or when the speaker imagines possible ways how the youth might betray him in his absence. In fact, all the eleven sonnets in the imagination cluster are also poems which address the young man's absence and how the speaker sees him in his dreams and attempts to invoke him through the power of imagination. However, unlike the poems on the speaker's unfulfilled desire and pain during the young man's absence, many of which I discussed in Chapter 6, the sonnets in this cluster place greater emphasis on the role and powers of imagination in dealing with this separation.

In Sonnet 27, for example, the speaker tells us that after a day's demanding work he falls into his bed to give his tired body its well-deserved rest. While his body rests, however, his mind begins to work: 'But then begins a journey in my head/ To work my mind, when body's work's expired' (27.3-4). His thoughts then '[i]ntend a zealous pilgrimage' (v. 6) to the absent lover and keep the speaker awake in the night ('keep my drooping eyelids open wide', v. 7). The image, 'shadow' (v. 10), of the youth which the speaker 'sees' in his soul occupies his mind. Paradoxically, the shadow image of the young man is also described as a 'jewel hung in ghastly night' (v. 11) which turns the night's darkness into light, thereby denying the speaker sleep (in Shakespeare's time it was believed that jewels could emit light, cf. Evans 1998: 140; KDJ 2010: 164; Booth 2000: 179).

The couplet 'Lo, thus by day my limbs, by night my mind,/ For thee, and for myself, no quiet find' (vv. 13-14) summarizes the crux for the speaker. While his body cannot get any rest during the day, it is his mind that cannot any 'quiet find' at night. The couplet also suggests that even the 'toil' (v. 1) of the day might be something that the speaker intentionally seeks in order not to make him think about the youth.

The main idea of the sonnet is developed through the clever use of oppositions. Day is contrasted with night, body with mind, seeing with blindness, light with darkness, and action with inaction. Each line of the poem contains at least one word that can be assigned to one of these aspects.

The brief discussion of Sonnet 27 once again illustrates the patchwork character of the entire sequence and how each poem engages not just with one but a number of themes that are interconnected. Sonnet 27 is also a poem about love and desire, imagination as a powerful creative force, the wish to preserve the memory of the absent youth, and the pain of separation.

Although the word 'imagination' and its inflections and variants appear more than seventy times in the plays and narrative poems (cf. Spevack 1974: 629), it appears nowhere in the *Sonnets* (cf. Roychoudhury 2014: 110). In *A Midsummer Night's Dream*, however, we find Shakespeare's probably most famous reflection on the power of imagination. When Theseus talks of 'imagination' (*MND* 5.1.8, 14) he has in mind the 'mental faculty that abstracts data from the senses into intelligible forms known as phantasms [. . .], judgment, and memory' (Roychoudhury 2014: 106). In Shakespeare's time, imagination was believed to be one of the five inner senses, or wits, whose function it is to unite 'the various reports of the senses into impressions that are in turn submitted to the examination of a rational power and then passed to memory which retains the impressions and reflects them back to the Imagination and Sensible Reason, should they turn to it to recall past incidents' (Rossky 1958: 51).

According to Theseus, this faculty is compromised and becomes pathological in the 'lunatic, the lover, and the poet' (*MND* 5.1.7). Each of them sees more or different things in his mind than exist. Therefore, what one sees with one's inner eye is different from what one sees with one's actual eyes: the madman 'sees more devils than

IMAGINATION

vast hell can hold' (*MND* 5.1.9), the lover sees beauty where there is none (*MND* 5.1.10-11), and the poet gives mental shape to something immaterial (*MND* 5.1.12-17; cf. Chaudhuri 2017: 247). Theseus derides 'strong imagination' (*MND* 5.1.18) as something that distorts and plays 'tricks' (*MND* 5.1.18) on the mind and can lead us to mistake a bush for a bear (*MND* 5.1.22), an understanding in line with the 'widespread disrepute of imagination as a falsifying and misguiding faculty' (Rossky 1958: 53) that existed at the time. The function of imagination 'in its healthy reproductive capacity' (ibid., 51) was limited to reflecting like a mirror 'accurate sensible impressions of the external world' (ibid.).

Suparna Roychoudhury points out that in 'late sixteenth-century physiological accounts, "fancy" is often used interchangeably with "fantasy" or "imagination"' (2014: 106) and that 'Renaissance discussions offer different and sometimes inconsistent definitions' (ibid.) of these terms. John Davies comments on this inconsistent use in his *Mirum in Modum* from 1602:

> *Imagination, Fancie, Common-sence,*
> In nature brooketh oddes or vnion,
> Some makes them one, and some makes difference,
> But wee will vse them with distinction,
> With sence to shunne the Sence confusion.
> (qtd. in Roychoudhury 2014: 106)

Theseus' speech reflects this inconsistency when he speaks of lovers' and madmen's 'shaping fantasies' (*MND* 5.1.5). According to Sukanta Chaudhuri, 'fantasy' can refer to 'fancy, love, especially light or passing love' (2017: 123) but also to 'the faculty whereby impressions of external objects are imprinted on the mind' (ibid.), which is more or less consistent with the meaning for 'imagination' offered by Roychoudhury above. 'Fancy' as another term for imagination is also used by Hippolyta in her reply to Theseus when she refers to 'fancy's images' (*MND* 5.1.25) regarding the lovers' account of their experiences in the forest.

For Theseus, the poet's imagination is even more dangerous than that of the lunatic and the lover. While the latter two only add to what is there, the poet creates things entirely new, 'bodies forth/ The forms of things unknown' (*MND* 5.1.14-15) and 'gives to airy nothing/ A local habitation and a name' (*MND* 5.1.16-17). While these lines by themselves are not yet a criticism of poetic imagination, the larger context of the speech and especially its conclusion reveal Theseus' critical stance: imagination can easily mislead and make us fear something that is not there.

Such a critical attitude is quite at odds with early modern poetics according to which the faculty of imagination distinguishes poetry from every other art form. Comparing the poet to those in other professions, such as the astronomer, geometrician, and philosopher, Philip Sidney argues in his *Defence of Poetry*: 'Only the poet, disdaining to be tied to any such subjection [of merely following nature], lifted up with the vigour of his own invention, doth grow in effect another nature, in making things either better than nature bringeth forth, or, quite anew, forms such as never were in nature' (2008: 216).

Sidney's understanding of the poet's 'vigour of his own invention' corresponds closely to our modern understanding of imagination as the 'power or capacity to form internal images or ideas of objects and situations not actually present to the senses, including remembered objects and situations, and those constructed by mentally combining or projecting images of previously experienced qualities, objects, and situations' (*OED*, 'imagination, n., 1.a').

While the first section of Chapter 5 focused on the technical side of imagination by exploring how the speaker navigates his way between the techniques of *imitatio* and *inventio* in his attempts to write truthfully about the youth, this final chapter will address the role of imagination in the speaker's attempts at coming to terms with the separation from the youth. It will also investigate the speaker's thoughts on how and where in the body the faculty of imagination operates. It will be shown that Shakespeare displays a similarly modern understanding of imagination as a mental power to conjure or generate objects and situations 'not actually present to the senses'.

In the next section I will discuss the sonnets addressed to the youth, beginning with those eleven sonnets (27–31, 43–47, 61) in which imagination, its workings, source and effects, take centre stage, before turning to those from other clusters, in which imagination also plays a prominent role. In the final section of this chapter, I will explore imagination's role in the poems addressed to or about the mistress.

The imagined youth

Sonnet 27, discussed in the previous section, is the first of a series of five sonnets in which the speaker meditates on the absent youth. While it centres on the speaker's ability to evoke the youth with his 'soul's imaginary sight' (27.9) to his 'sightless view' (27.10), Sonnet 28 describes the energy and 'toil' (28.8) such an imaginative effort requires from the speaker during the sleepless nights. The speaker complains that during the night he is not able to find the rest required to recover from the day's work: 'day's oppression is not eased by night' (v. 3) as he becomes aware of how far away he is from his lover (v. 8). In the third quatrain and the couplet, the speaker reflects on his futile attempts to master his situation by way of his imagination. Although he knows that 'clouds do blot the heaven' (v. 10) during the day and stars do not shine in the night (v. 12) he imagines the youth in the 'bright' (v. 9) sun and the 'sparkling stars' (v. 12). But, as he concludes, the power of imagination is not sufficient to compensate for his 'sorrows' and 'grief' (vv. 13-14) of being separated from the young man.

The next sonnet shows an altogether more optimistic view of the healing powers of imagination. In the first two quatrains of Sonnet 29, the speaker still finds himself in a hopeless situation: he curses his 'outcast state' (29.2) and the fact that he is 'in disgrace with fortune and men's eyes' (v. 1). He envies those who are 'more rich in hope' (v. 5) than he is, who look better and are more popular (v. 6) as well as more talented than him (v. 7), and he finds himself unable to be content with what he 'most enjoy[s]' (v. 8). It has been suggested that the speaker is here referring to 'his poetry' (Evans 1998: 141), which he is unable to appreciate enough. I believe, however, that the following sestet provides the answer as to what the speaker enjoys most, namely his imaginative powers.

Although the speaker has reached a low point in his life, he realizes that by thinking about the youth (v. 10) and remembering his 'sweet love' (v. 13), his spirit ('state', v. 10) is lifted and '[l]ike to the lark at break of day arising,/ From sullen earth sings hymns at heaven's gate' (vv. 11-12). KDJ has noted a moment of doubt in the phrase 'sweet love remembered' (v. 13), as 'if the speaker remembers his friend as loving him, but may not be in a position to know whether this love continues in the present' (2010: 168). Leaving this playful ambiguity aside, it becomes nevertheless clear that the

162 A COMPREHENSIVE GUIDE TO SHAKESPEARE'S SONNETS

speaker's imagination does have the power to change and to improve his state of mind.

The following Sonnet 30 addresses the faculties of memory and imagination and engages with the positive and negative effects of the 'power or capacity to form internal images or ideas of objects and situations not actually present to the senses' (*OED*, 'imagination, n., 1.a'). On the one hand, thinking about 'things past' (30.2) makes the speaker aware of past longings (v. 3) and 'old woes' (v. 4). He recalls and mourns for dead friends ('precious friends hid in death's dateless night', v. 6), laments 'many a vanished sight' (v. 8) and relives 'grievances' (v. 9) long 'foregone' (ibid.) which he now 'new pay[s], as if not paid before' (v. 12). On the other hand, these sessions of 'silent thought' (v. 1) are 'sweet' (ibid.), not the least because in the end mental images of the youth can dispel the negative effects of painful memory so that '[a]ll losses are restored, and sorrows end' (v. 14).

Recollecting past grievances by way of imagination also brings back old woes and pain, but at the same time restore the speaker to an 'enlivened emotional selfhood' (Vendler 1999: 165) which he had lost, as the phrases 'unused to flow' (v. 5), 'cancelled woe' (v. 7) and 'grievances foregone' (v. 9) imply.

Although the sonnet has been regarded by some as a 'simple poem' (Paterson 2010: 91), I agree with Vendler, who thinks that this 'is not only one of the richest sonnets of the sequence, but also one of the most searching, in its analysis of inevitable emotional phases, and of the dangerous delectation (whether morose or not) of reexperienced grief' (1999: 167). She praises the 'ingenuity' (ibid.) and 'exactness of Shakespeare's psychological portraiture' (ibid.) and identifies five levels or 'panels of time' (ibid., 165) in the sonnet.

In receding order, before the weeping 'now' (T5, where T = Time), there was the 'recent' dry-eyed stoicism (T4); 'before that,' the frequent *be-moanèd moan* (T3) of repeated grief; 'further back in the past,' the original loss (T2) so often mourned, and 'in the remote past' (T1), a time of achieved happiness, or at least neutrality, before the loss. (ibid., 165)

The sonnet with its 'moany Os and sighing sibilants' (Paterson 2010: 91) contains various rhetorical figures and devices which

IMAGINATION

serve to establish a heightened sense of tonal as well as semantic density, the most prominent being alliterations, consonances and assonances. The alliterations of the sounds /s/, /w/, /l/ and /m/ are probably the most striking feature: 'sessions of sweet silent thought' (v. 1), 'sigh'/'sought' (v. 3), 'woes'/'wail'/'waste' (v. 4), 'death's dateless' (v. 6), 'love's long', 'weep'/'woe' (v. 7), 'moan'/'many' (v. 8). But we also see instances of polyptoton (a rhetorical figure which repeats 'a word or words by varying their word-class (part of speech) or by giving different forms of the same root or stem' (Preminger and Brogan 1993: 967)) and word repetitions like 'grieve at grievances' (v. 9), 'from woe to woe' (v. 10), 'fore-bemoaned moan' (v. 11), 'pay, as if not paid' (v. 12). All these figures serve the purpose of creating a tighter structure and drawing attention to the sonnet's key concepts such as 'grieving', 'woe' and 'moan'.

Lastly, the sonnet is characterized by using language from legal and financial domains. Terms like 'sessions', 'summon', 'cancelled', 'expense', 'grievances', 'account', 'pay', 'losses [...] restored' underscore the rational and analytical attitude of the speaker towards his mental faculty of forming images, taking stock, as it were, of its positive and negative features.

It is interesting how Shakespeare introduces an idea in one sonnet and then develops and expands it in the following poems. After reflecting on his powers to invoke the youth in his mind in Sonnet 27, the speaker argues in Sonnet 28 that his imagination is not powerful enough to make up for the absence of the youth. Sonnet 29 then displays a more optimistic view when the speaker claims that mental images of the young man can in fact lift his spirits. This is followed by comparing the advantages and disadvantages of imaginative faculties in Sonnet 30 and the realization that thinking about the youth can heal and restore the loss of 'precious friends' (30.6) and 'love's long since cancelled woe' (30.7).

The last poem in this first mini-sequence on imagination, Sonnet 31, adds yet another perspective. It shows how the youth serves as a storehouse for the speaker to imagine and, as it were, bring back to life the friends and loves he lost. The sonnet thus provides more detailed information on how the recovery of the lost friends and loves referred to in the couplet of the previous sonnet ('But if the while I think on thee, dear friend,/ All losses are restored, and sorrows end', 30.13-14) can be achieved through imagination.

164 A COMPREHENSIVE GUIDE TO SHAKESPEARE'S SONNETS

The sonnet begins with the speaker stating that the youth now has 'the love of all those who used to love me; and because they don't love me any more, nor I them – I assumed they were dead' (Paterson 2010: 94). But the youth not only stores the love of the speaker's former lovers or friends but also 'all the aspects and capacities of love' (KDJ 2010: 172) in general: 'And there reigns love, and all love's loving parts' (31.3). The speaker realizes that all the loves for whom he mourned are not dead, not 'removed' (v. 8), but only 'hidden' (v. 8) in the youth. The volta after the second quatrain introduces a striking conceit. While in the first eight lines the speaker argues that his friends are not dead but saved in the 'bosom' (v. 1) of the young man, he now reverses the perspective. The youth becomes the 'grave where buried love doth live' (v. 9), a walking tomb, which houses the 'trophies of my lovers gone' (v. 10). The image explains why some critics have ascribed 'metaphysical effects' (Schiffer 2000: 36) to the *Sonnets*. By taking the loves away from the speaker and storing them in his breast, the young man both preserves and kills them (as well as the speaker's capacity for love in general). The loves are preserved since they are only hidden from sight and not dead, but in hiding them and taking them from the speaker, the youth has also killed them for the speaker. The speaker, however, enacts a final turn of argument when he concludes that even this act of burying his former lovers alive is something positive: by seeing (and by implication also thinking about) the youth, the speaker simultaneously brings to life his former loves by using his imagination. The young man's 'theft' of the speaker's loves has not only enriched him but also the speaker, who with the help of his imagination is able to 'find' their 'images' (v. 13) in the youth.

The next mini-sequence of poems focusing primarily on the theme of imagination are sonnets 43 to 47. The first three of these return to the narrative of the speaker missing and thinking about the absent youth. In Sonnet 43, Shakespeare uses a series of paradoxes based on the oppositions 'seeing/not seeing', 'light/darkness', 'day/night' to emphasize the speaker's powerful desire for the young man. The sonnet begins with one of these paradoxes and catches the reader virtually by surprise by stating in the first line 'When most I wink, then do mine eyes best see', meaning 'When my eyes are most closely shut, they see best' (E/W 2020: 270). The speaker goes on to explain why this is the case: 'when I sleep, in dreams they look on thee,/ And darkly bright, are bright in dark

IMAGINATION

directed' (43.3-4). The meaning of these lines is not easy to grasp because of the paradoxes and oxymora employed. How can the speaker's eyes be 'darkly bright' and 'bright in dark' (v. 4)? Since, as pointed out before, in early modern England 'eyes were generally thought of as giving off light' (Booth 2000: 203), the line can be translated as meaning '(My eyes,) illuminated by the darkness (secrecy) of night, are guided by or towards light through darkness' (KDJ 2010: 196). But what is exactly meant by saying that the speaker's eyes are 'illuminated by the darkness' of night? Colin Burrow's interpretation is more conclusive: my eyes, 'able to see more clearly in the dark [. . . are] directed piercingly towards their object [the absent youth], although it is night' (2002: 466). The darkness of night makes the speaker's eyes see more clearly than during the day in directing their rays of light at the beloved and thereby also making the dark night bright.

Where the first quatrain introduces the main paradox of the sonnet (the speaker can see clearer in the night), the second quatrain elaborates on it by the use of polyptotons. We already find one example in the verse just discussed with 'darkly' and 'dark' (v. 4) but more follow in the next three lines: 'shadow' and 'shadows' (v. 5), 'form' and 'form' (v. 6), and 'clear' and 'clearer' (v. 7). These repetitions enforce the highly condensed argumentation of the speaker which couples opposite ideas and concepts. While the repetition in the fifth verse can be explained easily (the shadow (image) of the youth is so bright that it illuminates shadows), the next two lines with their word play have puzzled readers. Paterson, for example, thinks these lines are a 'semi-coherent, oxymoronic, horribly inverted madness' (2010: 129).

How are we then to understand the lines 'How would thy shadow's form form happy show/ To the clear day with thy much clearer light,/ When to unseeing eyes thy shade shines so?' (vv. 6-8)? Everything depends on which word one identifies as the main verb in verse 6. If one understands the second 'form' in the sense of 'to create', the lines read 'How (much more) would thy body ('shadow's form', v. 6) create a joyful show (or spectacle in daylight) when you are already that bright in the night?' If one identifies 'show' as the main verb, however, then the lines read 'How (much more) would thy body present (itself as) a happy form in daylight when you are already that bright in the night?' (for a discussion of both meanings see Paterson 2010: 129).

166 A COMPREHENSIVE GUIDE TO SHAKESPEARE'S SONNETS

The third quatrain repeats the second quatrain's argument by arguing that seeing the speaker in daylight (being reunited with him) would by far surpass the bright image the speaker sees of the youth in his dreams. But as long as the speaker is separated from him, the couplet concludes, nights will provide the speaker with a clearer image of the young man than days.

Shakespeare uses several additional rhetorical devices to enforce the oxymoronic quality of the sonnet. Apart from the paradoxes and polyptotons, he employs word repetitions (epanalepses) like 'bright' and 'bright' (v. 4), 'days' and 'days' and 'nights' and 'nights' in the final two verses. The couplet also features both a chiasmus and syntactical parallelism: while the words 'days' and 'nights' of line 13 are repeated crosswise in line 14, the syntactical structure of the penultimate verse is mirrored in the final line. All these devices serve to knit the opposing and contradictory concepts closer together and thereby underscore the strong antithetical character of the sonnet or, as Paterson argues, '[b]old antitheses – sight/blindness, day/night, asleep/awake, light/dark – underpin the whole awful-yet-exhilarating paradox' (2010: 128–9).

The next two poems, sonnets 44 and 45 (already discussed in greater detail in the third chapter), are a meditation on both the limits and possibilities of imagination. In Sonnet 44, the speaker treats the material aspect of his being and how, being made up of the two heavy elements earth and water, he cannot travel across distances to the youth like his thoughts. All that he can do is to lament the youth's absence and express his grief in tears. Sonnet 45 deals with the other two elements air and fire, which stand for the speaker's thoughts and desire. These, the speaker concludes, can travel across distances while he himself remains in place. Thought and desire are 'present absent' (45.4) and can 'with swift motion slide [. . .]/ In tender embassy of love to thee' (45.4, 6), the absent lover. While the speaker's body stays fixed in one place, his thoughts are mobile and can move freely across time and space.

In the final two sonnets 46 and 47 in this mini-sequence the speaker addresses the relation between his eyes and heart in his perception of the youth. According to Suparna Roychoudhury, these two poems illustrate the early modern preoccupation with trying to find out how the mind abstracts 'data from the senses into intelligible forms known as phantasms' (2014: 106) and where this interaction was believed to take place in the human body.

IMAGINATION

At stake was an understanding of how the soul's faculties could be mapped onto a physiological body whose contours were coming into increasingly sharp focus. In one sense, the early modern discourse of imagination was conjectural and inconclusive; this was an 'anatomy' of synthetic approximations. Yet, in part because of its positional instability, imagination provides a conceptual space for theorization in which ideas about the body and brain can be tested and explored. (ibid., 108)

Both sonnets offer such 'a conceptual space for theorization' and explore the roles of sight and the heart as 'the seat of cognition' (ibid., 111) in the construction of 'phantasms'. Sonnet 46 presents the connection between eyes and heart as a conflict. Eyes and heart are 'at a mortal war' (46.1) in a legal dispute over which of them is entitled to the true image of the youth ('How to divide the conquest of thy sight', v. 2). While the eyes want to withhold the sight of the lover from the heart (v. 3), the speaker's heart wants to bar 'mine eye the freedom of that right' (v. 4). Both parties, heart and eyes, claim ownership of the youth's 'appearance' (v. 8), his image. A jury (a 'quest of thoughts', v. 10) which reports directly to the heart is called to decide on the outcome of this legal battle. It decides that while the eye is granted the right to behold the outward part of the youth, the speaker's heart, representing the 'power of imagination' (Roychoudhury 2014: 112), owns the young man's 'inward love of heart' (v. 14).

Roychoudhury suggests that we view heart and eye in this poem not so much as mutually exclusive alternatives but as representing 'different facets of consciousness, perception and contemplation, the eye being a window to the world and the heart being the closet of interiority. These are not alternatives: they are distinct yet connected aspects of ordinary cognitive experience' (2014: 112). The following Sonnet 47 corroborates this reading in that it describes a kind of 'out-of-court settlement' (Paterson 2010: 138) between eye and heart. While in the previous sonnet the two agents of perception and contemplation were at 'mortal war' (46.1), eyes and heart have now entered a 'league' (47.1), a truce of some kind, inviting each other to share their privileges and recall the youth: the eyes, when looking at a 'picture' (v. 5) of him, 'to the painted banquet bid [. . .] my heart' (v. 6), but are also invited to be 'my heart's guest' (v. 7), to turn inward as it were to visualize the young

168 A COMPREHENSIVE GUIDE TO SHAKESPEARE'S SONNETS

man. The cooperation between heart and eyes thus ensures that the absent youth is 'present still with' (v. 10) the speaker.

> Instead of legalistic wrangling, the sonnet cites rituals of hospitality, such as 'feast,' 'banquet,' and 'guest.' Heart and eye indulge together in 'the painted banquet' of 'my love's picture,' while the eye shares in the heart's 'thoughts of love.' [. . .] 'Picture' and 'thought' evoke the faculties of imagination and understanding, shown here in seamless and serene collaboration.
>
> Roychoudhury 2014: 113

In the sonnets immediately following this mini-narrative about imagination the focus shifts to the themes of deception, desire and writing, but in Sonnet 61 the speaker returns to the subject of imagination and how the image of the youth keeps him awake at night. While the earlier sonnets discussed in this group are concerned with the workings and effects of imagination, this poem posits the question as to what fuels the imaginative process. In the octave, the speaker implies that the jealous youth is responsible for his sleepless nights by sending images of himself ('shadows like to thee', 61.4) to the speaker to keep him awake at night and to 'find out shames and idle hours' (v. 7) in him. But in the sestet the speaker refutes that idea and concludes that it is his 'own true love' (v. 11) which keeps his 'eye awake' (v. 10) and makes him 'play the watchman' (v. 12). It is therefore not the 'spirit' (v. 5) of the jealous youth who pries into the deeds of the speaker which keeps him awake, but his own (jealous) concern for the absent young man who 'wake[s] elsewhere' (v. 13) with 'others all too near' (v. 14). (For a discussion of the different meanings of waking and watching in lines 10-13 see Ingram and Redpath [1964] 1978: 142 and Vendler 1999: 288–90.)

Later in the sequence addressed to the youth, in sonnets I have placed in the primary theme cluster of desire, the speaker returns to the roles of eye and heart in the production of mental phantasms, this time focusing again on the dysfunctional relationship between these agents. In Sonnet 113, the 'league' (47.1) between eye and heart, so much celebrated in Sonnet 47, and the clear division of labour between them in producing images of the youth, is disturbed once more and the speaker's 'eye is *in* his [. . . the speaker's] mind' (113.1; my emphasis). The speaker's eyes, which should govern him 'to go about' (v. 2), are now partly blind and do not transport any 'form' (v. 5) of what they see to the heart. Instead of conveying images of 'bird, of flower, or shape' (v. 6) to the heart, the eyes distort what they see and, because they see with the speaker's heart, turn everything into the youth's 'feature' (v. 12). A rupture occurs between eye and heart, the 'speaker is physically intact, and yet something is not right. He can still see and still form mental images, but the two processes are no longer connected. This can only occur if function and form can indeed part ways' (Roychoudhury 2014: 115–16).

As dysfunctional and inhibiting as this relationship between eyes and heart is in the speaker's engagement with the world, the couplet 'Incapable of more, replete with you,/ My most true mind thus maketh mine untrue' (vv. 13-14) suggests that this distorting effect of imagination on the speaker's senses is still something positive and 'even pleasurable, for the lover easily absolves the deceiving mind, calling it "most true"' (Roychoudhury 2014: 116).

In the following Sonnet 114, the speaker continues the discussion of this dysfunctional relationship between mind and eye and acknowledges that his mind allows itself to be corrupted by the eyes. After concluding in Sonnet 113 that his love for the youth affects his vision, the speaker is no longer so sure about this in Sonnet 114. In the first two quatrains, he asks himself whether his mind is betrayed by his eyes or his eyes by the mind. Is the mind flattered by the eyes into believing the false vision which the eyes create (114.1-2), or are his eyes truly transforming everything monstrous into something divine because they are under the influence of the youth's love (vv. 3-8)? In both cases, the eyes deceive the mind, the difference being that in the former case the eyes (and, to a certain degree, the mind) are aware of it while in the latter they are not.

The speaker concludes that it is the former and that his eyes do in fact know what they are serving the mind: 'Mine eye well knows what with his gust is greeing,/ And to his palate doth prepare the cup' (vv. 11-12). The eyes know what the mind likes to believe and provide it with the desired image of the youth. The speaker decides that even if that image is false and 'poisoned' (v. 13), it is excusable because the eye 'doth first' (v. 14) taste from it and protects the mind and because 'in his eagerness [. . .] he [the mind] drinks it [the poisoned cup] first – performing the tasting function normally exercised by a menial servitor' (KDJ 2010: 338).

The imagined mistress

Although all the sonnets in which imagination takes centre stage are from the youth sequence, there are a few poems addressed to or about the mistress which also treat the theme of imagination, albeit in a more cursory and slightly different manner. In Sonnet 137 from the deception group and discussed in Chapter 4, for example, the speaker's attitude is much less forgiving and more accusatory than in the poems addressing the interplay between vision and imagination in the speaker's relationship with the youth. In this poem addressed to the 'blind fool love' (137.1), the speaker accuses Cupid of having corrupted his eyes, which are led by mere sexual desire to be 'anchored in the bay where all men ride', v. 6). '[E]yes' falsehood' (v. 7) has 'forged hooks' (ibid.) clouding the speaker's judgement although he well knows the mistress and her body to be the 'wide world's common place' (v. 10). Ending on an acrimonious and intransigent note, the speaker concedes that both his 'heart and eyes have erred/ And to this false plague [the woman] are they now transferred' (vv. 13-14).

A similarly accusatory tone can be detected in Sonnet 141 in which the speaker acknowledges that he has become the mistress's 'proud heart's slave and vassal wretch' (v. 12). The speaker registers not only with his eyes but with all his five senses the faults of the mistress: he does not love her with his 'eyes' (v. 1) and sees her 'thousand errors' (v. 2); his ears are not with her 'tongue's tune delighted' (v. 5), and he neither wants to touch (v. 6), nor smell or taste her (vv. 7-8). Even his five wits, which comprise the faculties of common sense, imagination, fantasy, estimation and memory (cf. Booth 2000: 486–7), cannot dissuade his 'foolish heart from serving' (v. 10) the mistress. Although the speaker sees and knows about the corrupted nature of the mistress, he remains under her spell and submits willingly to her and the emotional or physical pain she causes him: 'Only my plague thus far I count my gain,/ That she that makes me sin, awards me pain' (vv. 13-14).

Roychoudhury draws attention to the way the sonnet inverts the Petrarchan blazon and redirects it at the speaker, and not the mistress:

Enumerating the senses one by one, the poem reduces the speaker to his eyes, ears, and tongue; the fragmentation is different from the customary partitioning of the *blazon*, in which the lady is segmented into the components of her beauty – hair, cheeks, neck, and so on. Here we see the confounding of corporeal functions rather than bodily parts; the body in question, moreover, belongs to the lover, not the love object.

Roychoudhury 2018: 40

While in the poems addressed to and about the young man the speaker displays a more forgiving attitude towards the youth's influence on his imagination, often defending the heart as the seat of cognition against the deceiving senses, in the sonnets about the mistress, eyes and heart are not disconnected but seem to be powerless in the face of the speaker's overpowering (sexual) attraction to her. The speaker does not try to explain or excuse the irrational quality of his relationship with the object of desire by invoking the dysfunctional collaboration of eye and mind, as he does in the sonnets about the youth. Instead, the blame is shifted to an agency outside the speaker, namely the mistress, to whom his foolish heart is enslaved, who threatens his selfhood, and against whose overpowering influence even the mental faculty of imagination becomes powerless.

Further reading

Early modern concepts of imagination: Cocking 1991; Haskell 2011; Nauta and Pätzold 2004; Rossky 1958; Schlutz 2009. **Imagination in the *Sonnets***: Healy 2011; Roychoudhury 2014; Roychoudhury 2018.

9

By Way of a Conclusion

For its relatively young age (compared to, for example, the epos, ode or epyllion), the sonnet form can look back on a very successful past. Apart from the late seventeenth and eighteenth century, when this form 'fell on hard times' (Hirsch and Boland 2009: 119), it has enjoyed great popularity and still does so today, as the collections by Levin (2001) and Hirsch and Boland (2009) and the adaptation history demonstrate.

Although this popularity has a lot to do with the fact that the sonnet form combines 'heart and the head, feeling and thought, the lyrical and the discursive' (Hirsch and Boland 2009: 40), it can also be attributed to the reception of Shakespeare's sonnet collection. As the contributions in Kingsley-Smith and Rampone Jr. (2023), Kingsley-Smith (2019) and the seventy-three contributions on the reception of the *Sonnets* on six continents in Pfister and Gutsch (2009) document, Shakespeare's *Sonnets* have made a lasting impact on poets, novelists, dramatists, translators, film makers, composers and artists worldwide.

As Vendler's pastiche of sonnets 80, 81, 83 and 84 (1999: 4–5) illustrates, merely complying to the metrical and rhyme scheme of the English sonnet without 'structural coherence, [. . .] logical development, and [. . .] unity of play' (ibid., 5) cannot explain its popularity. Neither can its aesthetic value be reduced to the semantic level, as Basil Bunting's two-line paraphrase of Sonnet 87 shows (cf. ibid., 9).

Instead – and as this *Comprehensive Guide* has attempted to show – the *Sonnets*' specific qualities reside in a combination of factors. The most striking of these is their impressionistic character and their refusal to be interpreted as a linear narrative, which has become evident not only in the constant changing of and returning to themes, but also in the fact that the speaker comes up with inconclusive and contradictory arguments as, for example, when he attempts to rationalize his deceitful behaviour towards the youth, or when he tries to figure out how and where precisely the faculty of imagination operates in his body. The *Sonnets'* 'anti-narrativity' (Schiffer 2007: 48) and 'impressionistic' (E/W 2013: 46) quality invite – and challenge – readers to identify links and establish coherence between them by way of 'deep reading' (Wolf 2018: 58), a practice which 'requires observation, hypotheses, and predictions based on inference and deduction, testing and evaluation, interpretation and conclusion, and when possible, new proof of these conclusions through their replication' (ibid.).

The *Sonnets* demand such a deep reading for their secrets and meanings to be revealed. However, while this deep reading may appear to stand in the way of their full appreciation, it is in fact an integral part of the aesthetic experience. Inferring meanings from the collection's gaps on various levels, from their 'gappiness' (Smith 2020: 2), is ultimately what the *Sonnets* are all about. Although Shakespeare assists us in these 'inferential processes' (Wolf 2018: 42) of creating coherence and meaning by providing unity through the use of recurring words, motifs and themes, gaps remain. These pockets of indeterminacy, ambiguity and contradiction engage, puzzle but also dazzle the reader and are one reason of the genre's popularity and longevity.

I also hope to have shown that, apart from their engaging gappiness, Shakespeare's *Sonnets* are highly relevant and topical texts that can tell us a lot about our own time, and in particular how we think and speak about issues of gender, race, and diversity. The speaker's shifting desires between youth and mistress, the 'master mistress['s]' (20.2) fluid sex and gender, and the homoerotic quality of the speaker's relationship with the youth can help us realize that what some only believe to be fashionable trends has in fact a history. Engaging with Shakespeare's *Sonnets* can therefore help us deepen our understanding of the history of gender as a social and performative practice. Instead of viewing these texts as merely confirming and 'enacting binary male/female or homo/hetero desires, we can instead recognize them as resisting precisely the binaries usually understood to structure modern gender, desire and marriage' (Sanchez 2019b: 88). The *Sonnets* may even, as some

BY WAY OF A CONCLUSION 175

scholars hope, enable 'us to unlearn our habits of perception[, . . .] learn to look differently' (Joubin 2023a: 68) and 'refine our understanding of identification and desire in the present as well as the past' (Sanchez 2019b: 2).

Learning to look differently is also required when addressing the figure of the mistress in the *Sonnets*. Although it is eventually not clear whether she is in fact Black, black or 'black', we have seen that Shakespeare's use of colour when referring to the mistress as 'dark' or 'black' and to the youth as 'fair' is a semantic distinction indicative of early modern racecraft. Contrasting the relationship with the 'black' (132.13) mistress who is a 'worser spirit' (144.4), 'coloured ill' (144.4), a 'bad angel' (144.14) and 'as black as hell, as dark as night' (147.14) with that to the 'fair' (144.3) youth who is a 'better angel' (144.3) and a 'saint' (144.7) therefore not only casts the black/'black'/Black mistress as a threat to the whiteness represented by youth and speaker, but also makes us reassess Shakespeare's position as a canonical writer, as 'the quintessence of Englishness and a measure of humanity itself' (Loomba and Orkin [1998] 2008: 1).

We have also seen how the syllogistic quality of the sonnets can facilitate and at the same time complicate our engagement with the poems. In Sonnet 55, for example, the structure seems to support and sustain the logic of the speaker's argument. The first quatrain introduces the main hypothesis that poems about the youth ('this powerful rhyme', v. 2) will outlive any 'monuments' (v. 1). The second quatrain explains why the material monuments are inferior to the poems: 'wasteful war' (v. 5) will destroy the 'statues' (v. 5) and 'masonry' (v. 6), but not '[t]he living record of your memory' (v. 8). The third quatrain elaborates why the poems' 'praise' (v. 10) of the young man will outlast the monuments: they will preserve the youth beyond 'death' (v. 9) and decay ('oblivious enmity', v. 9) and preserve him for 'posterity' (v. 11) until Judgement Day, when, as the final couplet concludes, he will be resurrected in his own body.

At a second glance, however, the logic is less convincing than it first appears. After all, even the 'powerful rhyme' (v. 2) written or printed on paper, for it to be passed on to future generations and to be read by the 'eyes of all posterity' (v. 11), has a material nature and can also be destroyed by 'sluttish time' (v. 4) and 'wasteful war' (v. 5), the difference admittedly being that multiple copies of the

176 A COMPREHENSIVE GUIDE TO SHAKESPEARE'S SONNETS

poems are more likely to survive than single monuments (cf. my discussion of Sonnet 15 in Chapter 4).

In 2016, on the quarter centenary of Shakespeare's death, The Arden Shakespeare published *On Shakespeare's Sonnets: A Poets' Celebration*. The editors, Hannah Crawford and Elizabeth Scott-Baumann asked thirty poets 'to respond to Shakespeare's sonnets in their own form, voice and style' (2016: xiii). The result is a remarkable and highly original collection of intertextual engagements with Shakespeare's *Sonnets* by poets such as Roger McGough, Douglas Dunn, Jackie Kay and Wendy Cope, to name but a few. In the foreword, Colin Thubron applauds the reworkings for their 'own idioms of irony, passion and playfulness, which sometimes break out from the sonnet form that generated them' (ibid., xi). In the *Sonnets*, we identified a similar originality and self-reflexivity, with Shakespeare creatively and subversively playing with and stretching the boundaries of the sonnet form. By substituting the adoration and veneration for the unreachable, distant beloved in the Petrarchan tradition with the sexual longing for male and female love objects who are placed in a triangle of desire with the speaker, Shakespeare not only modulates but also redefines the sonnet form. In his *Sonnets*, he reflects on, plays with and questions traditional Petrarchan beauty ideals, tropes and concepts like the fair and innocent mistress, the blazon and the Platonic quality of the speaker's longing, investing them with a new, raw physicality and urgency. In appropriating forms and contents of Petrarchism, the *Sonnets* acquire not an anti-Petrarchan, but a meta-Petrarchan quality, comparable with the way in which sonnets after Shakespeare continued to engage with his legacy.

The main concept of this *Guide* has been to treat the *Sonnets* not as a narrative sequence but as a collection, and to approach their patchwork character by grouping them into the five dominant theme clusters of preservation, writing, desire, deception, and imagination. As emphasized throughout this book, in having done so I by no means suggest that each of the sonnets can be clearly assigned to only one of these five themes. As I have shown, every sonnet is in fact concerned with more than one theme including those beyond the five suggested in this book. The five theme clusters are therefore meant to be understood as dominant, primary themes that organize the *Sonnets*' non-linear narrative structure and constitute each sonnet's main concern, at the same time allowing room for secondary themes. Like the secondary features that Franz K. Stanzel describes for each of the three narrative situations for novels in his typological circle (*Typenkreis*), these secondary themes inhabit 'areas of transition' (Bode 2011: 115; cf. Stanzel 2001) which connect each sonnet with sonnets in other theme clusters.

To use another, more adequate model to illustrate the five theme clusters, we can imagine a pyramid with the four corners of the base and the corner at the top representing our five themes. While every theme at the base is directly connected to its two neighbouring corners and the top of the pyramid, the latter is directly connected to all the corners of the pyramid's base and would therefore in our case represent the theme of desire which is, as we have seen, to different degrees, present in all the sonnets.

By placing the sonnets inside this three-dimensional pyramid model in corresponding proximity to their primary and secondary themes, the final figure would give us a visualization of the clustered quality of the *Sonnets*. For example, Sonnet 1 with its plea to the youth to preserve his beauty by begetting children would be placed in this model close to the corner of preservation and halfway along the line towards the top corner desire (since the speaker's wish to have the young man preserved in his children is also an expression of his desire for him). Sonnet 55, however, discussed earlier in this chapter, focuses on the speaker's conviction that his 'powerful

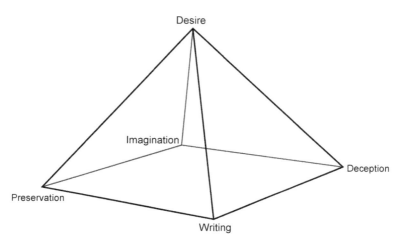

FIGURE 9.1 *Pyramid model of theme clusters.*

rhyme' (v. 2) will be able to preserve the youth for posterity. Accordingly, in our model this poem would be placed left of the corner of writing, somewhere along the line to the corner of preservation. Since the speaker's desire for the youth is only expressed in a reserved and indirect manner ('you shall shine more bright', v. 3; 'your praise', v. 10; 'dwell in lovers' eyes', v. 14), the sonnet would be positioned in the lower half of the pyramid. Conversely, Sonnet 61 about how the speaker's imagination keeps him awake at night in making him think about the absent lover would find a place close to and right of the corner of imagination on the axis towards the corner of deception, since the speaker cannot sleep because of his suspicions that the young man might deceive him, might 'wake elsewhere,/ [. . .] with others all too near' (61.13-14). Since the speaker's desire for the absent youth is articulated in a much more explicit manner than in Sonnet 55 ('my love', 61.10; 'Mine own true love', v. 11; 'For thee watch I', v. 13), it would find a place in the top half of the pyramid; and so on.

Regardless of which model one prefers in visualizing the *Sonnets'* network of interlocking primary and secondary themes, distinguishing between these five dominant theme clusters provides a useful approach to navigate one's way through the collection and to unlock its idiosyncrasies and secrets. The discussion of the preservation sonnets has shown, for example, that the speaker is not only interested in the conservation and passing on of the youth's beauty and character for posterity. He also has in mind the young man's (and his own) happiness and also more pragmatic ends like fulfilling the obligation to procreate and saving his reputation as a (good) writer in that the youth's beautiful children will prove the speaker's poems right.

But the collection also shows that procreation as a strategy of preservation has its limits, and that writing might be a more suitable and successful way of eternalizing the youth (and the speaker). The sonnets that focus primarily on the theme of writing reflect on the speaker's struggle with tradition and originality, his relationship with other poets, and what he can achieve by writing about the young man.

The wish to preserve and write about the youth and the mistress is a consequence of the speaker's strong desire for both personae. Although desire is the underlying theme in the entire collection, we identified a group of sonnets that focus on desire itself, its physical and raw, but also irrational and contagious qualities, as well as its paradoxical nature. We also identified a small group of sonnets in which the speaker compares his desire for the youth with that for the mistress and in which the latter is described as being more powerful than the former, and thus less controllable and consequently also more threatening to the fabric of the self and society.

As the brief discussion of Sonnet 61 above has reminded us, the speaker's desire for the youth is closely interlinked with suspicion and fear about acts of betrayal and deception. A group of sonnets focuses on how the speaker finds himself in a conflicted state of abjectness and suspicion and admits to colluding with both youth and mistress in acts of deception against himself. As with the speaker's desire for both love objects, we were able to notice that the speaker exhibits different attitudes toward the deceptions of youth and mistress. While he tries to rationalize and excuse the young man's acts of betrayal by testing out various argumentative strategies, the speaker's attitude towards the mistress's deception is less conciliatory. In the end, the speaker even accuses poetry itself of deception, thereby ironically undermining the project of praising the youth in his sonnets.

Finally, another small group of sonnets investigates the power and limits of imagination and the role it plays in the speaker's relationship with the youth. These sonnets also discuss the mechanics of imagination and the question where in the body (and how) the faculties of perception, cognition, and contemplation are involved in conjuring and reproducing the young man in the speaker's mind.

When Stephen Burt identifies five characteristics that distinguish the 'most original recent uses of sonnet form' (2011: 246), he is in fact describing the qualities we have identified in Shakespeare's collection. First, the *Sonnets* engage in 'formal play' (ibid.), stretching the form of the sonnet to its limits. Secondly, they display a 'sense of history' (ibid.), reflecting on, processing, and modulating the genre's history. Thirdly, the *Sonnets* show a 'commitment to dailiness' (ibid.) in that they deal with impressions, experiences and events readers can relate to. Fourthly, each sonnet, as a 'unit in series' (ibid.) and within its fourteen lines, sets narrative against recurring patterns. This results in the fifth characteristic, the sonnet form's ability to 'register the tension' (ibid.) between elevated discourse and the 'uninflated language of conversation and of diaries' (ibid.).

It is these features of the *Sonnets*, and the innovative ways in which Shakespeare adapted the sonnet form to engage with the complex relationships between speaker, youth, and mistress that contributed to the sonnet's ability to 'travel [. . .] remarkably well [. . .] down the centuries' (Hirsch and Boland 2009: 39). Moreover, as my discussion of desire, sex, gender and race in the *Sonnets* has shown, these poems still speak to us today and will, I am certain, continue to do so in the future.

Further reading

Anthologies of sonnets: Hirsch and Boland 2009; Levin 2001. **Reception of Shakespeare's *Sonnets*:** E/W 2013: 131–44; Kingsley-Smith 2019; Pfister and Gutsch (eds) 2009. **Translations of Shakespeare's *Sonnets*:** Pfister/Gutsch (eds) 2009; Kingsley-Smith and Rampone 2023: 17–179; Pfister 2012; Greiner 2016. **Rewritings and adaptations of Shakespeare's *Sonnets*:** Ackermann 2009; Crawforth and Scott-Baumann 2016; Kingsley-Smith and Rampone 2023: 183–316; Rupp and Gertich 2009; Springfeld, Greiner and Leopold 2016; Terry 2010. **Sonnet writing after Shakespeare:** Burt 2011; Campbell 2011; Howarth 2011; O'Neill 2011; Petzold 2022: 79–274; White 2011.

Appendix

1 Pairs, Sequences, Groups and Theme Clusters

The two tables 'Connected Pairs and Sequences' (Table 1) and 'Separated Pairs and Groups' (table 2) below summarize (by no means exhaustively) some of the attempts at identifying links and parallels between different sonnets in the sequence. While the first table focuses on neighbouring pairs and connected mini-sequences, the second provides an overview of some of the pairs and groups scattered across the sonnet collection. The range and diversity of links (thematic, verbal, structural, stylistic, and tonal) as well their overlapping nature reveal the difficulties in establishing a narrative structure in the collection and illustrate the complex patchwork character of the sequence pointed out in this *Guide*.

The two tables are followed by a tabular summary of the five theme clusters and the allocated sonnets as proposed in this book.

Table 1 *Connected pairs and sequences*

Sonnets	Common theme or link
1–126	Addressed to a male youth (cf. Malone 1780)
1–20	'"marriage poems" and their immediate aftermath' (Rudenstine 2015: 11)
1–19	'growth of love' (Pequigney 1985: 5)

[Continued]

184 A COMPREHENSIVE GUIDE TO SHAKESPEARE'S SONNETS

Table 1 *[Continued]*

Sonnets	Common theme or link
1–17	'Persuasion to procreate' (E/W 2013: 33)
5–6	Linked by *Then* (cf. E/W 2020: 18)
9–10	Linked by *shame* (cf. E/W 2013: 33)
15–17	'Writing for eternity' (E/W 2013: 33)
15–16	Linked by *But* (cf. E/W 2020: 18)
20–99	'maturity' of love (Pequigney 1985: 5)
20–21	'Love and appearances' (E/W 2020: 18) and linked by *So*
21–32	'Poems of praise in which the poet also reveals his misgivings about the friend's faithfulness' (Rudenstine 2015: 11)
23–24	'Eyesight' (E/W 2013: 33)
27–31	'five sonnets in which the solitary poet meditates on his friend' (KDJ 2010: 164)
27–28	'Sleeplessness' (E/W 2020: 18) and linked by *How can I then*
30–31	'Grief and memory' (E/W 2020: 18)
33–36	'"estrangement" sonnets' (Evans 1998: 144); 'friend [. . .] betrays and abandons the poet' (Rudenstine 2015: 11); 'Mistakes in love' (E/W 2020: 18)
33–34	'Weather and relationship' (E/W 2013: 33); 'treat of disappointment and betrayal, expressed in imagery of sun and cloud' (KDJ 2010: 176)
37–39	'Poems of longing and of praise when the two men are separated' (Rudenstine 2015: 12)
40–42	'The friend and the poet's mistress are jointly unfaithful to the poet' (Rudenstine 2015: 12); 'Attacking, love triangle' (E/W 2013: 33); 'A man takes away the poet's female loved one' (E/W 2020: 19)

1 PAIRS, SEQUENCES, GROUPS AND THEME CLUSTERS   185

43–75	'The poet ventures to discover and define the nature of the friend's character' (Rudenstine 2015: 12)
43–45	'three sonnets on absence' (KDJ 2010: 196)
44–45	'The four elements' (E/W 2020: 19) and linked by *The other two*
46–47	'Eyes and heart' (E/W 2020: 19); cf. also KDJ 2010: 202
50–51	'journey' (E/W 2013: 33); 'On horseback' (E/W 2020: 19) and linked by *Thus*; cf. also KDJ 2010: 212
55–60	'Different experiences of Time when in love' (E/W 2013: 33)
57–58	'emotional slavery' (Kerrigan [1986] 1999: 8); 'tone of apparent servility' (Evans 1998: 165); 'Slavery in love' (E/W 2020: 19)
62–63	on the speaker's 'decrepitude' (KDJ 2010: 234)
63–68	'Time and beauty' (E/W 2013: 33)
64–65	'Time' (E/W 2020: 18) and linked by *Since*
67–68	'Male beauty' (E/W 2020: 18) and linked by *Thus*
69–70	'Blamed for being beautiful' (E/W 2020: 18) and linked by *That thou art*
71–74	Speaker's 'proximity to death' (Cousins 2011: 128)
71–72	'Forgetting poet after his death' (E/W 2020: 18) and linked by *lest* and *World* (cf. also E/W 2013: 33)
73–74	'Mortality and poetry' (E/W 2020: 18) and linked by *But*
76–86	'The friend entertains the possibility of choosing another favored writer' (Rudenstine 2015: 12)
78–88	'play to some degree on the word *in* [. . .]; moreover, the idea of inherence figures in each of them' (Booth 2000: 269)
78–86	'Other poets writing about the loved one' (E/W 2020: 19)

[Continued]

186 A COMPREHENSIVE GUIDE TO SHAKESPEARE'S SONNETS

Table 1 *[Continued]*

Sonnets	Common theme or link
80–81	'An unidentifiable poet' (E/W 2020: 19); linked by *Or* (cf. ibid.)
82–83	'Being truer than other poets' (E/W 2020: 19)
87–96	The speaker, between hope and despair, attacks the youth's character (cf. Rudenstine 2015: 12)
88–90	'*Against myself*, hate' (E/W 2013: 33)
89–90	'on the readiness to sacrifice the self, however innocent, to the interests of the false beloved' (Evans 1998: 196); 'A loved one leaving' (E/W 2020: 18) and linked by *Then*
91–93	'falsity' (E/W 2013: 33); 'Loyalty' (E/W 2020: 18) and linked by *But* and *So*
97–108	After a lengthy separation the speaker returns to and reconciles with the young man (cf. Rudenstine 2015: 12)
97–99	'"separation" sonnets' (Evans 1998: 205); 'Seasons' (E/W 2013: 33); 'Absence' (E/W 2020: 18); cf. also KDJ 2010: 304
100–126	'decline' of love (Pequigney 1985: 5)
100–103	'offer apology and excuses for a period of silence on the poet's part' (Evans 1998: 208; cf. also Kerrigan [1986] 1999: 302); 'Muse sonnets' (E/W 2013: 33); 'Poetic Muse and poetry' (E/W 2020: 18)
106–109	'Echoes on writing, peace, and time' (E/W 2013: 33)
109–120	The speaker is unfaithful but eventually reunited with the youth (cf. Rudenstine 2015: 12)
109–112	'Temporary absences and distractions' (E/W 2020: 19)
109–110	'Contradiction of constancy and falsity' (E/W 2013: 33)
111–112	'Pity' (E/W 2013: 33); cf. also KDJ 2010: 334

1 PAIRS, SEQUENCES, GROUPS AND THEME CLUSTERS   187

113–114	'conflict between eye and mind' (Evans 1998: 224); 'Imagination and eyesight' (E/W 2020: 19) and linked by *Or* and *mind* (cf. also E/W 2013: 33)
115–116	'cooperate to demonstrate an inconsistency in traditionally approved attitudes toward mutability in love' (Booth 2000: 378)
118–120	'Sickness in love' (E/W 2020: 19)
118–119	'Sickness/Fever' (E/W 2013: 33)
121–126	'self-affirmation by the poet, with renewed professions of love, [. . .] now defined in a new way' (Rudenstine 2015: 12)
123–125	'graduated "No" pattern' (Evans 1998: 236) in 123.1, 124.5 and 125.9
125–126	Linked by 'render' (cf. E/W 2013: 33)
127–154	Addressed to a mistress (cf. Malone 1780); cycle of lust, 'moving from desire to gratification, then to abeyance of desire and aversion, then to the renewal of desire' (Pequigney 1985: 165); 'Poems to the mistress, with increasing indications of the poet's deep self-betrayal and lack of control in the face of lust' (Rudenstine 2015: 13)
128–136	'celebrating the erotic power of the "dark lady"' (KDJ 2010: 388)
129–130	'Stand alone sonnets, work almost antithetically, unusual so close together' (E/W 2013: 33)
131–136	'Love triangle' (E/W 2013: 33)
131–133	'Groaning sonnets' (E/W 2013: 33)
133–134	'Triangular relationship' (E/W 2020: 18) and linked by *So*; cf. also KDJ 2010: 382
134–135	'*Will*' (E/W 2013: 33)
135–136	'Play on poet's name, "Will"' (E/W 2020: 18) and linked by *If*; 'elaborate the idea of the woman's sexual voracity' (KDJ 2010: 384)

[Continued]

188 A COMPREHENSIVE GUIDE TO SHAKESPEARE'S SONNETS

Table 1 *[Continued]*

Sonnets	Common theme or link
137–142	'Lies, dishonesty' (E/W 2013: 33)
139–142	'Power of a loved one's eyes' (E/W 2020: 18)
140–142	Linked by *eyes* and *sin* (cf. E/W 2013: 33)
141–142	'Love and Sin' (E/W 2020: 18) and linked by *sin*; cf. also KDJ 2010: 398
149–150	'Power of a loved one' (E/W 2020: 18)
153–154	'Classical allusions, Cupid, translations' (E/W 2013: 33); cf. also KDJ 2010: 422

Table 2 *Separated pairs and groups*

Sonnets	Common theme or link
8, 128	Music imagery (cf. KDJ 2010: 126, 370)
12, 20, 49, 52, 60, 63, 70, 71, 126, 144	Numerological sonnets (cf. Burrow 2002: 108; KDJ 2010: 100–1; Booth 2000: 545–6)
19, 123	'To Time' (E/W 2020: 28)
26, 77	'Sonnet letters' (E/W 2020: 28)
40–42, 133, 134, 144	Love triangle (cf. KDJ 2010: 190); on 'a relationship with a male and female' (E/W 2020: 28)
56, 137	'To Love' (E/W 2020: 28)
57, 89, 134–136, 143	Play on the name 'Will' (cf. E/W 2020: 18). E/W also include Sonnet 22 in this list, but I do not see how the two 'will' (vv. 10, 11) in this poem refer to the name (cf. also KDJ's and Burrow's notes in their editions).
60, 64, 65	'On time' (E/W 2020: 29)

Sonnets	Common theme or link
66, 123–125, 129	General reflections on love and desire in a changing or corrupted world
76–80, 82–86	Rival poet group (cf. Booth 2000: 546); 'Rival poet/s' (E/W 2013: 33)
77, 122	Speaker mentions notebook (cf. KDJ 2010: 264, 354)
117–119, 120	'the poet's "transgression" [120.3] or "unkindness" [120.5]' (Evans 1998: 232)
33–35, 40–42, 48, 49, 57, 58, 61, 69, 78–96, 109–112, 117–120, 133–144	'jealousy sonnets' (Pequigney 1985: 102)

Table 3 *Theme clusters (as identified in this Guide)*

Theme	Sonnets
Preservation	1–17, 126, 146
Writing	18, 19, 21, 23, 26, 32, 38, 54, 55, 59, 60, 63, 65, 71, 72, 74, 76–86, 100–108, 122, 152
Desire	20, 22, 24, 25, 36, 37, 39–42, 50–53, 56–58, 62, 64, 66–70, 73, 75, 87–99, 109–117, 123–125, 127–136, 144, 145, 147–151, 153, 154
Deception	33–35, 48, 49, 118–121, 137–143
Imagination	27–31, 43–47, 61

2 Conjectured Dates of Composition for the Sonnets

Table 4 *Conjectured dates of composition*

Year(s)	Sonnets	
	(Burrow 2002)	**(E/W 2020)**
Pre-1582		153–154
1582	145	145
1591–1595 (Burrow) / 1590–1595 (E/W)	127–144, 146–154	127–144, 146–152
1594–1595	61–103	61–77, 87–103
1595–1596 (Burrow) / 1595–1597 (E/W)	1–60	1–60
1598–1600		78–86
1598–1604 (Burrow) / 1600–1604 (E/W)	104–126	104–126

3 Addressees of the Sonnets

Although there is 'an astonishing number of sonnets that do not make the gender of the addressee explicit' (de Grazia 2000: 97), a closer look at the poems reveals that in many cases they actually do provide us with either explicit information or clues that help us in identifying the gender. The following five tables differentiate between sonnets with a male addressee (table 1), a female addressee (Table 2), a male *and* female addressee (Table 3), a male *or* female addressee (Table 4) and no specific addressee (Table 5). For each sonnet I quote the respective evidence and indicate whether we are dealing with explicit or contextual information. While explicit information refers to words and phrases like 'sweet boy' (108.5), 'his' (3.8) or 'my mistress' eyes' (127.9), contextual evidence is inferred from context, which can either be relations to or within a group of sonnets like the procreation sequence (sonnets 1–17) or links to neighbouring sonnets. For example, although the gender of the addressee in Sonnet 34 is not explicitly given, the fact that it continues the theme of Sonnet 33 in which the gender is referred to as 'him' (vv. 12, 13), strongly suggests that the addressee in Sonnet 34 is also male. Similar contextual evidence can be found in Sonnet 134, which elaborates the idea of the black/'black'/Black mistress in sonnets 127, 130 and 133. Other types of contextual evidence for the addressee's gender are phrases and expressions with specific gendered meanings ('seal' and 'print' in Sonnet 11, v. 13, v. 14; 'youth' in Sonnet 54, v. 13) and puns and sexual innuendo ('she pricked thee out' in Sonnet 20, v. 13; 'is admitted here' in Sonnet 136, v. 3; 'the bay where all men ride' in Sonnet 137, v. 6).

Applying the term 'addressee' to the *Sonnets* in the sense of 'a person to whom words are directed' (*OED*, 'addressee, n.') is,

192 A COMPREHENSIVE GUIDE TO SHAKESPEARE'S SONNETS

however, slightly misleading since some of the sonnets are not directed at any person and are yet about someone. Sonnets 19, 123 and 125, for example, are addressed to Time, sonnets 56, 137 and 148 to Love, Sonnet 100 to the Muse, Sonnet 146 to the Soul, and sonnets 64, 65, 94, 116, 121, 124 and 129 to no one in particular. In most of these sonnets the speaker still reflects on his relationship with the youth and/or the mistress. Consequently, the term addressee is here understood as the speaker's love object which is the central focus of the poem.

The tables reveal that only eight of the 154 sonnets do not mention a significant other. The remaining 146 sonnets are all about at least one desired other, with thirty-six about a male love object, twenty-one about a female lover, five about both the youth and mistress, and eighty-four sonnets about someone of unspecified gender, although contextual analysis would in some of the sonnets lead to further clues about the addressee's gender (cf. the table in E/W 2013: 30). It is important to note, however, that the findings show that none of the sonnets 1–126 are explicitly or implicitly about (only) the mistress, and none of the sonnets 127–154 deal explicitly or implicitly with (only) the youth. One should also not forget that it was not unusual in early modern love poetry not to always identify the gender of the desired other.

Table 5 *Male addressee (thirty-six sonnets)*

Sonnet	Evidence	
1	Explicit	*His* (v. 4), *churl* (v. 12)
2	Contextual	context of surrounding sonnets
3	Explicit	*unbless some mother* (v. 4), *tillage of thy husbandry* (v. 6), *he* (v. 7), *his* (v. 8)
4	Contextual	context of surrounding sonnets
5	Contextual	context of surrounding sonnets
6	Explicit	*Make sweet some vial, treasure thou some place/ With beauty's treasure* (vv. 3-4)

3 ADDRESSEES OF THE SONNETS

7	Explicit	*strong youth in his middle age* (v. 6)
8	Contextual	context of surrounding sonnets
9	Contextual	context of surrounding sonnets
10	Contextual	context of surrounding sonnets
11	Contextual	*She carved thee for her seal* (v. 13), *Thou shouldst print more* (v. 14)
12	Contextual	context of surrounding sonnets
13	Explicit	*You had a father; let your son say so* (v. 14)
14	Contextual	context of surrounding sonnets
15	Explicit	*men as plants increase* (v. 5)
16	Explicit	*many maiden gardens [. . .] would bear your living flowers* (vv. 6-7)
17	Contextual	context of surrounding sonnets
19	Explicit	*Him* (v. 11), *beauty's pattern to succeeding men* (v. 12)
20	Contextual	*master mistress* (v. 2), *a man in hue* (v. 7), *for a woman wert thou first created* (v. 9), *by adding one thing to my purpose nothing* (v. 12), *she pricked thee out for women's pleasure* (v. 13)
26	Explicit	*Lord of my love* (v. 1)
33	Explicit	*him* (vv. 12, 13)
34	Contextual	context of surrounding sonnets
35	Explicit	*All men make faults* (v. 5)
36	Contextual	context of surrounding sonnets
39	Explicit	*him* (v. 14)
40	Contextual	reference to procreation sonnets (vv. 7-8)

[Continued]

194 A COMPREHENSIVE GUIDE TO SHAKESPEARE'S SONNETS

Table 5 *[Continued]*

Sonnet	Evidence	
51	Contextual	context of surrounding sonnets
53	Contextual	*Adonis* (v. 5)
54	Contextual	*lovely youth* (v. 13)
63	Explicit	*his* (3)
67	Explicit	*he* (v. 1),
68	Explicit	*his* (v. 1)
97	Contextual	*unfathered fruit* (v. 10)
101	Explicit	*he* (v. 9), *him* (vv. 11, 14)
108	Explicit	*sweet boy* (v. 5)
126	Explicit	*lovely Boy* (v. 1)

Table 6 *Female addressee (twenty-one sonnets)*

Sonnet	Evidence	
127	Explicit	*my mistress' eyes* (v. 9), *her* (v. 10)
130	Explicit	*my mistress' eyes* (v. 1), *her* (vv. 2, 3, 4, 6, 9), *my mistress* (v. 8), *My mistress* (v. 12), *she* (vv. 12, 14)
131	Contextual	context of surrounding sonnets
132	Contextual	context of surrounding sonnets
135	Explicit	*her* (v. 1)
136	Contextual	*is admitted there* (v. 3), *fill it full with wills, and my will one* (v. 6)
137	Contextual	*the bay where all men ride* (v. 6), *the wide world's common place* (v. 10)

3 ADDRESSEES OF THE SONNETS

Sonnet	Evidence	
138	Explicit	*she* (vv. 1, 2, 3, 5, 6, 9, 13), *her* (vv. 2, 7, 13)
139	Explicit	*Her* (v. 10), *she* (v. 11)
140	Contextual	context of surrounding sonnets
141	Explicit	*she* (v. 14)
142	Contextual	*scarlet ornaments* (v. 6)
143	Contextual	*housewife* (v. 1), *mother's part* (v. 12)
145	Explicit	*her* (vv. 3, 5), *she* (vv. 4, 9, 13)
147	Contextual	context of surrounding sonnets
148	Contextual	context of surrounding sonnets
149	Contextual	context of surrounding sonnets
150	Contextual	context of surrounding sonnets
151	Explicit	*Her* (v. 14)
153	Explicit	*my mistress' eye* (vv. 9, 14)
154	Explicit	*my mistress' thrall* (v. 12)

Table 7 *Male and female addressee (five sonnets)*

41, 42, 133, 134, 144

Table 8 *Male or female addressee (eighty-four sonnets)*

18, 21–25, 27–32, 37, 38, 43–50, 52, 55–62, 64–66, 69–93, 95, 96, 98–100, 102–107, 109–115, 117–120, 122, 128, 152

Table 9 *No specific addressee (eight sonnets)*

94, 116, 121, 123–125, 129, 146

4 A Step-by-step Approach to Sonnet 75

Understanding and appreciating a sonnet by Shakespeare requires time and effort, since a sonnet is usually a very dense and complicated affair that conveys meaning on several levels. It tells us about something (for example, a relationship, an argument, a proposition, a conflict etc.), confronts us with a specific communicative situation in which someone speaks to someone else in a specific moment in time and sometimes also in a particular space or place. It employs specific sound features such as metre, rhythm and rhymes which can (and must!) be related to the content, it uses a specific language and imagery, and it may also, as we have seen, refer to other sonnets in a sequence in that its themes, motifs or story continue in other poems. Lastly, a sonnet often enters a conversation with its own literary tradition, which may tell us something about the speaker's and implied author's perspective on the sonnet's themes and subjects.

The following step-by-step approach is intended to help those not yet familiar with Shakespeare's *Sonnets* discover, experience and appreciate the aesthetic and intellectual pleasure that these dense literary texts can provide. At the same time, this approach also shows what must be done before one attempts an interpretation of a sonnet. To produce an informed analysis of a sonnet, one must first collect the relevant data to prepare the ground for such an interpretation.

This step-by-step approach will use Sonnet 75 as an example, a poem that has not yet been discussed in this *Guide*.

4 A STEP-BY-STEP APPROACH TO SONNET 75

Sonnet 75
01 So are you to my thoughts as food to life,
02 Or as sweet seasoned showers to the ground;
03 And for the peace of you I hold such strife
04 As 'twixt a miser and his wealth is found:
05 Now proud as an enjoyer, and anon
06 Doubting the filching age will steal his treasure;
07 Now counting best to be with you alone,
08 Then bettered that the world may see my pleasure;
09 Sometime all full with feasting on your sight,
10 And by and by clean starved for a look,
11 Possessing or pursuing no delight
12 Save what is had, or must from you be took.
13 Thus do I pine and surfeit day by day,
14 Or gluttoning on all, or all away.

1   Before you look up any words or try to figure out what the sonnet might be about, read it, and read it out aloud. I firmly believe that there is something extremely valuable in one's first contact with a poem and the best way to experience and relish this moment is simply to speak and hear the words.

2   After reading the poem out loud you may already notice certain interesting sound features, such as the smooth, flowing quality of the poem which arises from the fairly regular metre, the fact that many verses end with a pause, and from the repetition of similar sounds at the end and in the middle of verses. You may have also noticed that occasionally your speaking flow was interrupted. For example, where you expected a stressed syllable, you did not find one (vv. 1, 5, 6) or where you expected a pause, there was none, or, conversely, you were surprised by a pause in the middle of a verse where you did not expect it (v. 5). As we will see, deviations from (and adherence to) the underlying metre can draw attention to important moments in and aspects of a sonnet and provide us with helpful information as to what is going on at what point.

3   In a next step try to define the main subject or theme of the poem. In doing so, it might be helpful to begin by

198 A COMPREHENSIVE GUIDE TO SHAKESPEARE'S SONNETS

establishing the communicative situation, i.e. who is talking to whom, when, where and about what. In our case, a speaker is addressing another person by telling him how much he desires him (as outlined above and in Appendix 3, I believe that this sonnet is addressed to the youth). Bearing in mind what you have learned about the syllogistic structure of the Shakespeare sonnet will help you see how the argument of the poem unfolds. While the first quatrain introduces the idea that the speaker's desire for the addressee is not something unequivocally positive ('strife', v. 3), the second quatrain specifies the speaker's reservations and conflicts. He is afraid that his 'treasure' (v. 6) might be taken from him, and he is torn between the desire of keeping the beloved all to himself and wanting to show him off to 'the world' (v. 8). In the third quatrain, the tone becomes more accusatory when the speaker describes the confining quality of his desire for the addressee and his total dependence on him ('starved for a look', v. 10; 'no delight/ Save what is had or must from you be took', vv. 11-12). In the couplet, the speaker summarizes the ambivalent and unsatisfactory nature of his relationship with the addressee: neither the presence nor the absence of the addressee brings the speaker happiness. In both cases he suffers from enjoying the addressee either too little ('pine', v. 13) or too much ('surfeit', v. 14). To get to the core argument of a sonnet, it might be helpful to summarize its main argument in just one sentence, which in our case could read 'In Sonnet 75, the speaker describes both the fulfilling and unfulfilling aspects of his desire for the addressee'.

4   Go through the sonnet verse by verse and look up words and phrases you do not know or understand. Although it is often not the actual words that pose problems, but the way they are connected and arranged in a verse or sentence, the meanings of words and the contexts they are used in have changed since the sixteenth century. Shakespeare is also known for his technique of 'conversion', the practice of, for example, using nouns as verbs, or verbs as adjectives. Annotated editions of the *Sonnets* (see References) provide useful information with their extensive commentary and

4 A STEP-BY-STEP APPROACH TO SONNET 75

notes, but also the (online edition of the) Oxford English Dictionary is of invaluable help here. Cases in point from our sonnet are, among others, the use of 'bettered' (v. 8) and the elliptical constructions in verses 5, 9-12 and 14. If you feel that the meanings of some of the words you looked up conflict substantially with your first perception of the sonnet, go through the poem again and adjust your idea of the main argument.

5 Having identified the most important points and arguments on the semantic level, we can now turn to the formal aspects of the sonnet, beginning with the sound qualities. On the basis of our first impressions in step 2 and taking a more detailed look at the metre, rhythm and rhyme patterns of Sonnet 75, we notice that the standard metre of the English sonnet, the iambic pentameter, is maintained throughout, with only a few minor deviations and adjustments: the first two feet in verse 1 contain no stresses, 'showers' in verse 2 is conflated to a monosyllabic word, and verses 6 and 8 with the feminine end rhymes 'treasure/ pleasure' contain an extra unstressed syllable. The resulting regular rhythm with only a few pauses and irregularities enhance the steady rhythm and support the idea that the nature and course of the speaker's relationship with the addressee is unalterable and outside the influence of those involved. Additionally, the use of alliterations ('sweet seasoned showers', v. 2; 'best to be', 'bettered', v. 7-8; 'Sometime . . . sight', 'full with feasting', v. 9; 'Possessing or pursuing', v. 11) and word repetitions ('by and by', v. 10; 'day by day', v. 13; 'all, or all away', v. 14) help to define the specific relationship between speaker and youth. The whispering and rustling effect produced by the triple repetition of the alveolar fricative /s/ in verse 2, for example, underscores the nourishing, but also tender quality the speaker ascribes to the youth. The sequence of soft voiced bilabial plosives /b/ in verses 7-8, followed by the harder, voiceless bilabial /p/ in 'pleasure' at the end of verse 8, establishes an effective contrast between the intimate and private relationship between the two men ('best to be with you alone', v. 7) on the one hand and the desire to announce this 'pleasure' (v. 8) in a more open and

aggressive way on the other. Similarly, the combination of voiceless plosives /p/ and sharp alveolar fricatives /s/ in 'Possessing or pursuing' (v. 11) support the forceful quality of the speaker's desire for the youth. Finally, the repetitions of 'day' and 'all' in the couplet support on the sound level the notion expressed in the poem (and the collection) that the speaker's desire for the youth is permanent and all-consuming.

6   When it comes to the language used in a sonnet, various aspects can and should be taken into consideration: the word classes employed (verbs, nouns, adjectives etc.), the style and register (archaic, colloquial, poetic, technical etc.), the syntax and imagery (tropes, semantic fields). For example, most of the main verbs in our sonnet (*are*, *hold*, *steal*, *see*, *pine*, *surfeit*) are of a mostly neutral character, except for the last two which reveal the speaker's heightened emotional investment in the final couplet. Other terms like 'miser' (v. 4), 'filching' (v. 6), 'starved' (v. 10) and 'gluttoning' (v. 14) are indicative of a similar emotional involvement. In this context it is also particularly useful to look at the semantic fields the words belong to. The most dominant field is associated with cultivation and nourishment, and words like 'food', 'seasoned', 'showers', 'ground', 'full', 'feasting', 'starved', 'pine', 'surfeit' and 'gluttoning' emphasize the great degree of urgency and dependency the speaker feels in his relationship with the addressee. This urgency is also reflected in the way the speaker describes his love for the addressee as a physical and life sustaining desire, a hunger that needs to be stilled, as the pun on 'peace of you' (v. 3) and expressions like 'enjoyer' (v. 5), 'all full with feasting on your sight' (v. 9), '[p]ossessing or pursuing' (v. 11) and 'what is had' (v. 12) indicate. The straightforwardness with which the speaker addresses his situation is also illustrated by the kinds of tropes that are employed. Apart from the metaphors of nourishment used by the speaker in verses 9-10 and 13-14 to express the sustenance (or lack thereof) he receives from the young man's love, the first four verses use similes in which the similarity between vehicle and tenor is spelled out more directly than in a metaphor: the youth is to the

4 A STEP-BY-STEP APPROACH TO SONNET 75

speaker's thoughts *as* food to life or *as* the showers are to the ground, and the speaker experiences a conflict *as* between a miser and his wealth.

7 When dealing with sonnets from a sequence, it is advisable to consider the place the sonnet inhabits in the collection and connections to other sonnets in the sequence. Admittedly, this is not always possible because of limited time or access, but – as this *Guide* hopes to have shown – a poem like Sonnet 75 is part of a whole group of sonnets which thematize the physical, irrational, and uncontrollable aspects of desire.

8 Finally, a sonnet to varying degrees always engages with its own literary tradition. While this self-reflexive quality is not as prominent in Sonnet 75 as in, for example, sonnets 127 and 130, the Petrarchan tradition still serves as a foil against which the poem creates a counter model of an entirely different, much more physical and sexual notion of desire.

5 Model Interpretation of Sonnet 106

Sonnet 106
01 When in the chronicle of wasted time
02 I see descriptions of the fairest wights,
03 And beauty making beautiful old rhyme,
04 In praise of ladies dead, and lovely knights;
05 Then in the blazon of sweet beauties best,
06 Of hand, of foot, of lip, of eye, of brow,
07 I see their antique pen would have expressed
08 Even such a beauty as you master now:
09 So all their praises are but prophecies
10 Of this our time, all you prefiguring;
11 And for they looked but with divining eyes
12 They had not skill enough your worth to sing;
13 For we which now behold these present days
14 Have eyes to wonder, but lack tongues to praise.

This is a sonnet that connects the theme clusters of writing, beauty and preservation, with a predominant focus, however, on writing. It argues that the youth's beauty cannot be given adequate expression, neither in the past nor in the present. True to the syllogistic structure of the Shakespearean sonnet, the speaker develops his argument in a highly logical manner. In the first quatrain, the speaker invokes the attempts of earlier poets to praise 'fairest wights' (v. 2), i.e. 'ladies dead, and lovely knights' (v. 4), and to lend them beauty in 'beautiful old rhyme' (v. 3). However, as is argued in the second quatrain, the idea of perfect beauty that those past poets had in

5 MODEL INTERPRETATION OF SONNET 106 203

mind ('sweet beauties best', v. 5), and which they thought was represented by the 'wights', was not embodied until now in the young man (vv. 7-8; cf. also Burrow (2002: 592), who argues that 'would have' in verse 7 should translate as 'wished to'). This makes the speaker conclude in the third quatrain that the poets of the past can be understood as biblical prophets who with 'divining eyes' (v. 11) predicted the coming of true beauty in the image of the youth. But not only did those poets fail to see that the 'ladies' and 'knights' they were describing did not meet the criteria of ideal beauty, but they also lacked the skill to adequately prefigure the beauty and 'worth' (v. 12) of the youth. But, as the couplet concludes, the speaker-poet finds himself in a similar predicament, for he realizes that like those past poets he and every other living poet also lack the 'tongues to praise' (v. 14) the young man and can only marvel at his beauty.

As becomes evident in this short summary of the poem's main argument, the sonnet is more complex than it first appears. This has to do with the fact that the argument takes a few turns, thereby throwing the reader repeatedly off the scent. Whereas the stress on 'fairest wights', 'ladies dead' and 'lovely knights' in the first quatrain seems to suggest that this sonnet will be about past women's and men's beauty which is perceived as inferior to the youth's, the second quatrain shifts the focus to poetry itself and the representation of beauty. While the 'blazon of sweet beauties best,/ Of hand, of foot, of lip, of eye, of brow' (vv. 5-6) refers to the by Shakespeare's time already outdated Petrarchan beauty catalogue, employed by poets to take stock of the features of the desired other (cf. my discussion of this tradition in Chapter 1), the 'antique pen' (v. 7) is a metonymy for similarly antiquated modes of poetic expression.

The second quatrain then shifts the focus from the objects of representation ('the fairest wights') to representation itself, only to return to the object of representation in its final line and to what is in fact the sonnet's main concern, the beauty of the youth addressed as 'you' (v. 8). The decisive turn in the argument occurs in verse 7 when the speaker argues that when the poets of the past attempted to describe the perfect beauty they thought they were seeing in the ladies and knights, they were in fact writing about the youth.

This idea is further explained in the third quatrain when the speaker says that the poets, in praising the beautiful men and women of the past 'prefigur[ed]', offered a template as it were, of the young man's beauty. Critics have drawn attention to the theological implications (cf. Burrow 2002: 592) and even 'mild blasphemy' (KDJ 2010: 322) of this conceit in which 'the youth's appearance was forecast in old chivalric literature, as Christ's was in the Old Testament' (ibid.). The argument, however, takes yet another turn at the end of the quatrain, since this act of prefiguring the youth is without poetic 'skill' (v. 12). Not only does the speaker imply that all the people former poets praised were not as beautiful as the youth, but he also says that those poets were not good enough to do justice to this idea of perfect beauty. The sonnet's final conclusion involves yet another turn: while 'older writers, lacking the direct inspiration of the youth's beauty, could not do it justice' (KDJ 2010: 322), the poet and his contemporaries also do not succeed in expressing this beauty since they are so overwhelmed by the youth's presence: they '[h]ave eyes to wonder, but lack tongues to praise' (v. 14).

The phonetic qualities support and enhance the argument of the sonnet on various levels. Although the entire poem follows the iambic pentameter closely, there are moments where the metre is disturbed by additional or unrealized stresses as well as pauses, most of which occur after the argument's decisive turn at the end of verse 7 in the middle of the poem. While the regular metre and the absence of pauses in the first half of the sonnet mirror the conventional beauty of the 'wights' and 'ladies' as well as the repetitive and unsuccessful poetry of former times, the rhythmical disruptions in the second half draw our attention to the fact that the youth's beauty is of a different, i.e. unique kind which resists expression according to the conventions of metre and rhyme.

For example, the very first verse of the second half begins with a trochaic inversion, thereby emphasizing the fact that the beauty of the youth, who is mentioned here for the first time in the poem ('you', v. 8), is different and superior to previous beauties. Also, the pause after the comma in verse 10 stresses the contrast between the praises of the past on the one hand and 'this our time' and 'you' on the other, an effect which is also enhanced by the fact that the end rhymes 'prophecies/eyes' and 'prefiguring/sing' in the third quatrain are not as perfect as (and therefore more conspicuous than) the rhymes in the first two quatrains. In a similar manner, the pause after the comma in the last verse mirrors the speechlessness that the 'wonder' at the youth causes in the poet and his contemporaries.

5 MODEL INTERPRETATION OF SONNET 106   205

Without wanting to read too much into alliterations (one of their main purposes in foregrounding phonetic similarities, after all, is simply to create a greater sense of unity), the use of the sounds /w/, /b/ and /p/ also illustrates and supports the main argument of the sonnet. While the weak and voiced /w/- and /b/-sounds in the first two quatrains, and in particular in verses 1-5, emphasize and correspond to the ineffective attempts in the *wasted time* of the past at describing 'wights' and their 'beauties' in stale and outdated 'blazon[s]', the dominance of the harder and more forceful voiceless plosive sound /p/ in 'praises', 'prophecies', 'prefiguring', 'present', and 'praise' in verses 9-10 and 13-14 gives expression to the more powerful and convincing beauty of the youth.

On the lexical level the idea that the poetry and poets of the past are ineffective is reinforced by associating them with terms that are either archaic or emphasize lifelessness and outdatedness, such as 'chronicle' (v. 1), 'wights' (v. 2), 'old' (v. 3), 'ladies dead' (v. 4), 'lovely knights' (ibid.), 'blazon' (v. 5), and 'antique' (v. 7). Interestingly, but altogether not unusual for a Shakespeare sonnet, the poem is nearly devoid of tropes. Except for the even at Shakespeare's time already conventional and naturalized tropes 'wasted time' (v. 1), 'antique pen' (v. 7) and 'lack tongues' (14), the poem does not employ figurative language. This literalness accords with the clear and direct message of the poem: the young man's beauty cannot be expressed in words, neither by poets of the past, nor by the speaker-poet or his contemporaries.

The poem belongs to the group of sonnets addressed to a male 'you', as indicated in verses 8, 10 and 12, and supported by the defeminized blazon in verse 5 (the list of bodily features does not contain any of the typical parts usually addressed in sonnets to or about women, such as skin, cheeks, or voice). Sonnet 106 can also be seen as part of a mini-sequence (sonnets 106–109) on 'writing, peace, and time' (E/W 2013: 33; cf. also Appendix 1 above); it is not, however, connected to its neighbouring sonnets by any thematic or verbal links, nor does it share any motifs with them.

REFERENCES AND COMMENTARY ON KEY WORKS

The following references are divided into four sections. In the first part I comment on those editions and collections from which I have benefited most in the writing of this book and which I think are most helpful when engaging with the *Sonnets*. This is followed by a list of the editions and collections of the *Sonnets* consulted for this *Guide*. In the third section, I briefly comment on what I believe to be the most valuable general works on the *Sonnets*, including introductions, companions, and collections of essays. The last section lists every work quoted from in this book, excluding the editions and collections of Shakespeare's *Sonnets*, listed in the second section.

Comments on key editions

Of the 'fabulous five' (Post 2018: 209) editions of Shakespeare's *Sonnets* (by Booth, Kerrigan, Vendler, KDJ, and Burrow) Booth's, published in 1977, was the first. Each sonnet is reproduced in facsimile from the 1609 Quarto and in an edited text in modern spelling on the opposite page. The notes on each sonnet are detailed and extensive, sometimes comprising more than fifteen pages, amounting in total to more than 400 pages of helpful commentary. Unlike other editions (see below), the comments are separate from the poems, which makes for a rather cumbersome reading. The edition also includes a short, but nevertheless informative appendix on 'Facts and Theories about Shakespeare's Sonnets', as well as two useful indices, one of words and concepts touched upon in the commentary, the other of the sonnets' first lines.

Kerrigan's Penguin edition, first published in 1986, also includes *A Lover's Complaint* and stresses its importance for a fuller understanding and appreciation of the *Sonnets*. As in Booth's edition, the notes are printed separately from the sonnets. They are, however, less detailed, probably owing to the fact that Kerrigan also includes the text of and commentary on *A Lover's Complaint*.

Vendler's collection, first published in 1997, constitutes an interesting hybrid form between edition and interpretation. As in Booth's edition, each sonnet is first printed in facsimile and then in modern spelling, followed by interpretations of varying length. Vendler focuses on the structural pattern of the sonnets and the words, which she believes to be the 'true "actors"' (3) rather than the characters. She defines key words and 'Couplet Ties' (passim) in each poem, the latter signifying 'the significant words from the body of the poem that are repeated in the couplet' (28). The semantic, phonetic and syntactical patterns are illustrated with intricate and at times 'terrifying diagrams' (Orgel 2007: 143).

KDJ's Arden edition, which was first published in 1997 and, like Kerrigan's edition, includes *A Lover's Complaint*, offers the reader not only the commentary on the opposite page of each sonnet, it also conveniently summarizes the main argument of each poem, which can be of great help on one's first contact with the poems. In her introduction KDJ focuses on the authority of the 1609 Quarto and emphasizes a biographical approach in relating the character constellation in the *Sonnets* to Shakespeare's personal life.

Burrow's edition from 2002 includes all Shakespeare's poems, and roughly half of the total 750 pages are devoted to the *Sonnets*. As in KDJ's edition, Burrow places the annotations on the page opposite to each sonnet, although without the helpful summary of the main argument. His introduction to the *Sonnets*, although shorter than KDJ's (understandably since he covers all of Shakespeare's poems), still comprises approximately fifty pages, with highly informative sections on the publication and circulation history, dating, sources, the structure and themes of the *Sonnets*.

Apart from Post's 'fabulous five', Evans' New Cambridge edition, first published in 1996, provides useful insights and helpful textual analysis. The notes for each sonnet, given separately from the poems, can be found at the end of the edition and are less extensive than Booth's, yet more comprehensive than KDJ's. Two sonnets in modern spelling are reproduced per page with detailed collations at the foot of each page, giving the most important emendations of the 1609 Quarto text.

REFERENCES AND COMMENTARY ON KEY WORKS 209

Paterson's book, first published in 2010, like Vendler's book takes on a hybrid form. Although it includes all the sonnets and provides notes on some words and phrases, this book lacks most of the trademarks one would expect from an edition. It does not include a lengthy introduction, footnotes and bibliography, or any notes on the textual history. What makes this edition stand out, however, is its tone. Paterson's interpretations of the sonnets are characterized by an informal, irreverent and, at times, polemical style. As refreshing as such an approach may be, it does, however, come at the cost of accuracy and neglect of established rules of literary criticism, as, for example, when Paterson without hesitation and factual backup equates the speaker with Shakespeare.

The most recent edition of Shakespeare's *Sonnets* is provided by E/W (2020). It contains not only the 154 sonnets of the sequence, but also those that appear in his plays and narrative poems. They are ordered chronologically, with one sonnet per page, including a few, brief annotations, and a short comment. It also includes helpful 'Literal Paraphrases' (233) of every sonnet and an introduction with tables listing the 'Mini-Sequences' and 'Direction' of the *Sonnets*.

For brief overviews of the main features of, and differences between some of the more recent editions cf. E/W 2013: 124–30; Orgel 2007: 142–4; Paterson 2010: xviii–xxi.

Editions

Benson, John (1640), *Poems: Vvritten by Wil. Shake-Speare. Gent,* London: By Tho. Cotes, and are to be sold by Iohn Benson, dwelling in St. Dunstans Church-yard. Available online: *ProQuest*, https://www. proquest.com/books/poems-vvritten-wil-shake-speare-gent/ docview/2248575672 (accessed 16 October 2023).

Booth, Stephen, ed. ([1977] 2000), *Shakespeare's Sonnets: Edited with Analytical Commentary*, New Haven: Yale Nota Bene.

Burrow, Colin, ed. (2002), *The Complete Sonnets and Poems*, by William Shakespeare, Oxford: Oxford University Press.

Burto, William, ed. ([1964] 1999), *The Sonnets*, by William Shakespeare, Introduction by W. H. Auden, 2nd rev. edn, New York: Penguin Putnam.

Duncan-Jones, Katherine, ed. ([1997] 2010), *Shakespeare's Sonnets*, rev. edn, Arden Shakespeare Third Series, London: A&C Black.

210 REFERENCES AND COMMENTARY ON KEY WORKS

Edmondson, Paul and Stanley Wells, eds (2020), *All the Sonnets of Shakespeare*, Cambridge: Cambridge University Press.

Evans, G. Blakemore, ed. (1998), *The Sonnets*, by William Shakespeare, Introduction by Anthony Hecht, Cambridge: Cambridge University Press.

Gildon, Charles, ed. (1710), *The Works of Mr. William Shakespear. Volume the Seventh*, London: Printed for E. Curll at the Dial and Bible against St. Dunstan's Church, and E. Sanger at the Post-House at the Middle-Temple Gate. Available online: *Internet Archive,* https://archive.org/details/worksofmrwilliam00shak/page/n7/mode/2up (accessed 25 April 2024).

Ingram, W. G. and Theodore Redpath, eds ([1964] 1978), *Shakespeare's Sonnets*, 3rd impression (with amendments), London: Hodder and Stoughton.

Kerrigan, John, ed. ([1986] 1999), *The Sonnets and A Lover's Complaint*, by William Shakespeare, London: Penguin.

Malone, Edmond, ed. (1780), *Supplement to the Edition of Shakespeare's Plays Published in 1778*, vol. 1, London, Bodleian Library. Available online: http://purl.ox.ac.uk/uuid/38fda6bf785d45f28b9165d0c5c7363 (accessed 16 October 2023).

Malone, Edmond, ed. (1790), *The Plays and Poems of William Shakespeare*, vol. 10, London, Hathi Trust Digital Library. Available online: https://hdl.handle.net/2027/nyp.33433074971965 (accessed 16 October 2023).

Mowat, Barbara A. and Paul Werstine, eds (2004), *Shakespeare's Sonnets and Poems*, New York: Washington Square Press.

Paterson, Don (2010), *Reading Shakespeare's Sonnets: A New Commentary,* London: Faber and Faber.

Proudfoot, Richard, Ann Thompson, David Scott Kastan and H. R. Woudhuysen, eds (2021), *William Shakespeare: Complete Works*, Arden Shakespeare Third Series, London: Bloomsbury.

Steevens, George, ed. (1793), *The Plays of William Shakespeare*, London: Hathi Trust Digital Library. Available online: https://hdl.handle.net/2027/hvd.hxkenh?urlappend=%3Bseq=15 (accessed 16 October 2023).

Vendler, Helen (1999), *The Art of Shakespeare's Sonnets,* Cambridge: Harvard University Press.

REFERENCES AND COMMENTARY ON KEY WORKS   211

Comments on introductions and essay collections

This section comments on the general works on Shakespeare's *Sonnets,* his poems and the sonnet form in general, which have influenced me the most in the writing of this *Guide.* All titles referred to can be found with full bibliographical information in the list of "Other works cited" below.

While Innes' monograph *Shakespeare and the English Renaissance Sonnet: Verses of Feigning Love,* first published in 1997, focuses on the procreation sonnets and the three personas of speaker, youth and mistress, Blades' *The Sonnets* (2007) and Callaghan's *Shakespeare's Sonnets* (2007) are more interested in the collection's themes and contexts. While Blades includes chapters on love, time, art, the rival poets, the mistress, the Elizabethan sonnet, humanism and critical responses, Callaghan concentrates on the themes of identity, beauty, love, numbers, and time. Unlike Matz's *The World of Shakespeare's Sonnets: An Introduction* (2008), which has a strong interest in literary and social contexts, such as gender and racial dimensions, both Rudenstine's *Ideas of Order: A Close Reading of Shakespeare's Sonnets* (2014) and Monte's *The Secret Architecture of Shakespeare's Sonnets* (2021) are more concerned with identifying intricate structural patterns in the sequence. The strength of E/W's *Shakespeare's Sonnets* (2004) lies in its combination of a historical, theoretical, thematic and formal approach. It includes chapters on the publication and literary context, biographical aspects, the sonnet's (and *Sonnets'*) form, their 'concerns' and their critical and artistic responses, but also on the sequence's relation to *A Lover's Complaint.*

The last decades have also seen the publication of various essay collections on the *Sonnets.* The most recent of these, Fielitz's *Shakespeare's Sonnets: Lovers, Layers, Languages* (2010), is a collection of papers given at a conference in 2009 to mark the 400th anniversary of the *Sonnets'* publication. It is divided into three sections as indicated by the volume's subtitle, with papers focusing on gender and sex, different layers of meaning, and linguistic aspects of the *Sonnets.* Cheney's *Cambridge Companion to Shakespeare's Poetry* (2007) includes essays on various poems and aspects of Shakespeare's poetry, including those of his plays. The essays focus

212   REFERENCES AND COMMENTARY ON KEY WORKS

on a range of topics, such as style and form, manuscript circulation and publication contexts, political, religious and sexual concerns, and different aspects of their critical reception. Schoenfeldt not only contributed the essay on the *Sonnets* to Cheney's *Companion*, but in the same year he also published his own *Companion to Shakespeare's Sonnets*. Still seen by many as the most relevant and comprehensive essay collection on the *Sonnets*, this anthology consists of nine sections with essays on the sonnet form and the sequence, Shakespeare's influences, editorial and biographical theories, the *Sonnets* in manuscript and print, the themes of desire, darkness, memory, and repetition, as well as two sections on the sonnets in the plays and the *Sonnets'* relation to *A Lover's Complaint*. Another substantial anthology, Schiffer's *Shakespeare's Sonnets: Critical Essays*, first published in 1998, provides a collection of recent essays focusing on aspects such as sexuality, homoeroticism, the sequence's structure, Petrarchan influences, issues of religion, maternity and race, plus a very detailed and helpful survey of criticism on the *Sonnets*.

The last twenty years have also witnessed a number of introductions to Shakespeare's poetry in which the *Sonnets* are discussed alongside the narrative poems. The most recent of these, Callaghan's *Reading Shakespeare's Poetry* (2022), discusses the poems in a chronological order and focuses on the specific features of Shakespeare's poetic language. One chapter deals with the *Sonnets*. Post's *Shakespeare's Sonnets and Poems*, first published in 2017 in Oxford University Press's *Very Short Introduction* series, includes two chapters on the *Sonnets* with sections on, among others, the sonnet form, Shakespeare's engagement with the Petrarchan tradition, the central characters, and the *Sonnets'* reception. Three years after his *Companion to Shakespeare's Sonnets*, Schoenfeldt in 2010 published his monograph *The Cambridge Introduction to Shakespeare's Poetry*. Three chapters are devoted to the *Sonnets*, with one discussing the questions surrounding the dedication, their publication, and the central characters, and the other two exploring the themes of time, mortality, and desire. Hyland's *An Introduction to Shakespeare's Poems* from 2003 includes general sections on the emerging literary marketplace, classical sources and the development of the Elizabethan sonnet, as well as two chapters on the *Sonnets* with a focus on the theme of immortality, gender issues, and the characters of the mistress and the rival poet. An earlier study, Dubrow's *Captive Victors: Shakespeare's Narrative Poems and Sonnets* (1987), supplies a rhetorical analysis of the poems, focusing in the chapter on the *Sonnets* on the different formal strategies that Shakespeare employs to explore power relations.

As regards introductions to the sonnet, Petzold's recent *A History of the Sonnet in England: 'A little world made cunningly'* (2022) offers a historical overview from the Italian origin of the form to the present, including a section on the sonnets in Shakespeare's plays and the *Sonnets*. While Regan's *The Sonnet* (2019) includes chapters on the Irish and American tradition, Spiller's *The Development of the Sonnet: An Introduction* (1992) focuses on the early centuries and only traces the development of the sonnet up to Milton. *The Cambridge Companion to the Sonnet*, edited by Cousins and Howarth (2011), includes essays on a range of topics, such as the form's lyric mode, European beginnings and transmissions, Shakespeare's *Sonnets*, as well as the Victorian and contemporary sonnet.

Levin's *The Penguin Book of the Sonnet: 500 Years of Classic Tradition in English* (2001) and Hirsch and Boland's *The Making of a Sonnet: A Norton Anthology* (first published in 2008) are highly useful anthologies of sonnets from the early modern age to the present with helpful introductory essays, introductions, and appendices on the history, development and main features of the sonnet.

Other works cited

Acker, Faith D. (2021), *First Readers of Shakespeare's Sonnets, 1590–1790*, London: Routledge.

Ackermann, Zeno (2009), 'Sounding the Sonnets in Popular Music', in Manfred Pfister and Jürgen Gutsch (eds), *William Shakespeare's Sonnets Global: For the First Time Globally Reprinted. A Quartercentenary Anthology 1609–2009*, 97–120, Dazwil: Edition SIGNAThUR.

Adelman, Janet (1999), 'Making Defect Perfection: Shakespeare and the One-Sex Model', in Viviana Comensoli and Anne Russell (eds), *Enacting Gender on the English Renaissance Stage*, 23–52, Urbana: University of Illinois Press.

Akhimie, Patricia (2018), *Shakespeare and the Cultivation of Difference: Race and Conduct in the Early Modern World*, London: Routledge.

214 REFERENCES AND COMMENTARY ON KEY WORKS

Al-Dabbagh, Abdulla (2012), 'Race, Gender and Class in Shakespeare's Sonnets', *International Journal of Arabic-English Studies (IJAES)*, 13 (1): 23–32. Available online: ijaes.net/article/fulltext/view?volume=13&issue=1&id=2 (accessed 16 October 2023).

Alexander, Catherine M. S. and Stanley Wells, eds (2000), *Shakespeare and Race*, Cambridge: Cambridge University Press.

Andrews, Michael Cameron (1982), 'Sincerity and Subterfuge in Three Shakespearean Sonnet Groups', *Shakespeare Quarterly*, 33 (3): 314–27.

Archer, John Michael (2012), *Technically Alive: Shakespeare's Sonnets*. New York: Palgrave Macmillan.

Ascham, Roger (2004), 'On Imitation', in Brian Vickers (ed.), *English Renaissance Literary Criticism*, 140–61, Oxford: Clarendon Press.

Bacon, Francis ([2002] 2008), *The Major Works*, ed. Brian Vickers, Introduction and Notes, Oxford: Oxford University Press.

Bates, Catherine (2011), 'Desire, Discontent, Parody: The Love Sonnet in Early Modern England', in A. D. Cousins and Peter Howarth (eds), *The Cambridge Companion to the Sonnet*, 105–24, Cambridge: Cambridge University Press.

Bell, Ilona (2007), 'Rethinking Shakespeare's Dark Lady', in Michael Schoenfeldt (ed.), *A Companion to Shakespeare's Sonnets*, 293–313, Oxford: Blackwell.

Berensmeyer, Ingo (2020), 'Methods in Hermeneutic and Neo-Hermeneutic Approaches: A Reading of Shakespeare's Sonnet 73', in Vera Nünning and Ansgar Nünning (eds), *Methods of Textual Analysis in Literary Studies: Approaches, Basics, Model Interpretations*, 59–83, Trier: Wissenschaftlicher Verlag.

Blades, John (2007), *Shakespeare: The Sonnets*, Basingstoke: Palgrave Macmillan.

Bode, Christoph (2011), *The Novel*, trans. James Vigus, Hoboken: Wiley-Blackwell.

Booth, Stephen (1969), *An Essay on Shakespeare's Sonnets*, New Haven: Yale University Press.

Booth, Stephen (2007), 'The Value of the Sonnets', in Michael Schoenfeldt (ed.), *A Companion to Shakespeare's Sonnets*, 15–26, Oxford: Blackwell.

Boyd, Brian (2012), *Why Lyrics Last: Evolution, Cognition, and Shakespeare's Sonnets*, Cambridge: Harvard University Press.

Braden, Gordon (2000), 'Shakespeare's Petrarchism', in James Schiffer (ed.), *Shakespeare's Sonnets: Critical Essays*, 163–83, New York: Garland.

Bray, Alan (1982), *Homosexuality in Renaissance England*, London: Gay Men's Press.

REFERENCES AND COMMENTARY ON KEY WORKS   215

Brennan, M. (1988), *Literary Patronage in the English Renaissance: The Pembroke Family*, London: Routledge.

Brinton, Laurel J. (1985), 'The Iconic Role of Aspect in Shakespeare's Sonnet 129', *Poetics Today*, 6 (3): 447–59.

Brown, David Sterling, Patricia Akhimie and Arthur L. Little, Jr. (2022), 'Seeking the (In)Visible: Whiteness and Shakespeare Studies', *Shakespeare Studies, 50:* 17–23.

Burrow, Colin (2007), 'Editing the Sonnets', in Michael Schoenfeldt (ed.), *A Companion to Shakespeare's Sonnets*, 145–62, Oxford: Blackwell.

Burt, Stephen (2011), 'The Contemporary Sonnet', in A. D. Cousins and Peter Howarth (eds), *The Cambridge Companion to the Sonnet*, 245–66, Cambridge: Cambridge University Press.

Callaghan, Dympna (2007), *Shakespeare's Sonnets*, Oxford: Blackwell.

Callaghan, Dympna (2022), *Reading Shakespeare's Poetry*, Hoboken: Wiley Blackwell.

Campbell, Matthew (2011), 'The Victorian Sonnet', in A. D. Cousins and Peter Howarth (eds), *The Cambridge Companion to the Sonnet*, 204–24, Cambridge: Cambridge University Press.

Chaucer, Geoffrey (1953), *Troilus and Criseyde,* ed. John Warrington, London: J. M. Dent.

Chaudhuri, Sukanta, ed. (2017), *A Midsummer Night's Dream*, by William Shakespeare, Arden Shakespeare Third Series, London: Bloomsbury.

Cheney, Patrick, ed. (2007), *The Cambridge Companion to Shakespeare's Poetry*. Cambridge: Cambridge University Press.

Chess, Simone (2019), 'Queer Residue: Boy Actors' Adult Careers in Early Modern England', *Journal for Early Modern Cultural Studies,* 19 (4): 242–64.

Chess, Simone, Colby Gordon and Will Fisher (2019), 'Introduction: Early Modern Trans Studies', *Journal for Early Modern Cultural Studies*, 19 (4): 1–25.

Clarke, Danielle (2007), 'Love, Beauty, and Sexuality', in Patrick Cheney (ed.), *The Cambridge Companion to Shakespeare's Poetry*, 181–201, Cambridge: Cambridge University Press.

Cocking, J. M. (1991), *Imagination: A Study in the History of Ideas*, London: Routledge.

Cousins, A. D. (2011), 'Shakespeare's Sonnets', in A. D. Cousins and Peter Howarth (eds), *The Cambridge Companion to the Sonnet*, 125–44, Cambridge: Cambridge University Press.

Cousins, A. D. and Peter Howarth, eds (2011), *The Cambridge Companion to the Sonnet*, Cambridge: Cambridge University Press.

Crawforth, Hannah and Elizabeth Scott-Baumann, eds (2016), *On Shakespeare's Sonnets: A Poets' Celebration*, The Arden Shakespeare, London: Bloomsbury.

Crawforth, Hannah, Elizabeth Scott-Baumann and Clare Whitehead, eds (2018), *Shakespeare's Sonnets: The State of Play*, The Arden Shakespeare, London: Bloomsbury.

Crewe, Jonathan (1995), 'Out of the Matrix: Shakespeare and Race-Writing', *The Yale Journal of Criticism: Interpretation in the Humanities*, 8 (2): 13–29.

Crosman, Robert (1990), 'Making Love Out of Nothing at All: The Issue of Story in Shakespeare's Procreation Sonnets', *Shakespeare Quarterly*, 41 (4): 470–88.

Crystal, David and Ben Crystal (2004), *Shakespeare's Words: A Glossary and Language Companion*, London: Penguin.

Dadabhoy, Ambereen (2021), 'Barbarian Moors: Documenting Racial Formation in Early Modern England', in Ayanna Thompson (ed.), *The Cambridge Companion to Shakespeare and Race*, 30–46, Cambridge: Cambridge University Press.

de Grazia, Margreta (2000), 'The Scandal of Shakespeare's Sonnets', in James Schiffer (ed.), *Shakespeare's Sonnets: Critical Essays*, 89–112, New York: Garland.

Dickson, Andrew (2009), *The Rough Guide to Shakespeare: The Plays. The Poems. The Life*, London: Rough Guides.

Donne, John (2007), *John Donne's Poetry: Authoritative Texts. Criticism*, ed. Donald R. Dickson, Norton Critical Edition, New York: W. W. Norton.

Dubrow, Heather (1987), *Captive Victors: Shakespeare's Narrative Poems and Sonnets*, Ithaca: Cornell University Press.

Dubrow, Heather (1996), '"Incertainties now crown themselves assur'd": The Politics of Plotting Shakespeare's Sonnets', *Shakespeare Quarterly*, 47 (3): 291–305.

Dubrow, Heather (2007), '"Dressing old words new"? Re-evaluating the "Delian Structure"', in Michael Schoenfeldt (ed.), *A Companion to Shakespeare's Sonnets*, 90–103, Oxford: Blackwell.

Dutton, Richard (2007), 'Shake-speares Sonnets, Shakespeare's Sonnets, and Shakespearean Biography', in Michael Schoenfeldt (ed.), *A Companion to Shakespeare's Sonnets*, 121–36, Oxford: Blackwell.

Edmondson, Paul (2013), 'The Plurality of Shakespeare's Sonnets', *Shakespeare Survey: An Annual Survey of Shakespeare Studies and Production*, 65: 211–20.

Edmondson, Paul and Stanley Wells ([2004] 2013), *Shakespeare's Sonnets*, Oxford Shakespeare Topics, Oxford: Oxford University Press.

Eklund, Craig (2021), 'Shakespeare's Love-Triangle Poems', *Essays in Criticism*, 71 (3): 269–82.

Ellmann, Richard (1988), *Oscar Wilde*, London: Penguin.

Empson, William ([1930] 1995), *Seven Types of Ambiguity*, London: Penguin.

REFERENCES AND COMMENTARY ON KEY WORKS   217

Erasmus (1518), 'Excerpts from Erasmus's "Encomium Matrimonii" in English translation from Thomas Wilson, *The Arte of Rhetorique* (1553), fols. 21v–34v', *Folger Shakespeare Library*. Available online: https://shakespeare.folger.edu/shakespeares-works/shakespeares-sonnets/appendix-of-intertextual-material/ (accessed 6 November 2023).

Erickson, Peter and Kim F. Hall (2016), '"A New Scholarly Song": Rereading Early Modern Race', *Shakespeare Quarterly*, 1 (67): 1–13.

Espinosa, Ruben (2016), 'Diversifying Shakespeare', *Literature Compass*, 13 (2): 58–68.

Faas, Ekbert (1986), *Shakespeare's Poetics*, Cambridge: Cambridge University Press.

Fielitz, Sonja, ed. (2010), *Shakespeare's Sonnets: Lovers, Layers, Languages*, Heidelberg: Winter.

Fleissner, Robert F. (1973), 'That "Cheek of Night": Toward the Dark Lady', *CLA Journal*, 16 (3): 312–23.

Fleissner, Robert F. (2005), *Shakespeare and Africa: The Dark Lady of his Sonnets Revamped and other Africa Related Associations*, Bloomington: Xlibris Corporation.

Fowler, Alastair (1970), *Triumphal Forms: Structural Patterns in Elizabethan Poetry*, Cambridge: Cambridge University Press.

Franssen, Paul (2010), 'How Dark is the Dark Lady?', in Sonja Fielitz (ed.), *Shakespeare's Sonnets: Lovers, Layers, Languages*, 31–42, Heidelberg: Winter.

Garber, Marjorie (2004), *Shakespeare After All*, New York: Anchor Books.

Gardner, C. O. (1974), 'Some Reflections on Shakespeare's Sonnets Nos 33, 34 and 35', *Theoria: A Journal of Social and Political Theory*, 42: 43–55.

Garrison, John S. (2023), *The Pleasures of Memory in Shakespeare's Sonnets*, Oxford: Oxford University Press.

Gascoigne, George (2004), 'A Primer of English Poetry', in Brian Vickers (ed.), *English Renaissance Literary Criticism*, 162–71, Oxford: Clarendon Press.

Goldberg, Jonathan (1992), *Sodometries: Renaissance Texts, Modern Sexualities*, Redwood City: Stanford University Press.

Goldberg, Jonathan (1994), *Queering the Renaissance*, Durham: Duke University Press.

Gordon, Colby (2020), 'A Woman's Prick: Trans Technogenesis in Sonnet 20', in Jennifer Drouin (ed.), *Shakespeare / Sex: Contemporary Readings in Gender and Sexuality*, 268–89, The Arden Shakespeare, London: Bloomsbury.

Graziani, René (1984), 'The Numbering of Shakespeare's Sonnets 12, 60 and 126', *Shakespeare Quarterly*, 35: 79–82.

Gray, Ronald (2011), *Shakespeare on Love: The Sonnets and Plays in Relation to Plato's Symposium, Alchemy, Christianity and Renaissance Neo-Platonism*, Newcastle upon Tyne: Cambridge Scholars Publishing.

Greenblatt, Stephen (1990), *Shakespearean Negotiations: The Circulation of Social Energy in Renaissance England*, Oxford: Clarendon Press.

Greene, Roland (1995), 'Petrarchism among the Discourses of Imperialism', in Karen Ordahl Kuppermann (ed.), *America in European Consciousness 1493–1750*, 130–65, Chapel Hill: University of North Carolina Press.

Greiner, Norbert (2016), 'Die übersetzerische Rezeption von Shakespeares Sonett 66', in Sara Springfeld, Norbert Greiner and Silke Leopold (eds), *Das Sonett und die Musik: Poetiken, Konjunkturen, Transformationen, Reflexionen*, 255–74, Heidelberg: Universitätsverlag Winter.

Grier, Miles P. (2023), 'Books of the Unlearned: Shakespearean Iconicity and Black Atlantic Critique', *Shakespeare Quarterly*, 74 (3): 247–63.

Gross, John J., ed. (2003), *After Shakespeare: An Anthology*, Oxford: Oxford University Press.

Gurr, Andrew (1971), 'Shakespeare's First Poem: Sonnet 145', *Essays in Criticism*, 21: 221–6.

Guy-Bray, Stephen (2020), 'The Sonnets', in Stephen Guy-Bray, *Shakespeare and Queer Representation*, 127–47, London: Routledge.

Habib, Imtiaz (2000), *Shakespeare and Race: Postcolonial Praxis in the Early Modern Period*, Lanham: University Press of America.

Habib, Imtiaz (2008), *Black Lives in the English Archives, 1500–1677: Imprints of the Invisible*, Farnham: Ashgate.

Hall, Kim F. (1996), *Things of Darkness: Economies of Race and Gender in Early Modern England*, Ithaca: Cornell University Press.

Hall, Kim F. ([1998] 2008), ' "These bastard signs of fair": Literary Whiteness in Shakespeare's Sonnets', in Ania Loomba and Martin Orkin (eds), *Post-Colonial Shakespeares*, 64–83, London: Routledge.

Hamilton, Walter, ed. and tr. (1951), *The Symposium*, by Plato, London: Penguin.

Hammond, Paul (2002), *Figuring Sex between Men from Shakespeare to Rochester*, Oxford: Oxford University Press.

Harvey, Elizabeth D. (2007), 'Flesh Colors and Shakespeare's Sonnets', in Michael Schoenfeldt (ed.), *A Companion to Shakespeare's Sonnets*, 314–28, Oxford: Blackwell.

Haskell, Yasmin Annabel, ed. (2011), *Diseases of the Imagination and Imaginary Disease in the Early Modern Period*, Turnhout: Brepols.

Healy, Margaret (2007), ' "Making the quadrangle round": Alchemy's Protean Forms in Shakespeare's Sonnets and *A Lover's Complaint*', in Michael Schoenfeldt (ed.), *A Companion to Shakespeare's Sonnets*, 405–25, Oxford: Blackwell.

REFERENCES AND COMMENTARY ON KEY WORKS   219

Healy, Margaret (2011), *Shakespeare, Alchemy, and the Creative Imagination: The Sonnets and A Lover's Complaint*, Cambridge: Cambridge University Press.

Hebron, Malcolm (2008), *Key Concepts in Renaissance Literature*, Basingstoke: Palgrave Macmillan.

Herman, Peter C. (2000), 'What's the Use? Or, the Problematics of Economy in Shakespeare's Procreation Sonnets', in James Schiffer (ed.), *Shakespeare's Sonnets: Critical Essays*, 263–83, New York: Garland.

Hieatt, A. Kent, Charles W. Hieatt and Anne Lake Prescott (1991), 'When Did Shakespeare Write *Sonnets* 1609?' *Studies in Philology*, 88: 69–109.

Hirsch, Edward and Eavan Boland, eds (2009), *The Making of a Sonnet: A Norton Anthology*, New York: W. W. Norton.

Hope, Jonathan (1999), 'Shakespeare's "Natiue English"', in David Scott Kastan (ed.), *A Companion to Shakespeare*, 239–55, Oxford: Blackwell.

Howard, Henry, Earl of Surrey (2001), 'Love that liveth and reigneth in my thought', in Phyllis Levin (ed.), *The Penguin Book of the Sonnet: 500 Years of Classic Tradition in English*, 7, London: Penguin.

Howarth, Peter (2011), 'The Modern Sonnet', in A. D. Cousins and Peter Howarth (eds), *The Cambridge Companion to the Sonnet*, 225–44, Cambridge: Cambridge University Press.

Hühn, Peter, ed. (2010), *Eventfulness in British Fiction*, with contributions by Markus Kempf, Katrin Kroll and Jette K. Wulf, Berlin: De Gruyter.

Hunt, Marvin (2000), 'Be dark but not too dark: Shakespeare's Dark Lady as a sign of color', in James Schiffer (ed.), *Shakespeare's Sonnets: Critical Essays*, 369–89, New York: Garland.

Hyland, Peter (2003), *An Introduction to Shakespeare's Poems*, Basingstoke: Palgrave Macmillan.

Innes, Paul (1997), *Shakespeare and the English Renaissance Sonnet: Verses of Feigning Love*, Basingstoke: Palgrave Macmillan.

Iyengar, Sujata (2005), *Shades of Difference: Mythologies of Skin Color in Early Modern England*, Philadelphia: University of Pennsylvania Press.

Jackson, MacDonald P. (1999a), 'Aspects of Organisation in Shakespeare's Sonnets (1609)', *Parergon: Journal of the Australian and New Zealand Association for Medieval and Early Modern Studies*, 17 (1): 109–34.

Jackson, MacDonald P. (1999b), 'Rhymes in Shakespeare's Sonnets: Evidence of Date of Composition', *Notes and Queries*, 46 (2): 213–19.

Jackson, MacDonald P. (2002), 'Dating Shakespeare's Sonnets: Some Old Evidence Revisited', *Notes and Queries*, 49 (2): 237–41.

Jackson, MacDonald P. (2005), 'Francis Meres and the Cultural Contexts of Shakespeare's Rival Poet Sonnets', *The Review of English Studies*, 56 (224): 224–46.

Jakobson, Roman (1960), 'Linguistics and Poetics', in T. A. Sebeok (ed.), *Style in Language*, 350–77, Cambridge: MIT Press.

Joubin, Alexa Alice (2023a), 'Shakespearean Performance through a Trans Lens', *Borrowers and Lenders: The Journal of Shakespeare and Appropriation*, 14 (2): 65–89.

Joubin, Alexa Alice (2023b), 'Trans as Method: The Sociality of Gender and Shakespeare', *Borrowers and Lenders: The Journal of Shakespeare and Appropriation*, 14 (2): 3–21.

Jowett, John (2011), 'Introduction', in John Jowett (ed.), *Sir Thomas More*, 1–129, by William Shakespeare et al., Arden Shakespeare Third Series, London: A&C Black.

Karim-Cooper, Farah (2021), 'The Materials of Race: Staging the Black and White Binary in the Early Modern Theatre', in Ayanna Thompson (ed.), *The Cambridge Companion to Shakespeare and Race*, 17–29, Cambridge: Cambridge University Press.

Kaufmann, Miranda (2017), *Black Tudors: The Untold Story*, London: Oneworld.

Keenan, Siobhan (2008), *Renaissance Literature*, Edinburgh: Edinburgh University Press.

Kennedy, William J. (2011), 'European Beginnings and Transmissions: Dante, Petrarch and the Sonnet Sequence', in A. D. Cousins and Peter Howarth (eds), *The Cambridge Companion to the Sonnet*, 84–104, Cambridge: Cambridge University Press.

Kennedy, William J. (2016), *Petrarchism at Work: Contextual Economies in the Age of Shakespeare*, Ithaca: Cornell University Press.

King, Helen (2013), *The One-Sex Body on Trial: The Classical and Early Modern Evidence*, Farnham: Ashgate.

Kingsley-Smith, Jane (2019), *The Afterlife of Shakespeare's Sonnets*, Cambridge: Cambridge University Press.

Kingsley-Smith, Jane and W. Reginald Rampone, Jr., eds (2023), *Shakespeare's Global Sonnets: Translation, Appropriation, Performance*, London: Macmillan.

Knecht, Ross (2021), 'Shakespeare's Sonnets as Reproductive Labour', *Shakespeare*, 17 (3): 279–95.

Kosofsky Sedgwick, Eve (1985), *Between Men: English Literature and Male Homosocial Desire*, New York: Columbia University Press.

Kullmann, Thomas (2010), 'Shakespeare and the Love of Boys', in Sonja Fielitz (ed.), *Shakespeare's Sonnets: Lovers, Layers, Languages*, 43–54, Heidelberg: Winter.

Laqueur, Thomas (1990), *Making Sex: Body and Gender from the Greeks to Freud*, Cambridge: Harvard University Press.

Lennard, John (1991), *But I digress: The Exploitation of Parentheses in English Printed Verse*, Oxford: Oxford University Press.

REFERENCES AND COMMENTARY ON KEY WORKS 221

Leishman, J. B. ([1961] 1963), *Themes and Variations in Shakespeare's Sonnets*, New York: Harper and Row.

Levin, Phyllis, ed. (2001), *The Penguin Book of the Sonnet: 500 Years of Classic Tradition in English*, London: Penguin.

Little, Arthur L., Jr. (2016), 'Re-Historicizing Race, White Melancholia, and the Shakespearean Property', *Shakespeare Quarterly*, 67 (1): 84–103.

Little, Arthur L., Jr. (2021), 'Is it possible to read Shakespeare through critical white studies?', in Ayanna Thompson (ed.), *The Cambridge Companion to Shakespeare and Race*, 268–80, Cambridge: Cambridge University Press.

Loomba, Ania (2000), '"Delicious traffick": Racial and Religious Difference on Early Modern Stages', in Catherine M. S. Alexander and Stanley Wells (eds), *Shakespeare and Race*, 202–24, Cambridge: Cambridge University Press.

Loomba, Ania (2002), *Shakespeare, Race, and Colonialism*, Oxford: Oxford University Press.

Loomba, Ania (2016), 'Identities and Bodies in Early Modern Studies', in Valerie Traub (ed.), *The Oxford Handbook of Shakespeare and Embodiment: Gender, Sexuality, and Race*, 228–46, Oxford: Oxford Academic.

Loomba, A. and M. Orkin, eds ([1998] 2008), *Post-Colonial Shakespeares*, London: Routledge.

Loughlin, Marie H., ed. (2014), *Same-Sex Desire in Early Modern England 1550–1735: An Anthology of Literary Texts and Contexts*, Manchester: Manchester University Press.

Lytle, G. F. and S. Orgel, eds (1981), *Patronage in the Renaissance*, Princeton: Princeton University Press.

MacDonald, Joyce Green (2021), 'The Legend of Lucy Negro', in Janell Hobson (ed.), *The Routledge Companion to Black Women's Cultural Histories*, 66–74, London: Routledge.

Marotti, Arthur F. (2007), 'Shakespeare's Sonnets and the Manuscript Circulation of Texts in Early Modern England', in Michael Schoenfeldt (ed.), *A Companion to Shakespeare's Sonnets*, 185–203, Oxford: Blackwell.

Marotti, Arthur F. (2014), 'John Donne and the Rewards of Patronage', in Guy Fitch Lytle and Stephen Orgel (eds), *Patronage in the Renaissance*, 207–34, Princeton: Princeton University Press.

Marotti, Arthur F. and Marcelle Freiman (2011), 'The English Sonnet: Manuscript, Print, Mass Media', in A. D. Cousins and Peter Howarth (eds), *The Cambridge Companion to the Sonnet*, 66–83, Cambridge: Cambridge University Press.

Matz, Robert (2008), *The World of Shakespeare's Sonnets: An Introduction*, Jefferson: McFarland & Company.

222 REFERENCES AND COMMENTARY ON KEY WORKS

McIntosh, P. D. (2013), *'Every Word Doth Almost Tell My Name': The Authorship of Shakespeare's Sonnets*, foreword by Rodney Croome, Jefferson: McFarland & Company.

Meller, Horst (1985), *Zum Verstehen englischer Gedichte*, Munich: Wilhelm Fink.

Monte, Steven (2021), *The Secret Architecture of Shakespeare's Sonnets*, Edinburgh: Edinburgh University Press.

Nauta, Lodi and Detlev Pätzold, eds (2004), *Imagination in the Later Middle Ages and Early Modern Times*, Leuven: Peeters.

Nubia, Onyeka (2019), *England's Other Countrymen: Black Tudor Society*, London: Zed Books.

Olusoga, David (2016), *Black and British: A Forgotten History*, London: Macmillan.

O'Neill, Michael (2011), 'The Romantic Sonnet', in A. D. Cousins and Peter Howarth (eds), *The Cambridge Companion to the Sonnet*, 185–203, Cambridge: Cambridge University Press.

Onions, C. T. ([1986] 1994), *A Shakespeare* Glossary, enlarged and revised throughout by Robert D. Eagleson, Oxford: Clarendon Press.

Orgel, Stephen (1989), 'Nobody's Perfect: Or Why Did the English Stage Take Boys for Women?', *South Atlantic Quarterly*, 88 (1): 7–29.

Orgel, Stephen (2007), 'Mr. Who He?', in Michael Schoenfeldt (ed.), *A Companion to Shakespeare's Sonnets*, 137–44, Oxford: Blackwell.

Oxford English Dictionary (2020), Oxford: Oxford University Press. Available online: http://www.oed.com (accessed 19 November 2020).

Palmer, Kenneth, ed. ([1982] 1994), *Troilus and Cressida*, by William Shakespeare, Arden Shakespeare Third Series, London: Routledge.

Park, Jennifer (2023), 'On Shakespeare's Legacy, Critical Race, and Collective Futures', *Shakespeare Quarterly*, 74 (3): 264–80.

Pequigney, Joseph (1985), *Such Is My Love: A Study of Shakespeare's Sonnets*, Chicago: University of Chicago Press.

Petrarch (1997), *Petrarch's Lyric Poems: The Rime Sparsi and Other Lyrics*, trans. and ed. Robert M. Durling, Cambridge: Harvard University Press.

Petzold, Jochen (2022), *A History of the Sonnet in England: 'A little world made cunningly'*, Berlin: Erich Schmidt.

Pfister, Manfred (2012), 'Made in Germany: Shakespeare's Sonnets', *Angermion: Yearbook for Anglo-German Literary Criticism, Intellectual History and Cultural Transfers/Jahrbuch für Britisch-Deutsche Kulturbeziehungen*, 5: 29–57.

Pfister, Manfred (2018), '"Love Merchandized": Money in Shakespeare's Sonnets', *Critical Survey*, 30 (3): 57–66.

Pfister, Manfred and Jürgen Gutsch, eds (2009), *William Shakespeare's Sonnets Global: For the First Time Globally Reprinted. A Quartercentenary Anthology 1609–2009*, Dozwil: Edition SIGNAThUR.

Plato (1951), *The Symposium*, tr. Walter Hamilton, London: Penguin.

Plato (2007), *The Republic*, ed. G. R. F. Ferrari, tr. Tom Griffith, Cambridge Texts in the History of Political Thought, Cambridge: Cambridge University Press.

Plett, Heinrich (1994), 'Renaissance-Poetik', in Heinrich Plett (ed.), *Renaissance-Poetik: Zwischen Imitation und Innovation*, 1–20, Berlin: de Gruyter.

Post, Jonathan F. S. (2017), *Shakespeare's Sonnets and Poems: A Very Short Introduction*. Oxford: Oxford University Press.

Post, Jonathan F. S. (2018), 'Regifting Some Shakespeare Sonnets of Late', in Hannah Crawforth, Elizabeth Scott-Baumann and Clare Whitehead (eds), *Shakespeare's Sonnets: The State of Play*, 209–28, The Arden Shakespeare, London: Bloomsbury.

Preminger, Alex and T. V. F. Brogan, eds (1993), *The New Princeton Encyclopedia of Poetry and Poetics*, Princeton: Princeton University Press.

Regan, Stephen (2019), *The Sonnet*, Oxford: Oxford University Press.

Richmond, Hugh (1986), 'The Dark Lady as Reformation Mistress', *The Kenyon Review*, 8 (2): 91–105.

Roberts, Josephine A. ([1983] 2000), 'Mary Wroth', in M. H. Abrams and Stephen Greenblatt (eds), *The Norton Anthology of English Literature*, 7th edition, volume 1, 1422–32, New York: W. W. Norton & Company.

Roe, John (2018), 'Unfulfilled Imperatives in Shakespeare's Sonnets', in Hannah Crawforth, Elizabeth Scott-Baumann and Clare Whitehead (eds), *Shakespeare's Sonnets: The State of Play*, 77–94, The Arden Shakespeare, London: Bloomsbury.

Rossky, William (1958), 'Imagination in the English Renaissance: Psychology and Poetic', *Studies in the Renaissance*, 5: 49–73.

Roychoudhury, Suparna (2014), 'Anatomies of Imagination in Shakespeare's Sonnets', *Studies in English Literature 1500–1900*, 54 (1): 105–24.

Roychoudhury, Suparna (2018), *Phantasmatic Shakespeare: Imagination in the Age of Early Modern Science*, Ithaca: Cornell University Press.

Rubinstein, Frankie (1984), *A Dictionary of Shakespeare's Sexual Puns and their Significance,* London: Macmillan.

Rudenstine, Neil L. (2015), *Ideas of Order: A Close Reading of Shakespeare's Sonnets*, New York: Farrar, Straus & Giroux.

Rupp, Susanne and Frank Gertich (2009), 'The Sound of Music: Shakespeare's Sonnets in the Concert Hall', in Manfred Pfister and Jürgen Gutsch (eds), *William Shakespeare's Sonnets Global: For the First Time Globally Reprinted. A Quartercentenary Anthology 1609–2009*, 81–96, Dozwil: Edition SIGNAThUR.

Salkeld, Duncan (2023), 'Black Luce and Sonnets 127–154', in Jane Kingsley-Smith and W. Reginald Rampone, Jr. (eds), *Shakespeare's Global Sonnets: Translation, Appropriation, Performance*, 335–51, London: Macmillan.

Sanchez, Melissa E. (2013), 'The Poetics of Feminine Subjectivity in Shakespeare's Sonnets and "A Lover's Complaint"', in Jonathan Post (ed.), *The Oxford Handbook of Shakespeare's Poetry*, 505–21, Oxford: Oxford University Press.

Sanchez, Melissa E. (2019a), *Queer Faith: Reading Promiscuity and Race in the Secular Love Tradition*, New York: New York University Press.

Sanchez, Melissa E. (2019b), *Shakespeare and Queer Theory*, London: Bloomsbury.

Sanghera, Sathnam (2021), *Empireland: How Modern Britain is Shaped by its Imperial Past*, London: Penguin.

Schalkwyk, David (2002), *Speech and Performance in Shakespeare's Sonnets and Plays*, Cambridge: Cambridge University Press.

Schalkwyk, David (2004), 'Race, Body and Language in Shakespeare's Sonnets and Plays', *English Studies in Africa*, 47 (2): 5–23.

Scheil, Katherine (2021), 'Millennial Dark Ladies', *Critical Survey*, 33 (2): 79–92.

Schiebinger, Londa (1989), *The Mind Has No Sex? Women in the Origins of Modern Science*, Cambridge: Harvard University Press.

Schiffer, James ([1998] 2000), 'Reading New Life into Shakespeare's Sonnets: A Survey of Criticism', in James Schiffer (ed.), *Shakespeare's Sonnets: Critical Essays*, 3–71, New York: Garland.

Schiffer, James, ed. (2000), *Shakespeare's Sonnets: Critical Essays*, New York: Garland.

Schiffer, James (2007), 'The Incomplete Narrative of Shakespeare's Sonnets', in Michael Schoenfeldt (ed.), *A Companion to Shakespeare's Sonnets*, 45–56, Oxford: Blackwell.

Schleiner, Winfried (2000), 'Early Modern Controversies about the One-Sex Model', *Renaissance Quarterly*, 53 (1): 180–91.

Schlutz, Alexander M. (2009), *Mind's World: Imagination and Subjectivity from Descartes to Romanticism*, Seattle: University of Washington Press.

Schmidt, Alexander (1971), *Shakespeare Lexicon and Quotation Dictionary: A Complete Dictionary of all the English Words, Phrases and Constructions in the Works of the Poet*, 3rd edn rev. and enlarged by Gregor Sarrazin, 2 vols, Mineola: Dover Publications.

Schneckenburger, Stefan (2023), *Garten-Theater: Shakespeares grüne Welten*, Darmstadt: wbg Academic.

Schoenbaum, Samuel (1980), 'Shakespeare's Dark Lady: A Question of Identity', in Philip Edwards, Inga-Stina Ewbank and G. K. Hunter (eds), *Shakespeare's Styles: Essays in Honour of Kenneth Muir*, 221–39, Cambridge: Cambridge University Press.

Schoenfeldt, Michael, ed. (2007), *A Companion to Shakespeare's Sonnets*, Oxford: Blackwell.

Schoenfeldt, Michael (2010), *The Cambridge Introduction to Shakespeare's Poetry*, Cambridge: Cambridge University Press.

Schwanitz, Dietrich (1985), *Literaturwissenschaft für Anglisten: Das studienbegleitende Handbuch*, Munich: Max Hueber.

Shyllon, Folarin (1977), *Black People in Britain 1555–1833*, Oxford: Oxford University Press.

Sidney, Philip (2008), *The Major Works including Astrophil and Stella*, ed. Katherine Duncan-Jones, Oxford World's Classics, Oxford: Oxford University Press.

Smith, Bruce R. (1991), *Homosexual Desire in Shakespeare's England: A Cultural Poetics*, Chicago: University of Chicago Press.

Smith, Bruce R. (2000), 'I, You, He, She, and We: On the Sexual Politics of Shakespeare's Sonnets', in James Schiffer (ed.), *Shakespeare's Sonnets: Critical Essays*, 411–29, New York: Garland.

Smith, Emma (2020), *This is Shakespeare: How to Read the World's Greatest Playwright*, London: Pelican.

Smith, Ian (2022), *Black Shakespeare: Reading and Misreading Race*, Cambridge: Cambridge University Press.

Spevack, Marvin (1974), *The Harvard Concordance to Shakespeare*, Cambridge: The Belknap Press of Harvard University Press.

Spiller, Michael R. G. (1992), *The Development of the Sonnet: An Introduction*, London: Routledge.

Sprang, Felix (2016), 'Die Beständigkeit des Wandels: die *volta* im italienischen und englischen Sonett', in Sara Springfeld, Norbert Greiner and Silke Leopold (eds), *Das Sonett und die Musik: Poetiken, Konjunkturen, Transformationen, Reflexionen*, 37–56, Heidelberg: Universitätsverlag Winter.

Springfeld, Sara, Norbert Greiner and Silke Leopold, eds (2016), *Das Sonett und die Musik: Poetiken, Konjunkturen, Transformationen, Reflexionen*, Heidelberg: Universitätsverlag Winter.

Spurgeon, Caroline F. E. ([1935] 1960), *Shakespeare's Imagery and What It Tells Us*, Boston: Beacon Press.

Standop, Ewald (1986), 'Shakespeares Sonett 73: Analyse einer Analyse anstelle einer Rezension', *Literatur in Wissenschaft und Unterricht*, 19: 227–38.

Stanivukovic, Goran (2020), 'Sex in the Sonnets: The Boy and Dishonourable Passions of the Past', in Jennifer Drouin (ed.), *Shakespeare / Sex: Contemporary Readings in Gender and Sexuality*, 171–94, The Arden Shakespeare, London: Bloomsbury.

Stanzel, Frank K. ([1979] 2001), *Theorie des Erzählens*, 7th ed., Göttingen: Vandenhoeck und Ruprecht.

Stapleton, M. L. (2004), 'Making the Woman of Him: Shakespeare's Man Right Fair as Sonnet Lady', *Texas Studies in Literature and Language*, 46 (3): 271–95.

Strier, Richard (2007), 'The Refusal to be Judged in Petrarch and Shakespeare', in Michael Schoenfeldt (ed.), *A Companion to Shakespeare's Sonnets*, 73–89, Oxford: Blackwell.

Stuart, David (2004), *Dangerous Garden: The Quest for Plants to Change Our Lives*, London: Frances Lincoln.

Sullivan, Garret A., Jr. (2007), 'Voicing the Young Man: Memory, Forgetting, and Subjectivity in the Procreation Sonnets', in Michael Schoenfeldt (ed.), *A Companion to Shakespeare's Sonnets*, 331–42, Oxford: Blackwell.

Sutphen, Joyce (2000), '"A dateless lively heat": Storing Loss in the Sonnets', in James Schiffer (ed.), *Shakespeare's Sonnets: Critical Essays*, 199–217, New York: Garland.

Terry, Philip (2010), *Shakespeare's Sonnets*, Manchester: Caracanet.

Tetzeli von Rosador, Kurt (2000), 'Die nichtdramatischen Dichtungen', in Ina Schabert, *Shakespeare-Handbuch: Die Zeit – Der Mensch – Das Werk – Die Nachwelt*, 4th ed., 575–606, Stuttgart: Kröner.

The Bible and Holy Scriptvres conteyned in the Olde and Newe Testament (1560), Geneva: Printed of Rowland Hall. Available online: https:// archive.org/details/TheGenevaBible1560 (accessed 2 November 2023).

Thompson, Ayanna (2021a), 'Did the Concept of Race Exist for Shakespeare and His Contemporaries? An Introduction', in Ayanna Thompson (ed.), *The Cambridge Companion to Shakespeare and Race*, 1–16, Cambridge: Cambridge University Press.

Thompson, Ayanna, ed. (2021b), *The Cambridge Companion to Shakespeare and Race*, Cambridge: Cambridge University Press.

Traub, Valerie (1992), *Desire and Anxiety: Circulations of Sexuality in Shakespearean Drama*, London: Routledge.

Traub, Valerie (2000), 'Sex without Issue: Sodomy, Reproduction, and Signification in Shakespeare's *Sonnets*', in James Schiffer (ed.), *Shakespeare's Sonnets: Critical Essays*, 431–53, New York: Garland.

Traub, Valerie (2003), 'The Sonnets: Sequence, Sexuality, and Shakespeare's Two Loves', in Richard Dutton and Jean E. Howard (eds), *A Companion to Shakespeare's Works, Volume IV: The Poems, Problem Comedies, Late* Plays, 275–301, Hoboken: Wiley-Blackwell.

Traub, Valerie (2016), *Thinking Sex with the Early Moderns*, Philadelphia: University of Pennsylvania Press.

Trevor, Douglas (2007), 'Shakespeare's Love Objects', in Michael Schoenfeldt (ed.), *A Companion to Shakespeare's Sonnets*, 225–41, Oxford: Blackwell.

REFERENCES AND COMMENTARY ON KEY WORKS   227

Vendler, Helen (2007), 'Formal Pleasure in the Sonnets', in Michael Schoenfeldt (ed.), *A Companion to Shakespeare's Sonnets*, 27–44, Oxford: Blackwell.

Vickers, Brian, ed. ([1999] 2004), *English Renaissance Literary Criticism*, Oxford: Clarendon Press.

Warley, Christopher (2005), *Sonnet Sequences and Social Distinction in Renaissance England*, Cambridge: Cambridge University Press.

Watson, Amanda (2007), '"Full Character'd": Competing Forms of Memory in Shakespeare's Sonnets', in Michael Schoenfeldt (ed.), *A Companion to Shakespeare's Sonnets*, 343–60, Oxford: Blackwell.

Weis, René, ed. (2012), *Romeo and Juliet*, by William Shakespeare, Arden Shakespeare Third Series, London: Methuen.

Wells, Stanley (2010), 'Shakespeare's Sonnets and Sex', in Sonja Fielitz (ed.), *Shakespeare's Sonnets: Lovers, Layers, Languages*, 9–20, Heidelberg: Winter.

White, R. S. (2011), 'Survival and Change: The Sonnet from Milton to the Romantics', in A. D. Cousins and Peter Howarth (eds), *The Cambridge Companion to the Sonnet*, 166–84, Cambridge: Cambridge University Press.

Wolf, Maryanne (2018), *Reader, Come Home: The Reading Brain in a Digital World*, New York: HarperCollins.

Zukofsky, Louis ([1948] 2000), *A Test of Poetry*, The Wesleyan Centennial Edition of the Complete Critical Writings of Louis Zukofsky, Preface by Robert Creeley, Middletown: Wesleyan University Press.

INDEX OF SONNETS

The index covers Chapters 1–9, Appendices 4 and 5, and relevant parts of the Introduction. Excluded are the Preface and Appendices 1–3. The following abbreviations are used in the index: m. = mistress, rp. = rival poet, rps = rival poets, Sh. = Shakespeare, sp. = speaker, y. = youth. Numbers in bold refer to a more detailed discussion of the respective sonnet.

Sonnet 1: logical structure **75–6**; placement in pyramid model 177; y. kills his beauty 79; y.'s obligation to procreate 79–80; y.'s reasons for not wanting children 75; y.'s self-love 75, 83

Sonnet 2 **73–4**; theme of death 74

Sonnet 3: imagery **76–7**; y.'s appreciation of his former beauty 81–2; y.'s obligation to procreate 76; y.'s self-love 83

Sonnet 4 **83–4**; y. kills his beauty, y.'s obligation to procreate 79

Sonnet 5: transience of y.'s beauty 78–9; y.'s vague beauty 77

Sonnet 6: transience of y.'s beauty 78–9; y.'s obligation to procreate 79; y.'s self-centredness; y.'s vague beauty 77

Sonnet 7: sun allegory **81, 115**

Sonnet 8 **82**; y. kills his beauty 79; y.'s unhappiness 82, 84

Sonnet 9: y. kills his beauty 79

Sonnet 10 **80**; sp. indicates his devotion to y. 78; y.'s self-hate 82, 84

Sonnet 11: y.'s obligation to preserve mankind 81; y.'s vague beauty 77

Sonnet 12 **84–5**; numerological reading 50; self-cancelling effect 85; sp. not young anymore 84; transience of y.'s beauty 78–9

Sonnet 13: sp. wants to preserve y.'s identity, vocatives of love **78**

Sonnet 15 **85–6**; self-cancelling effect 85

Sonnet 16 **86**; sp. as poet 91; sp. desires y.'s personality 77

Sonnet 17 **82–3**; sp. as poet 90–1

Sonnet 18: as English Sonnet **15–16**

Sonnet 19 **95–6**

Sonnet 20: argument against aristocratic dedicatee 40; non-binary gender 1–2, 125; numerological reading 50; sp.'s sexual incompatibility with y. 52; sp.'s sexual relationship with y. **124–5**; Steevens' reaction 36–7

INDEX OF SONNETS

Sonnet 21: as model of Shakespearean Sonnet 2–4

Sonnet 22 **116–17**; symbiotic relationship of sp. and y. 110

Sonnet 23 sp.'s faith in his poetic skills **99**

Sonnet 24 **117–18**; reference to 'table' (notebook) 89, 118; symbiotic relationship of sp. and y. 110, 117

Sonnet 27: multiple themes **127–8**; sp.'s evokes youth in his imagination 161, 163

Sonnet 28: imagination as 'toil' **161**; sp.'s insufficient imagination 163

Sonnet 29: healing powers of imagination **161–2**, 163

Sonnet 30: limits and possibilities of imagination **162–3**

Sonnet 31: function of imagination **163–4**

Sonnets 33 and 34: sp.'s forgiveness for y.'s betrayals **147–9**; y. unfaithful to sp. 53, 147

Sonnet 35: sp.'s collusion in y.'s betrayals **149–50**; y. unfaithful to sp. 53, 149

Sonnet 36: same couplet as Sonnet 96 66, 121; symbiotic relationship, transferral of flaws between sp. and y. **120–1**

Sonnet 38: poetry as expression of love **92–3**

Sonnet 39: separation of sp. and y. **110**

Sonnets 40, 41 and 42: triangular desire **131–3**; y. unfaithful to sp. 53, 133, 143

Sonnet 43: oxymoronic quality **164–6**

Sonnet 44 **49**; limits and possibilities of imagination 74, 166; sp.'s separation from y. 123

Sonnet 45 **49–50, 123, 166**; elements air and fire, limits and possibilities of imagination 166; sp.'s separation from y. 49

Sonnet 46: relation between sp.'s eyes and heart **167**

Sonnet 47 **167–8**; relation between sp.'s eyes and heart 168–9

Sonnet 48: sp.'s self-accusations **150**; y. unfaithful to sp. 53, 150

Sonnet 49 **69–70**; multiple themes 69, 72; numerological reading 50; sp.'s self-accusations 150

Sonnets 50 and 51: sp.'s separation from y. **123**

Sonnet 55: placement in pyramid model 177; syllogistic quality **175–6**

Sonnet 57: sp.'s abjectness and suspicion **143–4**

Sonnet 58: sp.'s jealousy and suspicion 124

Sonnet 59: anticipates rival-poet sequence 48

Sonnet 60: perfect sonnet **96–7**; sp. wants to protect y. from time 99

Sonnet 61: origins of imaginative process, placement in pyramid model **178**

Sonnet 62: sp. not young anymore 52; symbiotic relationship of sp. and y. 110, **118–19**

Sonnet 63: numerological reading 50; two voltas 61

Sonnet 64: anticipates y.'s death 124

Sonnet 66: irregular sonnet 66

INDEX OF SONNETS

Sonnet 69: accusations of deception and depravity 54; y.'s corrupted nature **121–2**

Sonnet 70: accusations of deception and depravity 54; sinister aspects of y. 109; sp. defends y. 121–122

Sonnets 71 and 72: sp. urges y. to forget him **100**

Sonnet 73 **60–3**

Sonnet 74: poetry as means of self-preservations **99–100**

Sonnet 75: step-by-step approach *see Appendix 4*

Sonnet 76: poetry as expression of love **91–92, 93**

Sonnet 77: writing in notebook **90**

Sonnet 78 **101–2**; artistic and emotional dependence 103; erudite rps 59; sp. dependent on y.'s love 48

Sonnet 79 **59–60, 102–3**; (literary) criticism, envy 103

Sonnet 80: comparison of sp.'s and rp.'s love for y. 48; sincerity and flattery 103

Sonnet 81: interrupts rp. sequence 48

Sonnet 82: comparison of sp.'s and rp.'s love for y. 48, 103

Sonnet 83: self-cancelling argument **103–4**; sp.'s plain but sincere style 48

Sonnet 84: sincerity and flattery 103; sp.'s no-win situation **103–4**; y. enjoys rps' praise 48

Sonnet 85: comparison of sp.'s and rp.'s love for y. 47–8

Sonnet 86: erudite rp. 59; envy 103

Sonnet 87: Bunting's two-line paraphrase 173

Sonnet 92: sp.'s abjectness and suspicion

Sonnet 93: sp.'s abjectness and suspicion 122; sp.'s self-delusion 144; y.'s faults can be forgiven **122, 144**

Sonnet 94: corrupted y. 122

Sonnet 95: y.'s beauty vs y.'s faults **122**

Sonnet 96: same couplet as Sonnet 36 66, 121; symbiotic relationship, transferral of flaws between sp. and y. **121**

Sonnets 97 and 98: separation increases sp.'s desire 123–4

Sonnet 99: irregular sonnet 34, 63; separation increases sp.'s desire 123–4

Sonnet 103: inadequacy of poetry **156**

Sonnet 104: sp. has known y. for three years 53

Sonnet 106: model interpretation *see Appendix 5*

Sonnet 108: Sidney's Sonnet 108 50; sp. struggles to express his feelings **98**

Sonnet 109 **145**; self-accusations of deception and depravity 54; sp. justifies his betrayal of y. 145–6, 150

Sonnet 110 **145–6**; self-accusations of deception and depravity 54; sp. justifies his betrayal of y. 150

Sonnets 111 and 112: sp.'s deception **146**; sp. justifies his betrayal of y. 150

Sonnets 113 and 114: relation between sp.'s eyes and heart **168–9**

Sonnet 115 **119**

Sonnet 116 **119–20**; expression of perfect love 69, 81; impersonal quality 81

Sonnet 117: pun on Sonnet 116, sp. justifies his betrayal of y. **146–7**; self-accusations of deception and depravity 54, 109

Sonnets 118, 119 and 120 **151–2**; self-accusations of deception and depravity 54

Sonnet 121 **152**; impersonal quality 81, 192; self-accusations of deception and depravity 54

Sonnet 122: writing in 'tables' (notebooks) **89–90**

Sonnet 123: impersonal quality 81

Sonnet 126: irregular sonnet **63–5**; 'non-sonnet' 50

Sonnet 127 **54–6, 127**; criticism of face painting 105–6; m.'s black eyes 54, 105; reflection on Petrarchan tradition 95, 105–7; two voltas 61; vague description of m. 127

Sonnet 128: musical m. 53; sp. competes with other suitors **128**

Sonnet 129: depicts orgasm **138–9**; epitomized stages of desire 43, 138; impersonal quality 81, 138

Sonnet 130 **106–7**; desire for m.'s blackness 54; m.'s appearance 54, 58, 106; inversion of Petrarchan ideals 56, 106

Sonnet 131 **128–30**; controlling m. 53

Sonnet 132: attractive m. 53; m.'s black eyes 54; m.'s corrupted character **130**

Sonnet 133: dominating m. 53; triangular desire **134–5**

Sonnet 134: triangular desire **134–5**

Sonnet 135: irregular sonnet 63; male sp. 52; name 'Will' 52,116; promiscuous, sexually insatiable m. 53

Sonnet 136: name 'Will' 52, 116; sexually insatiable m. 53

Sonnet 137: Cupid corrupted sp.'s eyes **70, 170**; depraved m. 53; multiple themes 70, 72

Sonnet 138: earlier version in *The Passionate Pilgrim* 29; m. lies 53; mutual self-deception **152–3**; sp. not young anymore 52

Sonnet 139: sp.'s collusion in m.'s betrayal of him **154**; unfaithful m. 53

Sonnet 140: proud and cruel m. 53; sp.'s self-deception **154–5**

Sonnet 141: inversion of Petrarchan blazon 170; irrational desire for m. 115; sp.'s powerless imagination 171; sp.'s self-deception **154, 170–1**

Sonnet 142: irrational desire for m. 115; sp.'s self-deception **153**; unfaithful m. 53

Sonnet 143 **115–16**; irrational desire 115, 153; name 'Will' 116; sp.'s dependency on m. 153

Sonnet 144: compares m. and y. 135, 175; earlier version in *The Passionate Pilgrim* 29; m. associated with venereal disease 53; m. coloured 'ill' 54, 59, 136; sodomitical erotic economy 139; triangular desire **135–136**

INDEX OF SONNETS

Sonnet 145: biographical reading **32**; dependence on m. 114, 153; 'inferior' first sonnet 32, 33; irrational desire for m. 114, 153; irregular sonnet 32, 63; m.'s volatile nature 114, 153; name 'Will' 52

Sonnet 146: absence of love-object, religious sonnet 74–5; impersonal quality 81; misprinted second verse 34

Sonnet 147 **114–15**; love-madness 114; m. referred to as dark and black 54

Sonnets 148 and 149: irrational desire for m. 114, 115

Sonnet 150: explicit criticism of m.'s 'blackness' **130–1**

Sonnet 151: couplet 'spoken by the penis itself' 135; sexual puns 52, 135

Sonnet 152: unfaithful and deceitful m. and sp., writing as betrayal **97–8**

Sonnets 153 and 154 **113–14**; bawdy revision of poem by Marianus Scholasticus 112; early sonnet 52, 135; syphilis/venereal disease 112–13, 114; urgent quality of desire 112, 114

GENERAL INDEX

The index covers Chapters 1–9, Appendices 4 and 5, and relevant parts of the Introduction. Excluded are the Preface and Appendices 1–3. The following abbreviations are used in the index: m. = mistress, rp. = rival poet, rps = rival poets, Sh. = Shakespeare, sp. = speaker, y. = youth.

#ShakeRace 7
1609 Quarto 29, 31, 33–5, 40

addressees in *Sonnets* 29, 35, 41–2, 45, 46–7, 51, 52–60, 69, 70, 104–5, *see also Appendix 3*
ambiguity (as feature of *Sonnets*) 34, 45, 62–3, 65, 76, 84, 89, 92, 97, 121, 125, 132, 150, 161, 174
Ascham, Roger, *The Schoolmaster* 94
atropa belladonna 7, 56

Baynam, Lucy (Lucy Negro, Black Luce) 42, 58
Beaumont, John 35
Benson, John 35
black/Black/'black' 2, 7, 42, 54–9, 72, 105, 107, 114–15, 127, 129–30, 135–6, 145, 175, *see also Preface*
blazon 25–6, 106, 170–1, 176, 203, 205
British Black and Asian Shakespeare Project 7
buggery, *see* sodomy
Burgess, Anthony, *Nothing Like the Sun* 58

Carey, Henry, First Lord Hunsdon 42
Caxton, William 101
Chapman, George 42
Chaucer, Geoffrey, *Troilus and Criseyde* 19
cis-sexism 5–6, *see also* heteronormative
class 2, 57, 136, *see also* rank
colonial(ism) 57–9
compositor 33
conceit 75, 78, 106, 118, 128, 148, 155, 164, 204
conversion (linguistic) 198
correlatio 90
cosmetic practices 3, 7, 55–6, 105–6
couplet tie 97, 208
Cupid (god of love) 45, 47, 70, 112–14, 170, *see also* Eros

da Lentino, Giacomo 16–17, 19, 23
Daniel, Samuel, *Delia* 24
Dante 18, 19
dark/'dark' 2, 7, 47, 54–9, 105, 107, 114–15, 127, 129–31, 136, 145, 175, 212, *see also* black/Black/'black'

GENERAL INDEX

Dark Lady 54, 58–9, 107, *see also* black/Black/'black'
Davies, John, *Mirum in Modum* 159
dedicatee of *Sonnets* 39–41
deep reading 174
disease 52, 135, *see also* venereal disease, syphilis, plague
Donne, John 96; *Holy Sonnets* 24; *La Corona* 24; *The Canonization* 19
Drake, Nathan 40
Drayton, Michael, *Ideas Mirrour: Amours in Quatorzains* 24
Dunbar, William 58

Eld, G. 30, 33
Elizabeth I 41
Empson, William, *Seven Types of Ambiguity* 62–3
English sonnet 16–17, 19–21, 23, 96
Erasmus, *Encomium Matrimonii, The Praise of Marriage* 79–80
Eros 79, *see also* Cupid
Ewart, Gavin 37
Exodus, Book of 152

fairness 2, 54–6, 58, 77, 105–6, 107, 129, 136, 145, 175
Fibonacci sequence 17
First Folio 35, 40
Fitton, Mary 41
Fletcher, Giles, *Licia* 24, 37

Galen 137, 139
gappiness (Emma Smith) 51, 65, 174
Gascoigne, George, *Primer of English Poetry* 15, 16, 20
gender: binary g. 1, 5–6, 47, 174; cross-gendered 6, 125; fluidity

of g. 1, 5–6, 125, 174; g. as social practice 1, 6, 125, 174; g. in Petrarchan poetry 112; g. of addressees 29, 34, 46–7, 125, *see also Appendix 3*; g.-transgressive desire 34, 127; g. transition 6; nonbinary g. 6; y.'s gender 124–7
Genesis, Book of 136
Gildon, Charles 35
golden mean (Pythagoras) 17
Greville, Fulke, *Caelica* 50
groups within *Sonnets*: death 48, 73–5; impersonal sonnets 81, 138; jealousy 48, 124; love/desire in changing/corrupted world 110, 119–20; love triangle/triangular desire 45, 48, 70, 109, 131–41, 143; m. sequence 32, 45–7, 53–9, 70, 107, 127; numbers 50–1, 70; pairs 48–50, 70–1; procreation 46, 47, 50, 70, 73, 137, 157, 178; rival poet(s) 44, 47–48, 59–60, 70, 100–4; separation, absence, and reunion 44, 48, 52, 70, 109–10,122–4, 143–6, 150; suggestions of groups, overview 43–51, 70–2, 95, 109–10, 111, *see also Appendix 1*; symbiotic relationship of sp. and y. 109, 110, 116–19; 'Will' 52, 116, 135; y. sequence 45–7, 50, 52–3, 63, 65, 70

Harrison, G. B. 58
Hathaway, Anne 32, 42
Hathaway, William (Sh.'s brother-in-law) 41
Herbert, George 96; 'A Negress Courts Cestus, a Man of a Different Colour' 58

GENERAL INDEX

Herbert, Mary, Countess of Pembroke, *The Triumphs of Death* 26
Herbert, William, Third Earl of Pembroke 40, 41, 116
hermaphrodite 137
Herrick, Robert 35
heteronormative 5–6, 136, 139–40
homoerotic(ism) 2, 6, 34, 36, 40, 43, 124–7, 136–8, 139–40, 174
Howard, Henry, Earl of Surrey 20, 21–3, 61
Hughes, Willy 40

intransitive desire (Catherine Bates) 22, 112
irregular Sh. sonnets 34, 63–6
Italian sonnet 16–17, 18–19, 22–3, 61, 106

Jakobson, Roman 76
Johnson, Samuel 35
Jonson, Ben 29, 35, 57
Jordan, Wilhelm 58

Kyd, Thomas 57

Lanier, Emilia 42
Laqueur, Thomas *see* one-sex model
Lintot, Bernard 35
Locke, Anne, *Mediation of a Penitent Sinner* 19, 23–4
Lodge, Thomas, *Phillis* 24
Lucian of Samosata, *Amores* 139

Malone, Edmond 35–7, 40, 45, 46, 47
Marlowe, Christopher 42, 57
Meres, Frances, *Palladis Tamia, Wits Treasury* 31
Milton, John 6, 35
mimesis 155

mini-narratives, mini-sequences *see* groups within *Sonnets*
misogynistic, misogyny 70, 107, 138
More, Thomas, *History of Richard III* 111

Nashe, Thomas 42

one-sex model 5–6, 136, 137

patchwork character of *Sonnets* (lack of narrativity; impressionistic quality) 34, 41, 44–5, 48, 51, 65, 69, 71, 73, 84, 86, 158, 173–4, 176, *see also Appendix 1*
patron, patronage 42, 60, 100–4
Paul the Apostle, *Epistle to Ephesians* 136
Petrarch: *Canzionere* 19; English engagements with P. 19–26; Laura 19, 22, 23, 26 91; Petrarchism 22–3, 104–7, 111–12, *see also* Italian Sonnet; 'Rime 140' 20, 21–2; Sh.'s engagement with P. 32, 56, 95, 98, 105–7, 111–12, 129, 136, 170–1, 176, 201, 203; *Trionfo della Morte* 26
plague 70, 170, *see also* disease
Plato: *The Republic* 155–6; *The Symposium* 79, 136, 137–8, 139
Premodern Critical Race Studies (PCRS) 7
presentism 6–7

race, racism, racecraft 2, 5, 6–8, 54, 57–9, 135–6, 174, 175, 180
RaceB4Race Mentorship Network 7
rank, social 125, 136, *see also* class

GENERAL INDEX

Revett, Eldred, 'One Enamour'd on a Black-Moor' 58
reworkings of Sh.'s sonnets 176

Shakespeare, William: *A Lover's Complaint* 29, 35, 45–6; *A Midsummer Night's Dream* 158–60; *Cymbeline* 111; *Hamlet* 89; *Julilus Caesar* 128; *King John* 89; *Love's Labour's Lost* 29; *Othello* 7; *Sir Thomas More* 33; *The Merchant of Venice* 134; *The Passionate Pilgrim* 29, 31–2, 35; *Richard III* 89; *Romeo and Juliet* 128–9; *The First Part of Henry VI* 89; *The Phoenix and the Turtle* 35; *The Rape of Lucrece* 40; *The Two Gentlemen of Verona* 89; *Titus Andronicus* 7; *Troilus and Cressida* 113; *Venus and Adonis* 40
Sidney, Philip: *Astrophil and Stella* 24, 25, 50, 91, 129; *Defense of Poesy* 38, 155–6, 160; Sonnet 1 93–5; Sonnet 54 129; Sonnet 77 25–6
slavery 56–7
sodomy, sodomite, sodomitical 2, 138–40
sonnet cycles 19, 23–6, 37, 50
sonneteering craze 24
Southampton, Henry Wriothesley, Earl of 40, 126–7
Spenser, Edmund 42; *Amoretti* 24, 26
Stationers' Register 29, 33
Steevens, George 35–7
strambotto 17

syllogism, syllogistic quality of sonnets 3, 17–18, 49, 76, 175, 198, 202
syphilis 112–14, *see also* disease, venereal disease

theme clusters, definition of 5, 69–73, 176–8
Thorpe, Thomas 29, 31, 40–1, 65
Tottel, Richard, *Songes and sonnettes* 23

venereal disease 45, 53, 112–14, 129, 135, *see also* disease, syphilis
Vernon, Elizabeth 41
volta 18

Watson, Thomas 37, *The Hekatompathia, or, Passionate Century of Love* 24
W. H. *see* dedicatee of *Sonnets*
Whateley, Anne 41
whiteness 2, 5–7, 26, 55–6, 58, 77, 105, 107, 136, 175, *see also* fairness
white studies 7
Wilde, Oscar, *The Portrait of Mr. W. H.* 40
Wilson, Thomas, *The Arte of Rhetorique* 79
Wriothesly, Henry, Earl of Southampton, *see* Southampton
Wroth, Mary, *Pamphilia to Amphilanthus* 24, 26
Wyatt, Thomas 19–20, 23

xenophobia 57, *see also* racism